HEADLONG INTO THE SEA

HEADLONG INTO THE SEA

Robert Clarkson

The Pentland Press
Edinburgh—Cambridge—Durham—USA

© Robert Clarkson, 1995

First published in 1995 by
The Pentland Press Ltd
1 Hutton Close
South Church
Bishop Auckland
Durham

ISBN 1-85821-286-3

Typeset by Carnegie Publishing, 18 Maynard St., Preston
Printed and bound by Antony Rowe Ltd., Chippenham

In Endymion, I leaped headlong into the sea, and thereby have become better acquainted with the soundings, and the rocks, than if I had stayed upon the green shore, and piped a silly pipe, and took tea and comfortable advice.

Keats

Letters 1818

CONTENTS

ILLUSTRATIONS

ACKNOWLEDGEMENTS

My grateful thanks are owed to the following who have kindly lent me journals and photographs, and provided copies of official and unofficial records of some of the events described in the book

Lieutenant-Commander G. E. Bingham, R.N.

Monsieur C. Brechoire, Municipal Archivist, Cherbourg

Lieutenant-Commander D. C. Douglas, R.N.

Major E. A. Elbers, Assistant Defence Attaché, Embassy of the Federal Republic of Germany, London

Doctor Sir John Ellis, M.B.E., M.D., F.R.C.P.

Herr R. Gelbhaar

Lieutenant-Commander A. Hague, R.N.R.

The Imperial War Museum

Commander H. L. Jenkins, D.S.C., R.N.

Lieutenant-Commander R. J. Mordaunt, V.R.D., R.N.R.

Fregattenkapitan Albert Nitzschke, Deutscher Marinebund e.V.

Portsmouth City Records Office

The Public Record Office

Rear Admiral Sir David Scott, K.B.E., C.B.

PROLOGUE

This is an account of the life of a junior R.N. officer between 1939 and 1946, recorded with the benefit of hindsight and the years for reflection. I have tried to recall some of the atmosphere of those days, when the British world was changing for good.

In July 1939 thirty-one paymaster cadets left *Vindictive* for the Fleet; eight were killed by 1941, a rate of loss nearly twice that of seaman cadets. I hope this book may be some tribute to their memory.

R.A.C.
Crudwell
Wilts
1994

SPECIAL ENTRY

I entered the Royal Navy more or less by accident. In July 1938 a contemporary, also with Oxford in mind, gave it up for a short service commission in the R.A.F. He was soon being taught to fly Blenheims, the new twin-engined day bomber. I asked him what had brought on the death wish and he said that a war was coming and he would rather be fully trained than half trained. I found it hard to dispute the logic of this remark, or forget it. Why begin a university course to be whipped into the maelstrom, after a year perhaps, for cannon fodder? Better to make a virtue of necessity and become a regular officer while there was time. It was not as if it was all going to be a big surprise.

My generation were born in the twenties and the boys expected to be in uniform sooner or later. By 1938 it was apparent that the struggle with the Germans begun in 1914 would soon be re-started. We were raised in the shadow of the Somme and knew what we might be in for. It was not discussed, but it was there, like the next visit to the dentist. We were not put off by Sassoon or Owen; the unlucky would not see it out but it was fruitless to fret about war itself, a customary experience for the British, who owed their blessings to their warships and infantry, victorious for centuries; war was part of our scene. If you were for it there was nothing to be done; when the Chief said go, you gotta go.

> The Garden called Gethsemane,
> It held a pretty lass,
> But all the time she talked to me
> I prayed my cup would pass.
> The officer sat on the chair,
> The men lay on the grass,

And all the time we halted there
I prayed my cup would pass.

Munich came and went and Mr Chamberlain waved his one-sided gentleman's agreement. It was obvious that the class of '21 were to be in it—the question was, with whom? There was no way to a pilot's brevet with astigmatic eyesight. I was qualified medically for the army, naval engineer or paymaster. The sea had my vote so that it was to be either the maroon stripe of the engineer or the white of the paymaster.

Engineering cadets had to spend years ashore learning the job. I elected to be examined by the Civil Service Commissioners in March 1939 for entry as a paymaster cadet, intending to try for Sandhurst if I failed. It sounded nearer to a trade than the profession of arms; I had never met a paymaster and had little idea what he did. By the end of the summer holidays of 1938 I had crossed the Rubicon to a military career; provided I became a naval officer in a seagoing ship I was content to leave it to the Almighty to sort out the details. The dreaming spires vanished in the tremor of events. These were not the times for books.

I was given a refresher course in mathematics and told the English and History ought to be pushovers. I raked up two kind sponsors and hoped for the best.

There were nine papers to negotiate. I had prepared some notes and looked at them on the way to the contest. I saw no alternative to failure. By then my head was full of the Dreadnoughts, the Hero at Trafalgar, *Shark* at Jutland and Cradock at Coronel; I was awash with it. The economics of a service career were irrelevant. If pay and prospects troubled you, you had to be keen or, more accurately, transverging upon the lunatic, to volunteer for the traditional sea service of the Empire.

'What,' I read from the note, 'were the significant events in Gladstone's Second Ministry?' I digested these epic details from the Liberal past and entered the Institute of Civil Engineers in Great George Street. The first question greeted me like an old and dear friend. 'What were the significant events in Gladstone's Second Ministry?' My pen hurtled over the paper while stocks lasted. This must be the first leg of the pushover.

New Entry: 1939

The interview came on the last day. All five were in plain clothes but the sailors were easy to see. The Admiral in the middle began.

'I see you are in the first eleven and first fifteen, who do you play?'

We had had a good team that winter and had only been beaten by an Old Boys side led by a Cambridge international. I gave the answers. He seemed relieved. I suspected he had not heard much about us.

'Where do you play?'

That was better. He had his doubts about me. He was right. I was a scrawny number eight and lucky to get in.

This preliminary skirmish of a social nature was interrupted by a civil servant with a thin nose and striped trousers, anxious to get on with the agenda.

'You realize that it will not be heave-ho my lads on deck all day so far as you are concerned? What do you think that you will have to do?'

The correct answer would have been that I did not know but was prepared to give it a try.

'Naval law and courts martial, secretarial and accountancy'

It sounded brittle. I had been cornered. The interview ended on a friendly note. The Admiral asked me if my eyesight was good enough for the executive branch. I said it was not and went away to abide the result.

On 5 April I learned from the Daily Telegraph that I was in the list of seventeen successful applicants. One hundred and ninety-six had entered for all branches and seventy nine had been admitted. I was sixth from the bottom in English, one of my university subjects. Poetry did not seem to be a requirement.

It remained to say goodbye. I missed the four hundreth anniversary celebrations and captaincy of the first eleven. It mattered not. On 1 May 1939, one week after my eighteenth birthday, I joined H.M.S. *Vindictive* at Chatham for training.

CHAPTER 2

TRAINING CRUISER

Vindictive was laid down as a cruiser, altered to an aircraft carrier, and completed in 1918. Against the trend, she was converted back to a cruiser and then to a cadets training ship. Her last cruise before the war was planned for the Baltic but the gathering storm obliged us to make do with Iceland and the west coasts of Scotland and France.

Two hundred and seventy cadets embarked for instruction; owing to the shortage of seamen the Young Gentlemen had to keep her clean and cared for.

It was the great Drake no less who expected officers to haul and draw like the men. This meant a change in routine to which we adapted without difficulty, scrubbing decks and polishing flats while qualifying to take our places aft.

The ship was made for the job. Her armament had been replaced by classrooms and she was roomy in the right places. Two rundowns took the places of ladders between the waists and the quarter deck, discharging cadets in a high speed torrent when they were required to fall in. Thirty-nine officers in charge of us had been picked for it. The Cadet Gunner played the part of God in discipline and organization, making sure that we were in the right places at the right time.

The first two days were spent in gas drill, swimming tests, inoculations, checking kit and finding our way about. The tricks of slinging, lashing and stowing a hammock were explained, enabling us to sleep when it was permitted.

We gave each other the once over. Nearly all of my entry had eyesight bad enough to exclude them from the executive branch. Three were killed in *Hood*, *Southampton* and *Neptune* when those ships were sunk in 1941. One was wounded by a bullet from a

Zero while on the bridge of *Dragon*. One was captured by the Japanese when *Exeter* was sunk and another had to swim from two battleships, *Royal Oak* and *Prince of Wales*. All that lay ahead and when *Vindictive* left for Scapa Flow the consensus was that we had been lucky to find ourselves afloat at once, unlike our shipmates who had already served four years at Dartmouth or one term of basic training in the old monitor *Erebus*.

The Admiralty sent young paymasters straight to sea with no preliminaries onshore, considered essential for everyone else, officers and ratings alike. This may have been a legacy from the 74s when the Paymaster and his juniors were strictly businessmen, there for the perks, not the glory.

On the way downriver, I was surprised to see a coloured pin against my name on the Cadet Gunner's noticeboard indicating that part of my third night in the Navy was to be spent on the bridge with the middle watch. I persuaded myself that the authorities had to know what they were doing and climbed the ladders at ten minutes to midnight, unsure of my role in the conduct of a heavy cruiser travelling at 12 knots through a moonless night in the North Sea. Beyond an introduction to hammocks and gas masks, I had had no training of any kind. It was a relief to find that no contribution was expected from me beyond standing behind the Officer of the Watch, First Cadet of the Watch, Yeoman of Signals, Signalman and others who seemed to be there to take the air. The lights of Yarmouth appeared on the port beam and I was sent below to shake the fo'cstle officer for the morning watch.

The relief was an old hand who knew the risk in waiting for a Second Cadet of the Watch to arrive. I found him putting on a greatcoat when I appeared before the open curtain at his cabin door. He was a submarine captain carrying out his obligatory general service time; when he acknowledged my report that it was 0345 my naval career got underway. My first duty was completed and I was over the threshold between carefree youth and the rigours of the Naval Discipline Act; it had been a quick trip.

The next day we began initiation into the specialist branch we had joined. The instructor was a paymaster lieutenant with a place in the England and Navy rugby sides, at a loose end during the summer months, when he was turned out to train new entry officers. We gathered round to receive the first message—a résumé perhaps of the function of the Branch in the modern Navy, or some history—how Nelson's secretary at the Nile broke down in the bread room of the *Vanguard* leaving his master to write his own despatch, with blood running into his eyes; or his secretary at Trafalgar, the first casualty in the *Victory*. 'Is that poor Scott?' the Hero had asked as the shards of a man hit by a cannon ball were pushed over the side. Seventeen potential Scotts waited for the Word. They were disappointed. The International was dedicated to keeping an eye on the ball and wasted no time on preliminaries. He explained at length and not very well the rules for the award of Good Conduct Badges to the lower deck. We learned of the many ways in which the errant sailor lost his threepence a day for the good conduct stripe on his arm, from C for cells to the ultimate DD or discharged dead. We were spared nothing. There might be a price to pay for our headlong journey to the sea.

The ship bumped her way across the Pentland Firth during a seamanship lecture and we had Lesson One in seasickness; eight of the class limped over the heaving deck, hoping their legs would get them outside in time. The lecturer carried on without drawing breath or looking at them. Seasickness did not merit attention.

The Captain cleared lower deck and told us that we were going to Iceland to show the Flag. He had a drawling and fruity voice, easy to imitate, and the wags had a good time telling each other that we were going to Iceland etc., and rolling about when they got it right.

A military looking gentleman in plain clothes arrived and lived with the Captain. The word was that he was on his way to tell the Icelanders what HMG wanted them to say if the Germans tried to talk to them. There was nothing remarkable about a directive of that kind then. The Americans had the money but we had no doubts that otherwise we were top dog and it was up to the smaller fry to watch points and seek to please.

The passage was made in perfect weather and we learned about sea boats, which were hoisted by hand, involving both watches of cadets in a ritual with its own language. After the falls had been married and the long awaited 'Hoist Away' came the ship

7

drummed with the clump of 500 feet as the cadets hauled the boat out of the water. The upper deck was not long enough for the hoist to be made in a straight run. At the end of the available space each cadet had to drop the falls and sprint along the upper deck to take them up again at the nearest point to the davits, before the absence of manpower enabled the boat to take charge. The drill resembled other seamanship evolutions; it was all good fun until confusion reduced it to dangerous hysteria. A knot of fallen cadets, a wrong order and a cutter with its crew could dive back into the sea. The ship carried a crane but it was not used for boats; the drill of hoisting by hand was a Good Thing and not to be criticized, one of a kind with open bridges, Jackie Fisher and gunnery.

In bright and cold weather I entered my first foreign harbour at Reykajvik as one of the cable party. I remember the coloured houses, muddy streets and pink skins of the locals. They swarmed over the ship when she was opened to visitors. An overloaded canoe began to sink and the motor dinghy was called away at the double to show what Britannia could do for its small friends. The Icelanders onboard crowded to the guardrails to cheer. The dinghy coxswain was an engineering cadet of extreme height and thinness. They saw him run along the boom, swoop down the rope ladder, start the engine and let go the bow rope at a conjuror's speed. He put her in gear and shot off at maximum revolutions on his errand of mercy. The visitors became quiet in silent horror while the cadets cheered. The coxswain had forgotten to let go the stern rope. It was an extra long mooring and the crowd had its money's worth, as the line straightened and reduced the boats speed to zero. The coxswain sailed over her bows to the ecstasy of his messmates and the bewilderment of the guests at our barbarity. It would have been fruitless to explain that we were a rough lot at heart.

My entry gradually absorbed the routine and learned, like the victims of the press gang, that it was possible to get by in one of His Majesty's Ships without knowing much about the sea.

We were introduced to Jack, the naval rating upon whom all depended. The frontispiece in the Naval Staff Handbook used to be a photograph of a seaman in a Russian convoy. Snow and ice cover him and he is bowed down by the weather and heavy clothing. All that can be seen of his face under the round cap and muffler are a pair of grinning eyes. The caption provided Lesson One for staff officers—'The greatest single factor'.

Among the seamen's jobs we had was submerged flat sweeper, assisting the Able Seaman in semi-permanent residence there. In her cruiser days the ship had carried torpedoes and the space had become a lecture room. The job meant polishing the deck and listening to a monologue from the sweeper. He welcomed a chat. For some reason he associated officers with nannies and the conversation always came back to that. He was fascinated in the subject and asked us while we were polishing away, whether we had ever had a nurse and if so what was her name and how old. It could have been that he had had a walk out with one but I think not. He said one day that he had gone straight from an orphanage into the Navy. He was absorbed by the notion that for money a child could be provided with the attention he had never had.

The duty of cadet ST (Seaman Torpedoman) involved a day in the low power workshop where electrical repairs were done. One of the seamen was a persuasive communist who used the opportunity to rehearse the dialectic. The torpedo party had heard it all before but gathered round in case the solitary captive audience could provide a response which might amuse. We were all given the treatment. I had to wait twenty years, when I joined the Staff College, before I heard Marxism given such an airing.

The passage from Iceland to the west coast of Scotland brought the first heavy weather. The ship rolled for two days with the end of a south-west gale on her beam. Coincidentally, it was the turn of my mess to exercise broadside messing.

We were served our food by Royal Marines who brought plates to the end of each mess table. The full plates were passed from hand to hand. Had good manners prevailed the cadets sitting by the ship's side and furthest from the table's end would have been served first. Unhappily for them, the senior cadets occupied the inboard ends of the benches and were able, with a dexterity acquired over two cruises, to pick out the best helpings and pass on the rejects to the second eleven.

For one week this gentleman's life was interrupted and we messed like the ship's company. It involved a cadet, laughingly called the cook of the mess, collecting the food from the galley in a large tin and serving it to the rest. My turn came on a savoury mince night. I negotiated the ladders without losing any of the protein awaited by my twenty messmates but when crossing the bathroom flat she gave a roll, I slipped on sea water which had found its way below, and one third of the tin was ejected. Luckily for me the weather ensured some poor appetites and enough to go round. I wedged myself behind a water main and picked the debris out of a valve wheel assembly before the Cadet Gunner saw it. I still have a hesitant approach to savoury mince.

At dusk that day we raised the Flannen Islands, rocks in the deep Atlantic miles from the nearest shipping lane. In the gloom of the storm and scudding sea it was the loneliest place on earth.

We passed Mull, remembered by the Navy in the first war for Loch-na-Keal where Beatty hid the battle cruisers because there was no safe base for them, and ran through the Sound of Mull for Oban. Two capital ships in line ahead appeared through the haze miles away and turned south. They were the new French heavy ships *Strasbourg* and *Dunkerque*; one wore a rear-admiral's flag. We responded like Nelson's *Agamemnon* in sight of a French 74. Pipes shrilled, the gun's crew dashed to their gun, the upper deck thundered to the boots of a Royal Marine colour guard and the band took its position on the hurricane deck. The Captain of Marines with white helmet and sword called the guard to attention and to present arms. The band played and the gun fired the first round of the salute to the French admiral. The turnout of men, music and gunfire at the drop of a hat seemed perfectly done and we waited for the gun flashes and sound of music in reply from the great ships in view. The battle cruisers increased speed and disappeared. They gave no sign that they had noticed we were there. A Scottish journalist short of copy rang Fleet Street and the national dailies reporting that British and French warships had been engaged in joint manoeuvres off the West Coast.

We began boat work and learned how to rig and sail the Navy's three basic sailing craft, the Bermuda rigged cutter, the ketch rigged whaler and the 14ft RNSA dinghy. We picnicked in the coves of Kintyre and thought ourselves sailors of a kind. We dressed up in stiff shirts for guest night and wore our round jackets to march past the Captain at Sunday Divisions.

At Campbeltown two weeks of solid training began. Lectures, sailing, boat picnics and professional briefing filled the days, which began at 5.30. It was possible to sleep at the blink of an eye. The only requirement, like that of the fast worker, was opportunity. Few better than the top of the quarter deck awning when legitimately there to take up the slack on a frapping line. The canopy was warm in the afternoon sun, the harbour and the distant shore were co-conspirators, and save for the marching to and fro of a party at rifle drill on the quarter deck below, there was nothing to be heard save the murmurs of an afternoon in midsummer.

I was awakened by a jolt under the canvas two feet from my head. The tip of the bayonet showing there provided an electric start to my undetected escape, before the Gunner's Mate had warmed to his task of explaining to the cadet who had shouldered arms when he should have done something else, his view upon his suitability for a military life.

Our equable routine was broken by news of the sinking on her acceptance trials of the new submarine *Thetis* in Liverpool Bay, a day's steaming away. We were the nearest H.M. ship to the disaster and carried a 6½in wire rope. The submarine was in shallow water and the word was that we were bound to be called to help. Whether the Admiralty were not reminded that we had something to offer or it was thought that, despite the wire, our nearness to the scene and abundancy of manpower and boats, we would have been in the way in a very specialized situation, I do not know. We remained anchored in Campbeltown Loch and listened to the news, hour by hour, while the unsuccessful attempts to get her up went on. We were engrossed by the tragedy, which made us aware, suddenly and close by, that it was not all boat picnics and classrooms.

The date came for all to submit a compulsory essay, making the point that while we were not there to learn the violin, neither were we mere gladiators being prepared for the arena. The essay was the token cultural event in the syllabus. I had two runners, having been paid half a crown to write an entry for another cadet the night before the deadline. My patron was not a Philistine but disliked paper work. In later years he prospered in Royal Service.

At Guernsey the First Lieutenant took a boat picnic to Sark. Two cadets were left with the cutter while the rest of us walked through the honeysuckle hedges to the Seignurie and tea with the Dame de Sark. The boat's crew in serge trousers and blue jerseys with roughened hands and reddened faces, wandering around the beautiful garden, were agelong mariners on a strange shore, unlikely successors to *Bounty*'s crew gaping at Tahiti.

We went down the hill and found that the boatkeepers had brought the picnic ashore. The sausages were fried and we began. There was no second bite. The First Lieutenant swept the festivities aside and ordered us to the boat at the double. It was not a joke or an esoteric piece of training. We recovered the anchor and sailed her for St. Peter Port, eight miles away. It became apparent what the fuss was about. Although the wind was fair the tide had started to flood and we had no hope of stemming it without an engine or strong wind. The rise and fall in the Channel Islands is the biggest in the British Isles and when the flood got going we would be carried towards the Alderney Race and France.

Jimmy the One had either forgotten to look at the tide tables or his watch had stopped. He did not say which. This enabled him to give his bewildered crew a lesson in dealing with a Situation. (Lesson One for the seaman is to avoid Situations by developing a lively sense of impending disaster.) The sails came down at the rush and the grapnel anchor went over the side to hold us before the tide took her into deep water. The anchor failed to reach the bottom. We had already come too far. Again at the rush we took off the foresail and mainsail sheets and bent them on to the anchor cable to lengthen it and tried again. This time she just held. The First Lieutenant thought we had hooked a rock. The sheets tautened like violin strings and seemed sure to part. We sat back in the boat as she breasted the tide and awaited the next move. It seemed good fun. Jimmy had the responsibility (which makes the difference) and decided that the prospect of spending all night in an open boat with seven paymaster cadets was beyond the call of duty. By then it was dark. There was a lamp in the locker. We raised the lighthouse and asked for a tow.

An hour later a fishing boat puttered towards us. Simultaneously, a motor boat sent from the ship to look for us came round the point. We were towed back and turned in about 4 a.m. There was no guard and steerage (lie in) because we had not been on duty and we fell in as usual at 0530.

One of the lessons learned was the importance of neatness and accuracy when urinating over the side in an open boat. Another was the value to morale when in charge of a Situation of appearing bored and saying next to nothing. The first was soon acquired, given a sound bladder and a sense of the wind's direction. The second was not so easy, although Jimmy had made it seem otherwise.

We found Brest alive with brightly uniformed matelots and old warships in plenty among the new. The battleship *Paris* lay alongside, built in 1914 and unmodernized. We were to meet again. On the other side of the basin lay her sister ship *Bretagne*, shortly to be the grave of most of her crew at Mers-el-Kebir. Both were in full commission with pom-pom hatted sailors everywhere and boats scuttling about the basin. The scene was Gothic with soaring bridges, yards and masts and rank on rank of scuttles, torpedo nets and general impedimenta covering their sides. The two battleships were irrelevant to the submarine and air battles about to start, or indeed to any likely naval conflict. They might have been there since the Directory for any use they had now.

Brest was a home for sailors with bars and brothels to suit all tastes. The cadets were children of Victorian parents; trade was indifferent for the whores but modest for the wineshops. Some got drunk and were supported by their friends while their leave cards were collected under the eye of the Officer of the Watch. It was the custom that provided a libertyman did not make a nuisance of himself, and was attended by his friends, the Officer of the Watch looked the other way. This convenient, although unwritten, rule saved many a career.

The snails and the wine were diversions but there were no real get togethers. The French and the British did what was expected of them without enjoying it much. The talk among us was critical of our hosts and jokes were plentiful. They were the ancient enemy, obsessed by women and drink and not to be relied upon.

We were sons of the Great War generation and our fathers tended to blame the French for everything that had gone wrong.

The standard swimming test took place in the estuary. We jumped off the forward boom in overalls and swam with the tide to the after gangway, where we paddled about for fifteen minutes. The water was warm enough but the ship took on a remote and unfriendly look with the swell showing the rust around her boot-topping. It was good to haul our dripping bodies back over the grating aware of the disadvatages of being a non-swimmer in the open sea.

Douarnanez Bay provided two days' relaxation. The ship was illuminated and we were lowered on wooden stages over the side to secure the electric cable, fit the bulbs and check that they worked. Mine shone beautifully and I swung idly on the stage in the sun waiting for the Captain of the quarterdeck to spoil it with an order to do something else. He was a petty officer diver blessed by the Almighty with an awareness of the exact moment when hands became idle. I was suddenly and comprehensively showered with a disgusting surge from a pipe in the ship's side above my head. This lesson, like so many in the training cruiser, was of little practical use thereafter, never again being called upon to rig light bulbs from a stage.

The night before leaving Douarnanez was much enjoyed. The last boat from shore was loaded to capacity with cadets buzzing with cheap wine, or romance, and in some cases a lethal combination of the two. Singing began and grew louder as we neared the ship.

> Once I was slavey, down in Drury Lane,
> My master was so kind to me
> My mistress was the same,
> Until one day quite suddenly
> A sailor came to tea
> And that was the beginning
> Of all my misereee . . .

The engines stopped. The Leading Seaman coxswain put his head out of the cabin forward, the cadet coxswain being ignored for the business in hand. The leading hand had all the experience needed to deal with raucous libertymen. We were told that we were approaching the ship and all singing would cease. It did. By way of an encore the passengers swayed gently from side to side. This caused the boat in its loaded state to roll. The coxswain did not stop a second time. It was not his task to teach discipline to forty officers, albeit officers of the lowest order. He was responsible however for the safety of the boat and the lives of the clowns in it. He reduced speed to dead slow so that if she capsized there would not be enough way to drive her under. We went on with water sloshing over the gunwales. A cable from the ship sanity returned, speed was increased and we came alongside as if nothing had happened. The coxswain had other ideas. He was annoyed and had a right to be. He jumped on to the gangway and told the cadet coxswain to keep her there with everyone in her. Ten minutes later we were allowed up the ladder to face the Officer of the Watch. It was obvious that he was seriously displeased. Forty blazers, brown trilby hats and grey flannels lined up, dressed by the right and were called to attention.

The Officer of the Watch was a destroyer officer doing big ship time. Perhaps there were things he did not like about training in general and training officers in particular. This may have accounted for the heartfelt quality of his short address. We were glad when it was over and pleased to get away with one day's extra work. It was explained that we owed this leniency to his reluctance to waste the Commander's time by putting forty irresponsible idiots into his report. The coxswain watched the proceedings in silent embarrassment. He was popular and this episode changed nothing.

There were others besides those in the motor boat who had fallen foul of the Naval Discipline Act at Douarnanez and some fifty-eight of us mustered on the quarter deck at sea the following day to pay our debts. The punishment was one hour's physical training. There were two instructors and no break. We were all young and fit. Our sweat marked the teak. There were wardoom officers watching the show and the instructors made sure they got their money's worth. When it was over the exhaustion was real. We all knew what one day's No 16 punishment, within the powers of any officer of the watch to award, felt like when properly carried out.

The ship anchored for a few hours off Lee-on-the-Solent. A Sea Fox seaplane, a tiny reconnaissance aircraft on floats, landed alongside and the pilot came on board while trials with the crane went on. His uniform had the letter 'A' in the centre of the curl on his sleeve indicating that he was a short service officer entered for flying duties only. There had been a vigorous recruitment drive in 1937. In 1941 a lieutenant (A) told me that one intake included an ex-RN cook rating who had been discharged earlier because his services were no longer required. The story was probably a lie but it illustrates the uphill journey the new branch had to face. The 'A' was there not only to advertise a skill in aviation but also to mark an absence of full membership of the club.

We caught a distant glimpse of the new carrier *Ark Royal* at Spithead and had to be content with that, and the Air Branch officer with his toy aeroplane, as our introduction to the all out air war about to start.

An end of cruise concert was held at Sheerness. The heavy cruiser *York* was near by, about to leave for a two year commission in the West Indies. A midshipman running one of her boats came to the concert and sat with the Wardroom. We realized what it must be like to be a one-eyed man in the kingdom of the blind.

Next day our boats were sent ahead to await the ship before she entered dry dock at Chatham. I went with a motor boat, towing a cutter up river. We watched *Vindictive* come up and turn into the dock. The wind caught her and she crushed a wooden floating fender on the elbow at the entrance. Her side then went into the wall with a crunch, providing the spectators with a grandstand lesson in shiphandling and delaying the moment when she was secured.

The boat parties got back onboard five minutes before the Second Sea Lord arrived to present the end of cruise prizes. I was ordered to fall in on the quarter deck. I pointed out that I had been in a boat all day, was dressed in my working uniform and in a state of grubby disarray. It was a mistake to initiate a discussion when given a direct order. I found myself in the line somewhat quicker than I would have been had I kept my mouth shut and gone away to clean. I extended an oily hand to the Admiral who congratulated me on winning the Admiralty Essay

Prize. He said that there was no prize to give me because it had not arrived. It was that sort of day.

The senior cadets went on leave the following morning while the rest of us provisioned ship. It was then our turn to go and, as matters turned out, my training cruiser days were over. My pal in his bomber came to mind; I was not fully trained, but I was not just half trained either.

CHAPTER 3

HALIFAX ESCORT FORCE

My uncle took a house near to us by the sea that summer and I enjoyed my status as the sailor in the family. Come-uppance soon arrived; Cousin Pam, aged 10, got chicken pox and gave it to me. On 3 September I listened to Mr Chamberlain with my face in spots and under orders from the Admiralty to keep away until they had gone.

I reported that I was fit but nothing happened. My last order, now weeks old, had not been changed so I set out for Chatham where I had been told to re-join *Vindictive*. She had long gone and no one knew what to do with me. I attended a wardroom guest night in the barracks with band, mess undress, five courses and the Loyal Toast. This seemed a reasonable prelude to hostilities. I sat next to a midshipman from the Royal Indian Navy who had just finished his small ship time in a Chatham destroyer. He surprised me by saying that he had spent two nights that week laying mines off the North German coast.

The forenoon found me hanging about the wardroom and reading the magazines. The next move is recorded in a letter to my mother I found after my father's death. It ended: 'My papers have just come through. I am to join H.M.S. *Revenge*, a battleship, at Portland as soon as possible. I shall have lunch first.'

Nine hours later, and separated from my kit, I arrived at Portland to join the Fleet.

I could see her at a buoy in the half light while I waited for a boat. Next to her was *Resolution*, her sister ship, wearing the flag of the Rear-Admiral Third Battle Squadron. I was taken by the midshipman of the watch through the 6-in battery. The guns were surrounded by dwarf walls to contain the sea which came through the casemates in heavy weather. Each gun's crew lived within the walls, beside the ready use ammunition. The gundeck was a mass of seamen and marines round the mess tables, generating noise and smoke. I had *Victory* in my mind's eye. Muzzle loaders had given way to breech loaders, wooden walls to armour plate, but the men still ate and slept around the guns and dreamt of the girls they had left behind them.

I ate a solitary late dinner in the gunroom and one of my entry already there showed me round. He brought the good news that our pay had been increased 400% from 1 September, the day we were appointed to a ship of the Fleet. It was now four shillings a day.

It was too dark to see much of the upper deck. I was shown the midshipmen's flat where we stored our kit in five-drawer chests. We slept where we could in hammocks, as in the training cruiser, with the luxury here of a seaman boy to sling, lash and stow it for us. I felt honoured to be in the belly of this great steel whale, her name redolent with the bloody history of my country.

The first *Revenge*, under Drake, fought the Spanish in the Armada and was lost fighting them again under Grenville at the Azores. Another *Revenge* was in the lee column at Trafalgar where she had 28 killed and 51 wounded, including her captain.

My ship was the ninth *Revenge*, the third of the five R-class battleships laid down in 1913–14 and marginally the fastest, having achieved 21.9 knots on her trials. Her record was unsurpassed by the others. At Jutland she fired 102 15-in and 87 6-in shells at the enemy, an achievement only exceeded by *Marlborough* among the heavy ships of the main force. She engaged *Derfflinger* and *Von Der Tann* with 15-in and *Wiesbaden* with 6-in. She fired a torpedo at *Von Der Tann* which missed, and avoided 5 torpedoes aimed at her by enemy destroyers; 2 passed within thirty yards. One hit her but did not explode. She landed five 15-in shells on *Derfflinger*, four of which were of the kind that turn the scales. The first put out Y turret and killed the seventy-five in the crew. The second hit X turret, filled the engine room with gas and killed all the turret crew except six. The third and fourth hits devastated the main and quarter decks. The fifth passed harmlessly through her funnel. The second hit was the only one from the Grand Fleet during the battle to penetrate the armour on a German ship and burst inside.

The hit on the *Von Der Tann* landed on her armoured conning tower and killed or wounded the whole of the crew.

Between the wars she had been flagship in the Mediterranean, one of the twelve capital ships upon which the security of the British Empire depended. She was now nearly 25 years old and vulnerable, not only to submarine and air attack, but also to the latest German heavy ships, who could outrange and outrun her. For underwater protection she had waterline bulges which could not save her from an explosion under her hull; her air defence depended on eight .5-in machine-guns firing solid bullets for close range, and eight high-angle 4-in guns with manual fuze setting for high level attacks. Her fire control system was unmodernized.

In appearance she had a squat ferocity evolved over four centuries by the warship builders. The eight 15-in guns were moulded into her in two turrets forward and two aft. She was honeycombed with watertight doors and armoured hatches to enable her to survive another Jutland. The Captain fought her from the compass platform, an open bridge some seventy feet above the water line. The main and secondary armament was directed from the spotting top thirty feet higher with auxiliary control from an armoured Gunnery Control Tower above B turret. When the directors were knocked out the armament was designed to go into local control with the guns crews taking over the spotting and range correction as well as serving the guns. It was all glorious stuff with a 400 year pedigree. It might still work with but one proviso; the Germans had to play the game and fight from the surface and not over or under it.

Twelve hundred of us, nearly all regulars then, kept her going and we, too, had a long pedigree. Our organization was readily comparable with a 74-gun eighteenth-century line-of-battle ship. The command at all levels was the exclusive prerogative of the military, or executive branch, officers. They wore no colour betweeen the gold lace on their sleeves and were not slow to acknowledge, correctly, that they ran the show. Unlike officers of the military branches in the Army and Air Force, the naval executive officer in a big ship took no more risks in battle than his brother engineers and paymasters. His status was, however, that of the Gentleman compared with the Player.

Executive officers only were able to sit upon courts martial or award punishments. The highest ranks and membership of the the the Board of Admiralty were reserved to them. They enjoyed all the key jobs on the Naval Staff, except that of Secretary. They exercised an exclusive right to command, both ashore and afloat. It was a Bourbon system which encouraged many of the thicker ones to believe that their function entitled them to the status they enjoyed, however limited their ability.

A serious attempt was made to bring in the changes needed after the Great War but it was stifled. The officer structure bore some responsibility for the failure of the Navy to move with the times and prepare for both world wars; it discouraged change and led to bizarre results. By 1914 an admiral I served told me that executive officers could be divided into three groups. The first was inefficient through drink, the second regarded the Navy as a yacht club and the third provided the professionals to run it. Unfortunately, the professionals were unable to take care of everything. Thus no Naval Staff existed until 1910 because no need was seen for one. In 1939 the German gunnery, armour and ammunition were still much better than ours. The Fleet had no effective air defence until 1942. Communications suffered because the archaic flag lieutenant system encouraged the socially inclined into the signal branch and our cyphering was a joke. Anti-submarine warfare, upon which the nation's survival depended on two occasions within thirty years, was largely avoided by the high flyers. The whole caboodle had become hidebound.

Roskill attributes blame for this to the system of training naval cadets at Osborne and Dartmouth. Nearly all the senior officers in the Navy in 1939 had been through this mill . . .

> which forced cadets into pre-conceived and rigid moulds by the application of harsh, even inhuman discipline. Any signs of originality or independence were severely frowned on—if not actively suppressed; while intellectual accomplishments always came a bad second to athletics . . . it was not surprising . . . this system should have stifled any tendency to show originality.
>
> (*Earl Beatty* pp 21–22)

Dartmouth produced the best junior naval officers in the world;

in Whitehall, however, it was not the best preparation for taking on men like Churchill and Trenchard.

The signal 'Winston's Back', sent to the Fleet by the Board of Admiralty in September 1939 said it all in two words, with historical illiteracy, political naivety and a clarion call which might have come from a Women's Institute.

The enthusiasm in high places for the return of Winston Churchill to the post of First Lord at the outbreak of war is hard to justify. The First Sea Lord had resigned in 1915 rather than continue to serve him and his Admiralty record was at best controversial, at worst second rate. The Churchills had no connections with the Navy and were resposible for an unforgivable insult to it. In 1802, after receiving the Freedom of the city of Oxford, Nelson, with Sir William and Lady Hamilton, called at Blenheim. A footman was sent to the Admiral's carriage with a message that his party might picnic in the park upon food which would be sent out from the house. They were not invited inside and no member of the family came out to greet the national hero. The visitors left. Churchill was not responsible for the manners of his ancestors; but his record with the Navy was known to all. The Fleet paid the price in Norway, Greece, Crete, Kuantan and the Dodecanese. The public took it all without a murmur. There was a reason.

After Trafalgar the Navy could do no wrong. It had no *Times* correspondent, like Russell with the Army in the Crimea, to tell the world what was happening. It is doubtful whether it would have made a difference if it had. The Senior Service was beyond reproach. Incidents like the sinking of the *Victoria* by the *Camperdown* hardly raised a ripple. To criticize the Navy was to denigrate by association the nation's one true hero, Horatio Nelson; it was near to blasphemy.

Nelson's life had a Messianic pattern. The insignificant body and indifferent health; the years in the wilderness as a junior officer on foreign stations; the sudden conversion, revelation and dedication in the *Dolphin*, frigate, returning home from the East broken by fever. The miraculous battles of St Vincent, the Nile, Copenhagen and Trafalgar; the Band of Brothers, the wounds and scars and the sacrificial death in action. The toast on Trafalgar

Night is 'The Immortal Memory'. He is revered by the Navy with a sublime intensity; with Leonidas and Alexander his name will live for ever. His legacy ensures to this day that the Royal Navy is without blemish in the public eye. As a result some archaic nonsense enjoyed a charmed life.

These reflections were not upon my mind when I began my first day of duty. I reported to the Commander after Both Watches, bare footed in rolled up trousers with sea water swirling round him as the hands scrubbed the quarter deck. He carried a telescope under his arm and seemed feverishly occupied. He expressed pleasure that I had come from *Vindictive* and observed, optimistically, that I had been properly trained.

I reported to the Warrant Stores Officer, a young man in his early thirties who resembled Mr Pickwick. He shared a small office with the senior stores Chief Petty Officer, known by the lower deck as the 'Chief Pusser'. The Chief kept a large ledger, called the 'Pusser's Bible', in longhand. It is possible that the system, except for the change from a quill to a steel pen, had been unaltered since Trafalgar. He recorded in the ledger all the provisions issued each day to the ship's company and their value.

I attended my first grog issue as witnessing officer. It began with a descent into the bowels of the ship to the spirit room. The barrel of Jamaican rum was whisked through the hatches on a whip with me in hot pursuit. The cask was broached and the rum pumped out and thence from one copper jug to another at bewildering speed accompanied by a fast monologue from the Stores Petty Officer. The cooks of the mess were in a queue and the rum was diluted and the grog issued before I could get the hang of what was happening.

The intricacies of rum swindles formed part of lower deck lore and the variants were the stuff of legend. A simple trick was to leave rum in the copper pump and go back for it when the coast was clear. In one ship a means was found of recovering the grog poured down the scuppers at the end of the issue. A gunroom officer witnessing the ceremony provided no real challenge to fraudsters.

On the second day we went to sea with *Resolution* for 15-in firing practice and steamed up and down the Channel about ten miles off Portland Bill. Two days later the process was repeated; there was usually one battleship exercising in the Channel while the Squadron was at Portland. These sorties demonstrated the resolve of the Naval Staff to begin this war precisely like the last by operating capital ships off the south coast, and accepting the submarine risk.

The battleship *Formidable* while exercising in Lyme Bay on 1 January 1915 was torpedoed by U 24 with the loss of 35 officers and 512 men. The enemy was unable to send another U 24 to try her luck in September 1939 but did their best and sent U 26. This boat was stationed off Portland from mid-August to 16 September 1939 when she was recalled with ten other submarines operating round the British Isles, to be re-grouped in the Western Approaches. Happily for the 3rd Battle Squadron, her luck was out.

A ship's company concert was abandoned on the evening of 6 October and both watches were ordered to unload a lighter which had arrived alongside laden with yellow wooden boxes, stated by the Commander to contain margarine. It was apparent from the comments of the working party sweating with the weight that this was margarine of an unusual kind. The cargo was not stowed in a provision room but in the disused submerged torpedo compartment under the midshipmen's chest flat. When the lighter had been emptied and cast off the news was out that this was gold bullion from the Bank of England and we were taking it to Canada.

Accordingly, the 3rd Battle Squadron started its war on 7 October. The Squadron, consisting of *Resolution* wearing the flag of Rear-Admiral Sir Lancelot Holland, *Revenge* and 4 destroyers left Portland and rendezvoused with the 6-in cruisers *Emerald*, *Enterprise* and *Caradoc* with 2 more destroyers, and steered west.

The ship had only been brought up to full complement for the July 1939 Reserve Fleet Review and there had been little opportunity to practise for war, for which we had no sea night routine. At dusk we went to action stations and tried to sort ourselves out until the morning. I shared the Gunnery Control Tower with an able seaman and the Captain's secretary. He was the secondary 6-in Control Officer and I was the secondary 6-in Rate Officer. I had no idea what a rate officer had to do but felt sure that someone would tell me before the enemy appeared. We reduced to defence watches and divided the night between us. This was not a sustainable routine for long periods and thereafter the ship went to cruising stations on passage with only one part of the watch closed up.

The following day provided a full gale with green water over the forecastle and quarterdeck. The ship had not felt the raging of the seas for some time and her new company had not learned the tricks required to keep it out. Water found its way down trunkings into compartments deep inside her. The 6-in batteries were awash with gear of all kinds swimming about in the free surface water. The stinking air below caused seasickness among those who had not found their sea legs.

In the middle of the night we received a message that the pocket battleship *Admiral Hipper* and the heavy cruiser *Koln* had broken through the Northern Patrol in the gale. The Squadron opened out to search for the enemy at dawn but visibility in the heavy weather was poor and the search was called off.

The second night was devoted to an encounter exercise. *Emerald* and *Enterprise* went ahead and approached the battle squadron on opposite course. This was before radar and the weather was thick. Both divisions were in line abreast. *Emerald* appeared out of the murk and the searchlights by the funnel casing went on with a loud sizzle. The cruisers shot past and the show was over. The aircraft carrier *Courageous* had been sunk by U 29 in these waters on 17 September. She was one of eight boats then operating off south-west Ireland.

During the time on passage we shook down into some sort of routine although we had a long way to go to reach a standard for war. At night the Gunroom had to find an alternative to hammocks which got in the way in an emergency and might throw the sleeper out if there was an explosion. All thirty-five gunroom officers, therefore, slept in the mess when off watch. The gunroom was about forty feet long and twelve feet wide with cushioned seats on the outboard side. Some five square feet was taken up by a solid fuel stove with brass fittings. The senior midshipmen took the benches, the Sub-Lieutenant the sofa and the rest of us slept on oilskins on the deck. I found myself under the gunroom table in reasonable comfort. As the months and years went by the junior midshipmen acquired the bench seats and in the end by one means or another no one slept on the deck.

At night cruising stations I kept one watch in four in the cypher office. The Signal Branch had no responsibility for cyphering which fell to the paymasters. We sat in an office in the bridge superstructure and spent the night decyphering signals bought to us from the wireless office below. It was a hand operated system with an unchanged basic book and four figure re-cyphering tables which were altered monthly. After a short while it was easy to remember many of the number groups in the basic book for the words that were in frequent use. The system was elementary and it was unsurprising to learn after the war that the enemy had cracked it at an early stage,

I received instruction in one of the 6-in casemates, with the other control officers, into the duties of a rate officer. The rate of an enemy ship was the angle its course presented relative to our own course. It could vary from zero to red 180 and zero to green 180. The control and rate officers practised for war with a model warship in a frame that resembled a doll's house. The Second Gunnery Officer altered the model's course while the class corrected the fall of shot from the artificial splashes which our instructor simulated by pressing a key. The rate officers estimated the rate angle and we all pretended, with difficulty, that this is what it would be like. I found it hard to remember whether the rate was zero when the enemy was coming straight for us or going straight away. 'Easy', said the Gunner's Mate, 'think of a cat's arse.'

I had an opportunity to practise this esoteric skill during a 15-in throw-off shoot with *Resolution*. She was almost hull down and her rate was hard to guess. It was an odd experience to see the flash, hear the whistle of the salvo and see the shells land in our wake and then hear the sound of the guns.

We arrived at Halifax after a nine day passage. The bullion was checked into railway freight cars with Canadian Mounties watching the loading. Keeping the tally on hundreds of boxes each worth a king's ransom soon becomes tedious. I have not heard from the Treasury for fifty years so have confidence that the ones

I signed for got to their destination. One box slipped out of the hoist and scattered sovereigns over the submerged flat. The working party swept them together, lashed up the box, and hoped for the best.

Revenge carried bullion on five passages to Canada, more than any other warship had ever done so far as is known. The total value was £113½m. The greatest load on any one trip was worth £47m. The weight of it trimmed her down by the stern two feet six inches. Under the old rules codified in 1819 the Captain would have been entitled to claim 1% on the value of the treasure delivered safely by his ship. These rules were not cancelled until an Order in Council dated 26 October 1914. The treasure was not being sent abroad for safety, as we all thought at the time, but to pay for war materials bought in the USA under the Cash and Carry legislation of 1939. The known amount of gold shipped to Canada and the USA up to March 1941 was $931m together with securies of comparable value. The money then ran out and the Lend Lease Act brought to an end the arrangement which enabled the United States to be handsomely paid by the British for the satisfaction of fighting the American corner as well as their own.

Admiral Holland struck his flag on arrival. The North American end of the Atlantic convoy system was based on Halifax and it was his task to command the escorts from there. The Canadians were not excited by the prospect of a British admiral hoisting his flag on Canadian territory. Their feelings were massaged by the device of chartering the steam yacht *Seaborne* and berthing her alongside in Halifax harbour. The Admiral hoisted his flag in the yacht, his staff crowded onboard and the Halifax Escort Force was in business, more or less to everyones satisfaction.

On 24 October 1939, *Revenge* left Halifax as the ocean escort for convoy HX 6. The homeward bound convoys were numbered in sequence after the letters 'HX'. Outward bound convoys from the UK were similiarly numbered with the prefix 'OB'. The merchant ships collected in Bedford Basin, a large anchorage at Halifax. There were over fifty ships in our first convoy and we watched them pass us in their new grey paint. Some had guns but most were unarmed. Two Canadian Tribal class destroyers

honoured our standing as a capital ship for the first two days of
the voyage. There was little their presence could achieve beyond
training. German submarines did not reach Nova Scotia for another two years.

We took station in the middle of the convoy, which received
its orders from the convoy commodore in a ship at the head of a
column. All fifty ships endeavoured to keep station and zig-zag
together to deter submarines. The Navy were used to station-keeping but it was new to the merchantmen who had single screws
and modest power to call upon. All seemed to go pretty well on
that first convoy. The whole show could be wrecked by bad
weather, which made station-keeping something of a lottery. After
a sustained gale it was never certain whether the few ships near
us were the convoy or stragglers from it. Sometimes ships broke
down and were left behind.

We provided the ocean escort for over twenty convoys during
the next twenty months. We were not attacked by air, submarine
or surface vessel. We did not lose a ship and did not see the
enemy. It was our task to defend the merchantmen against German heavy ships. *Scharhorst*, *Gneisenau* and the pocket battleships
were in the Atlantic during this period. We developed a routine;
the ship left Canada and escorted the convoy to twenty degrees
west and then came back alone. The Canadian destroyers saw us
out and in. The crew of the boomgate vessels politely formed up
on the upper deck as we passed both ways. Each trip took between
two and three weeks. Most of it was monotonous and unexciting.

The crew of *Revenge* settled down as the ship worked up. In the
gunroom the Sub-Lieutenant ruled absolutely under customs established for generations. In harbour his bath was run by the Duty
Midshipman, known as 'the Duty Boy'. Thirty-three of us shared
two baths. When the temperature was exactly right, the Sub was
called and told that it awaited him. By custom he had the right
to beat midshipmen, and did so on at least one occasion when he
found a junior midshipman in a wrestling bout with a gunroom
steward. The punishment was carried out in the gunroom bathroom. Our Sub filled his Byzantine role with effortless ascendancy.
His authority over a potentially mutinuous mob was unquestioned.
It had nothing to do with rank or his charm and dark good looks;

he was a natural leader. When the Sub had something to say the racket stopped until he had said it. When he embarked upon a story we all listened. I do not remember one reference to the war, which seemed to have escaped his notice. He came from a family of generals and admirals and for his kind active service was unremarkable. He indulged in a running skirmish with the Captain; the midshipmen of the watch kept us abreast of these exchanges. In social terms the Sub and the Captain were Fletcher Christian and Bligh. He grew his hair at sea until it reached his collar and the Captain had to say something.

'Sub, do you intend to get a haircut before we return to harbour?'

'Yes, sir. I find that it is best to wait until it is hard to get my cap on.'

This was dangerous stuff but he got away with it.

The Captain was a large man who knew his job backwards and flattered his officers by assuming that they did too. He ascended from his day cabin to the quarter deck just before we left harbour dressed in sea boots, an old cap and a duffel coat. On the way to the bridge, and his sea cabin where he would stay for the next two weeks, he went out of his way to talk to everyone he met on his trudge forward. He wanted to be seen before he was obliged by his responsibility for the lives of all of us to be shut away in the superstructure round the bridge until we came back. The process was reversed on return to harbour when he was always in the best of moods and beamed with pleasure on his journey aft. He was nearing fifty and knew that these were the best years of his life. When the ship had shaken down she was happy and efficient and it all came from him.

He regarded defaulters with official contempt and saw the cases of absence over leave and drunkenness on the second day at sea, sitting in his duffel coat at a table outside his sea cabin. He had an abrupt and frightening way with old lags. While the Commander, Master-at-Arms and the divisional officers waited to hear the sentence, and the defaulter in bare-headed humility told himself that whatever happened now it had been a good idea at the time, the Captain called for the man's Service Certificate and wrote on the back of it in pencil in silence. He then pushed the document under the defaulter's nose. 'See that? Warrant next time!' The threat was against the rules but it worked. A warrant punishment was cells or worse, a permanent entry on the record and to be avoided. Discipline was excellent despite the harpies and the drink in Halifax.

He was proud of his ship and her company but seemed embarrassed to admit it. In the early days we attended Sunday morning service in Halifax Cathedral. Eight hundred officers and men marched in divisions through the seaport streets. We were a fine sight and the Captain, who was not marching, wanted to see us go by. Every time the leading division came up to him at the side of the road the order 'Eyes left' or 'Eyes right' was given. His embarrassment was intense and he waved his hand at the officer in charge to prevent attention being paid to him. He then disappeared and was sighted a few street corners ahead trying to watch us without being noticed.

He held extreme tactical views. He confided one night to the watch officers that he would like to take her into Hamburg to sink everything we could before they put paid to us. It had been proposed by Churchill that the R-class should be used on some such ride to destruction.

On one occasion when it was known that the pocket battleship *Scheer* was at sea, he cleared lower deck and announced that if we met her he intended to overcome the disadvantage of being outranged by sudden turns towards the enemy, with the object of using our ram to sink her if we could get close enough. From that moment he was known by all as 'Rammer'.

Despite his unsophistication he was well aware that he commanded 1,200 men who expected to sink German warships and spent their days wallowing about with convoy after convoy of merchantmen. He had to keep their expectations high and he knew how to do it. We wanted to serve him and the ship and both things seemed the same.

After our second convoy the Commander had a breakdown through overwork and was sent home. At sea at night he never turned in and went rounds of the ship every hour. Happily he recovered. He became a Commander-in-Chief after the war.

The battle cruiser *Repulse* entered harbour too fast shortly before we left for our third trip and the scend from her wash parted our wires and made her unpopular. She made peace by offering us fifty lifebelts in exchange for fifty tin hats. We had plenty of the latter but none of the former so the deal was struck.

The cruiser *York* left for Bermuda and a swarthy Air Branch officer arrived in the gunroom, having missed his ship on sailing. 'What is that brown job doing in the mess?' the Sub asked the Senior Midshipman. He was told that the visitor had been left behind. 'Someone had better put him on a train.'

The Australian lieutenant in charge of the midshipmen decided that the flesh pots of Halifax might be debilitating and ordered early morning physical training. On the second day three failed to get a shake and arrived late. When the PT was over and we came back on board, breathing easily after jumping over box horses in the shed, the Australian, who was on watch, decided to show who was boss. Warm and comfortable in his greatcoat he ordered us over the mainmast, guilty and innocent alike. The Canadian winter had started, with snow and ice everywhere.

We raced for the mast in gymn shoes, shorts and singlet. I happened to be nearest and first to start the climb. The iron ladder to the truck was simple enough but the wire rope ladder to the topmast was slimy with soot and ice and I was obliged to proceed with caution while the sweat froze and the Snotties' Nurse diminished in size on the quarter deck miles below. I heard the shouts and curses of my messmates clustered in shivering misery at the foot of the mast and unable to climb it until I came down. They were indifferent to my problems and content to see me fall if that meant they could get started and out of the cold. There were at least fifteen of them and the last one over must have been stiff before he started the climb. The general view at breakfast was that the Australian should be court-martialled for attempted murder.

A court martial of another kind was held in December. The Captain presided over the trial of an emergency list lieutenant-commander from one of the armed merchant cruisers in the Escort Force. Proceedings on the day opened with the firing of one round from the court martial gun to salute the President and arouse proper trepidation in the Fleet, hoisting of the Jack at the masthead and parading of the guard. The accused was brought in by the Officer of the Court with drawn sword and the Circumstantial Letter and Charge Sheet read by the Officiating Deputy Judge Advocate. This part of the trial involved a ritual of putting on and taking off hats which had to be observed with precision, the Paymaster acting as Officiating Deputy Judge Advocate whispering the drill into the President's ear.

The Gunroom off watch were directed to attend in the Captain's Day Cabin, where the trial was held, in order to further their education. Naval Law was part of our job so the three paymaster cadets expected to be there. The rest regarded it as a chore and would have made excuses for sliding off had the presence of the Captain not deterred them. All that changed when the Circumstantial Letter and Charge Sheet were read. The case was about an indecent assault upon an RNR midshipman. The accused was alleged to have gone to his cabin and awakened him with a rain of passionate kisses. The absorption of the Gunroom in the proceedings became total. The Captain was horrified. He stopped the trial and ordered the midshipmen out, save for the three of us who were there to fulfill an unpleasant duty. The Young Gentlemen had to be protected from such things. It mattered not that most of them had lived in an all male society away from home since the age of eight and heard Lower Deck talk every day of their service. They left with glum faces and waited for us to pass the word.

The accused was dismissed the Service and a boat from his ship came to take him away. He was seen over the side by one of the junior Dartmouth midshipmen who stood silently with his telescope under his arm to watch him leave. He was a tycoon in private life and not prepared to go quietly.

'I am waiting for your salute,' he said when he reached the top of the gangway.

'You are not entitled to one,' said the Mid.

On 21 December we left Halifax wearing the flag of Rear-Admiral Holland, as ocean escort for the second Canadian troop convoy. This time the freighters and oilers were replaced by seven ocean liners. The French battlecruiser *Dunkerque* and cruiser *Gloire* joined the escort for seven days. We did not give up as usual at twenty degrees west but went all the way to the Clyde. On Christmas Day an intrepid soldier in one of the transports shinned up the topmast in a gale to secure a Christmas tree to the masthead.

In the gunroom we listened to the King's broadcast. When the National Anthem was played the Sub, looking self conscious, stood up and the rest of us did the same. Nothing was said.

We had been given a stock of warm clothing by the Canadian Red Cross. The 4-in guns' crews and lookouts were to be seen in woolly hats, leather gloves and sheepskin coats when dawn broke the second day. After the usual blue greatcoats and round caps they looked warm, cheerful and convivial. This lasted until the Admiral arrived on the bridge. He was a gunnery officer by specialization and did not appreciate the tableaux. The Red Cross clothing came off and did not appear again while he was onboard.

We met thick and persistent fog, an ordeal for the Navigating Officer who had to rely on dead reckoning and soundings as we neared the Irish coast. The eleven Fleet destroyers of the escort appeared through the gloom and the convoy entered the Firth of Clyde as the fog lifted.

The Captain used the exchange of signals at the end of our escort duty to remind the soldiers what it was all about.

Revenge from *Duchess of Bedford*

On behalf of all ranks Canadian contingent onboard S.S. *Duchess of Bedford* and *Antonia* permit me to express our warmest thanks for your watchful care and sure protection during our voyage across the Atlantic. May the best of luck attend you.

Duchess of Bedford from *Revenge*

Very many thanks. It is our privilege to have such an important and model convoy. May the best of fortune be yours and may there be many notches on those rifle butts when the time comes to make the return trip.

For the veterans of 1914–18 the only good German remained a dead one.

The ship had some urgent defects and was overdue for a boiler clean. We entered the floating dock at Devonport on New Year's

Day 1940 for the work to be done. On the same day the three of us were rated Paymaster Midshipmen, four months ahead of the expected date, and our pay increased again, from four shillings to five shillings a day. We were on to a good thing.

CHAPTER 4

GUNROOM DAYS

Plymouth had some experience of the Navy and its needs. A Gunroom run ashore meant The Steam Reserve and the Duchess, an Edwardian lady who had seen a lot of the passing show. Her public house had not changed its style for a generation and once inside its convivial womb young men found it hard to leave. At the Hotel Royal drinks in the long bar were served by an enchanting blonde called Helen whom we adored from afar. Among the familiar faces was the cadet who towed us back from Sark, serving in the 'J' class destroyer in which he was to be lost.

Towards closing time the bar became solid with naval officers, with air force aircrew here and there. I do not remember many soldiers. We had an outrageous arrogance towards the others because we believed we were the only Service in the same league as the Germans. Army officers were 'brown jobs' or 'pongos' and the Air Force 'Brylcreem boys'. We welcomed onboard midshipmen from the engineering college at Keyham, sharing their dismay at the years of shore training before them.

There was a big change round in officers. The Navigating Officer became acting Commander, the navigation being taken over by an officer from *Adventure*, a minelayer, in drydock with a hole in her side big enough for a bus. The Sub left to begin a distinguished career in motor torpedo boats. The senior Mids went to their courses for sub-lieutenant. We got our first dead beat. A 'dead beat' was a retired officer brought back for the war. Thus reinforced, refreshed and repaired we left Devonport with another cargo of bullion and arrived at Halifax on 5 February 1940.

Our next convoy was ready two days later and we left in fog. I was in the chest flat and felt the ship shudder to port. We had collided with the 9,000 ton oiler *Appalachee*, from Trinidad loaded with benzine. The ships met on opposite courses, starboard bow to starboard bow and predictably the merchantman came off worst. Our starboard anchor opened up her forecastle in a shower of flame and rust. Happily for both of us, and for Halifax harbour, the ships parted before the oiler's foremost tank was punctured.

The damage to *Revenge* was evident. About twenty feet of her forecastle was open to the weather and the upper deck littered with debris from the other ship. Our sheet anchor had been carried away and the starboard bower bent. We increased speed for the entrance, intent upon our affairs. The ship was always wet forward and the water now had an easy way in. Luckily there was a following wind and sea and no heavy weather. We reported the collision and our intention to proceed, while the Warrant Ship-wright assessed the damage. It was unlikely that the Captain ever contemplated a return to harbour, whatever the technical findings. The shipwrights worked night and day to stop the leaks and we went as usual to twenty degrees west, returning to Halifax on 19 February, none the worse. It took two weeks for essential repairs.

Appalachee was put together at Halifax but her luck ran out on 1 December 1940 south of Greenland when HX 90 was attacked by a pack of seven submarines, with U 99 and Kretschmer, the bravest of the brave. *Appalachee* and ten others were sunk, including *Forfar* the armed merchant cruiser providing the ocean escort. Armed merchant cruisers were no match for submarines, or the surface warships they were likely to meet, and it was unclear why they were there.

HX 24, 30 and 36 were shepherded across without incident except for a storm. We were used to gales with the ship taking green seas onboard and rolling about in drunken impotence. Nevertheless, if one had to be in the North Atlantic in winter, a 30,000 ton battleship was as good a place as any. Because she ploughed on regardless the sailors called her the Halliwagon and were thankful for the comfort she provided.

This time there was too much for her to shake it all off and the steep Atlantic swept her from stem to stern. The forward 15-in were trained aft, presenting the back of the turret to the storm. The water came green over the fo'cstle round A turret gunhouse, some 120 tons, and lifted it. The startled crew heard it thump back on to its rollers. The hurricane wind whipped a sea into the window in the spotting top, 100 feet above the water line, and broke it. The 4-in gun deck and the boats got the worst. The iron ladders from the upper deck were carried away and the boats shifted out of their crutches and pounded. The forward part of the gun deck was twisted upwards and the guns could not be manned; although lifelines were rigged no one was allowed on the upper deck. The underground journey was by way of watertight doors and armoured hatches shut in second degree of readiness.

It was possible to stand up and face the storm on the bridge decks by ducking and holding tightly to the guardrails. The wind flattened the wave crests and the sea was white with flying spume. Conversation was reduced to shouting. The convoy largely vanished.

It was worse for the enemy. German Type VII C submarines were expected to remain on the surface in the North Atlantic. In a storm in February 1943, U 653 lost the whole of the conning tower watch of an officer and four lookouts.

The executive midshipmen were shorthanded until the reliefs joined and I helped out as midshipman in charge of the twenty lookouts at night; my eyesight was disregarded. Later on I became Midshipman of the Watch. Performance was judged by the ability to make cocoa for the three bridge officers, and write up the decklog. My contribution was appreciated by my messmates because they enjoyed an extra night in. One Mid asked me to shake him just before midnight, when I was taking his watch, to remind him that he did not have to turn out for the middle.

After the storm a heavy swell made her roll extravagantly. A thunderclap proclaimed that the wooden main topmast had carried away, being old and no doubt weary of the endless to-and-froing in the weather, added to the indignity of being climbed by idle midshipmen. The mast was taller than that of any of our sister ships, being a relic of her days when she wore the flag of the Commander-in-Chief Mediterranean. It fell aft on to the high angle control director, occupied in defence stations by a lieutenant and petty officer sitting side by side. The mast crushed the rangefinder and came to rest exactly between the two of them. Neither was scratched, though surprised.

The Sambro Light Vessel, marking the approaches to Halifax, broke adrift in the storm and entered harbour in company astern of us.

In harbour the Gunroom dined the Captain. After dinner he took over the sofa in the senior end of the mess and told a yarn about his young days in a sloop which rode out a hurricane by passing a wire round the dockyard boatswain's house. The story came from Bartimeus but he told it well and we hesitated to ask whether he had got it from the author or the author had got it from him.

The Captain liked a good yarn. He read Hornblower novels at sea and talked about the characters to the bridge watch. The word was that he saw himself as the Captain of a 74, ready to order the Commander to beat the hands to quarters and have the guns run out. The make believe ended there. The reality was that he would not have hesitated to take his ship headlong into action, whatever the odds, willing to sacrifice each and every one of us if he thought that his duty required it. That part of his job had not changed since the first *Revenge*.

The Halifax Escort Force was now commanded by Rear-Admiral Bonham-Carter who, as a lieutenant, had taken a block ship into Zeebrugge in 1918. Lower deck was cleared and the ship's company braced themselves for an exhortation to battle from their Admiral, accommodated like Cardigan in the Crimea, in a yacht.

He told us that he hoped we would soon have a chance to hit that bugger Hitler for six. Our only opportunity to cause Hitler problems arose in an action with a surface raider. *Schharnhorst* and *Gneisenau* were in dockyard hands after torpedo hits in Norway. *Bismarck* and *Tirpitz* were fitting out. *Prinz Eugen* was completing. *Hipper* tried a break out later in the year but had to return with engine trouble. *Admiral Scheer* also had engine trouble. The ring was empty of opponents. After an early attempt at a pack operation by six submarines in the North Atlantic, the main German effort stayed in Norway until the French bases were taken in June. These were dog days for everybody.

The Admiral and his staff challenged us to cricket. It was a bold move because we had a 1,200 men to pick from. The first four of the staff were out without delay. The Admiral was next, dressed in a bright cap with a strong belt round his middle. It did not seem cricket to fire away at such a nice old gent and I bowled him my slower one. It raced past mid-off to the boundary before the fielder could bend, let alone stop it. I put my all into the next, which went back over my head for six. He made fifty and walked out to give someone else a chance. We found out that he had been a county cricketer.

I was moved to the ship's pay office to get a ledger certificate, an essential step for an officer of my specialization. The pay account of everyone onboard was kept in the ship and sent to the Director of Navy Accounts for audit at the end of each quarter. The system was hallowed by use and no one thought it should be changed. Although small ships, without specialists, got on well enough with accounts on shore or in the depot ship, cruisers and above took the whole works with them, enabling everyone to know at any time exactly how he stood financially with the Admiralty. The disadvantage, apart from tying up space and effort in offices, was that chaos followed the loss of the ship. The pay records went down with her and the next of kin might have to wait months for the ledgers to be reconstructed ashore before they were paid what was owed to them.

After *Royal Oak* was lost Their Lordships became inspired. Big ships were directed to make ready a metal canister with a water-tight lid held on with four butterfly nuts. When the ship was hard hit the ledgers went into the canister and the Paymaster Commander, if able to do so, fulfilled his last duty and accompanied it into the water. I am confident that the big ship paymasters I knew would have risked their lives to carry out this tragi-comical task. They were aware of the pay and conditions on the lower deck and would have done their best to mitigate the hardship caused by an archaic system. It was not all gloom. I served with one paymaster captain, sunk at Crete, who found himself in the water with the ledger in its floating chrysalis, and having no lifebelt, was glad of it.

The summer was upon us and the Gunroom had two idyllic days in a rest camp by a lake near Halifax. The forest stretched unbroken northwards to the tundra. The water was warm and we swam all day and forgot the real world.

The fun was interrupted for a Mid from a Dominion Navy who had a brief encounter with a sporting amateur and developed clap. This was before penicillin and the victim had an uncomfortable course of treatment as well as the opprobrium of having a malady not stictly permitted to officers. A surgeon lieutenant was sent to the gunroom to restore order. He brought a set of genito-urinary instruments and laid them on the green baize cloth of the gunroom table. We looked in silent horror at the shiny probes and clamps. It was an old trick, but not ineffective, and our indifference was pretended. He reminded us that while the love diseases could be caught from lavatory seats, that peril was restricted to three social classes—Admirals of the Fleet, one's own relations and learned members of the clergy. The joke helped, but not a lot.

On 12 May we left for our sixth Atlantic convoy of that year, carrying Canadian troops in the liners *Duchess of Bedford* and *Antonia*. We led the way out of harbour in heavy rain and low visibility and worked up to 12 knots with the destroyer escort astern. A cable or so from the entrance it became apparent that the boom had not been opened. We never learned why. Full speed astern was ordered while the Captain considered the options. Stopping a battleship at 12 knots in the 200 yards between the ship and the boom was not one of them. She would never do it. He could charge the boom and hope that the screws would not be meshed in the net as our massive bulk took us through and over it; he could go for the boom gate vessel itself, being the softest target and the one likely to cause least damage to the ship, accepting that by so doing he might kill her crew.

His duty was to get *Revenge* to sea and escort the convoy behind him. He pointed her for the boom gate vessel. She was called *Ypres* and had a crew of twelve. As we got closer it was apparent that the boom had started to open and in an endeavour to find the narrow gap twenty degrees of port wheel was put on. The wheel was then put hard a starboard to straighten up, but she was going full astern and would not answer. A hand on *Ypres* upper deck got the message and yelled a warning to those below. The ship was about fifty yards away before they all came up. We had sailed at dusk and the light had almost gone. We saw two dive over the side and swim for the nearest buoy in the net. Mercifully we did not hit her head on with the ram which would have sent her to the bottom in seconds. Our stem glanced along her starboard side and heeled her over to port, carrying her along in front of us before she slipped away. It was an oblique blow which laid her on her beam ends. As she heeled over and filled the massive weight of the net slowed us up and gave her people a chance to save their lives before she sank. They all got away except one who became trapped somewhere between the two hulls. He was hauled to safety by one of our able seamen who had to lean right out over the ship's side to reach him. He survived, with eleven others who were taken to the sick bay and put ashore in a motor boat which had come out for them. The boat was well equipped with wardroom whisky and brandy to fortify them in their ordeal. *Ypres* sank with a sigh and we were clear and undamaged. The destroyers and the convoy followed us through the hole. Thereafter the crews of the boomgate vessels at Halifax gave up falling in to see us in and out of harbour.

Back in the Clyde, the cruiser *Penelope* was anchored near by, damaged by a rock in Norway. A French destroyer with her bows blown off by one of her own torpedoes made a dismal wreck. One of our boats recovered a body risen to the surface after three weeks below and the bowman manoeuvred it gently alongside with a boathook.

We were not allowed ashore in plain clothes and wore a cap and reefer with our flannels, even when on the way to play games. There were not enough service revolvers to go round and the Gunroom were encouraged to find their own sidearms when going on leave, so that we could play our part in repulsing the infantry and parachutists of the *Wehrmacht* in the unimaginable event of invasion. Some odd weapons appeared in the chest flat, from a long barrelled .22 rat pistol to a 9 mm Luger.

The summer of 1940 seems now to have been all sunshine; we had two days' leave from the Clyde. Mine was enlivened by the presence of my favourite cousin, to whom I explained that the war had not really started, but we were ready and willing in case it did. She assured me that whatever the Germans might do to me it had to be worth joining for the uniform.

The journey back to Glasgow was interminable. I wandered round Birmingham waiting for a connection. A well-dressed woman stopped me and asked whether I did not think it terrible the way the Belgians had let us down. It did not seem to matter very much to me, but before I could reply, she told me that her brother was a commander who had taken part in the Narvik battles and how wonderful we all were. She held my arm and wished me good luck. As she went away I saw that she was crying.

The boatswain and I were the only passengers in the boat. He was sitting on the starboard side aft and I was standing, looking at the ship. It was about an hour before sunset. I remember these details because I have not forgotten our short conversation.

'The bastards have done it,' the boatswain said.

'Done what? I have been in a train all day.'

'The Jerries have reached Boulogne.'

I suggested he had got it wrong. He told me that he had heard it from the Warrant Telegraphist, who had seen an intercepted signal. I knew then that it must be true and the brown jobs were in trouble. For the first time it occurred to me that the British Empire might not be able to win them all.

We left the Clyde on 30 May with bullion again and a fast convoy of the liners *Antonia* and *Duchess of Richmond*, carrying children to North America. We arrived in Halifax on 8 June and sailed three days later with another fast troop convoy for the Clyde. The band played 'Roll Out The Barrel' as usual, and as usual the troops massed on the upper decks of the transports cheering like mad. All concerned were now used to the routine.

In the Irish Sea *Revenge* broke off and arrived at Devonport on 21 June with little fuel left. The ship went to a buoy in the Hamoaze and I was sent ashore in the first boat, with the postman, carrying a personal letter from the Captain to the Chief of Staff to the Commander-in-Chief Plymouth. I was told to wait for the answer. It was a request to give leave and everyone knew it although the Captain had written the letter in his own hand. Information of that kind travelled with laser speed and no one knew how it happened.

Posty and I had to jump from the lower gangway grating into the boat because the ship was high out of the water. Her boot-topping was streaked with rust and weed and the bulges looked fat enough to walk on.

I delivered my letter and sat on a chair in the Admiral's office to await the reply, while two paymaster lieutenant-commanders worked on heaps of paper. Occasionally they spoke to each other. I waited there for about an hour and a half and they neither looked at, nor spoke to me. Midshipmen did not seriously exist. In later years I served with both of them and knew them to be charming and friendly men. The Chief of Staff wrote the answer and I sprinted back to the boat leaving the two staff officers to their writing. The answer was yes; four days to each watch.

We went alongside to fuel and begin the disembarkation of 15-in cordite, an essential step before going into dockyard hands. The harbour was cluttered with merchant ships who had straggled across the Channel before the German tide. The old battleship *Paris* had arrived from Brest, where I had seen her a year before; she was secured to a buoy with the submarine *Surcouf* alongside. *Surcouf* was then the largest submarine in the world, designed for commerce raiding. She displaced 4,300 tons and was armed with two 8-in guns, ten torpedo tubes, two 37 mm AA guns and an aeroplane. Her designed speed on the surface was 18 knots and 10 knots submerged. She had a range at 10 knots of 10,000 miles and a diving limit of over 400 feet. These were figures handed out by the French and were regarded with scepticism by our submarine service, particularly the claim that her great gasometer of a hull could be got under water in two minutes.

The Gunroom roared ashore and renewed its acquaintance with the Duchess and Helen. The shortage of trained seamen for the new ships coming forward cost us the crews of one of the two 6-in batteries. They filed over the side into the dockyard boat with their kitbags and hammocks, laughing and joking, the best of the nation, long service RN ratings from a happy ship. I honour the memory of those who did not see the end.

The Gunnery Officer decided that the Young Gentlemen needed instruction in the use of sidearms, to be ready if the invasion caught them on leave. The training was a day's pistol course, not to be compared with the indoctrination given to a trooper in the Grossdeutschland, but it was a start.

On a bright June day we marched through the dockyard, taking it in turns to pull a handcart with the Smith and Wesson revolvers, ammunition, lunch and beer. The party was in the charge of the Director Gunner. In the absence of higher authority, warrant officers could be said to be on our side, and we made the best of the day out. We fired off most of the ammunition before a long lunch in the range hut, while the Gunner entertained us with stories and repartee, the fruits of his years on the lower deck.

> Simple Simon met a pieman
> On the way home from the fair,
> Said Simple Simon to the pieman,
> 'Prithee Sir, what is your ware?'
> 'Pies, you daft bugger.'

On the march home, being cock-a-hoop, we sang.

> A poor old man
> Walked up and down
> To see what he could find in town.
> He came unto an eating place
> And entered in with humble grace.
> The bill of fare he scanned it through,
> To see what three halfpence could do.
> He beckoned to a waiter tall, and said
> 'I'll have sir, just one fish ball.'
> The waiter bawled back through the hall
> 'You get no bread with one fish ball.'
> The poor old man then went outside
> And shot himself and so he died.
> The moral is for one and all,
> You get no bread with one fish ball.

The streets seemed empty. The sun shone. The future would take care of itself. We were Lords of the Earth.

CHAPTER 5

THE FRENCH AFFAIR

Leave expired on 2 July 1940 and we were ready to go next day. The short refit had seen our damaged bow repaired and bullet proof shields fitted round the 4-in guns. We now had Sound Reproduction Equipment ('Tannoy' in the vernacular). Orders would no longer have to be piped by seaman call boys peregrinating the mess decks and flats as had been the custom for generations.

The armada in the dockyard had thinned out. *Revenge* lay alongside in No. 5 Basin with the River class submarine, *Thames*, outside her. *Paris* was on the opposite wall with *Surcouf* alongside. This symmetry might have put us on enquiry, but except for noting the generosity of the King's Harbour Master in giving plum berths to the French, we saw no significance in the moves.

It was a still summer evening. Three stokers in overalls were fooling about on the casing of *Thames* and one ended in the water. Some of us went ashore while we could and came back to find the gunroom in a bustle. *Revenge* had to provide seamen and Royal Marines to take *Paris* that night, while another of our platoons, led by the Captain of *Thames*, with officers and ratings from that submarine, would take *Surcouf*.

While the boarding went on the ship would go to general quarters with X turret closed up and ready to fire on the French battleship. The range was 300 yards; if the magazines in *Paris* were exploded, the effect on the dockyard and Devonport would be cataclysmic. Our guns would be loaded but their function restricted to repeated elevation and depression, in the hope of intimidating the French. It was that sort of plan. It must have been the first robbery under arms with 15-in guns.

The orders required one sailor in three to carry a loaded rifle

45

and stand clear while the other two, with unloaded rifles and bayonets fixed, shook the matelots, using enough force to get them out of their hammocks and on to the jetty. The language problem was diminished by introducing the boarding party to a few phrases; *levez*, to turn them out, and *montez sur le quai*, to get them ashore. Midshipmen were to be called at 0130 to shake the officers. A handwritten note from the Commander was given to each officer to be read to the ship's company when they mustered in the port 6-in battery.

To be read when lower deck has been cleared
The ship will not sail this morning.
Reason for early call is that we have been ordered to board the French ships in the hope that they will agree to remain pro-Ally.
Boarding is to take place at dawn to-day and owing to the shortness of notice and the absolute necessity for surprise it is essential that all hands should pay the most careful attention to their orders.
Silence is the watchword till we get on board.
We have to board the *Paris* and the S/M *Surcouf.*
The Captain will go first and will ask the Admiral in the *Paris* to comply with our wishes.
Simultaneously our parties will board and will take charge. Some will take charge of the upper deck, guns and bridges, some will go below and some will call the officers and men and order them to fall in on the jetty. They will be marched up to the barracks.
It is necessary that great politeness should be observed but at the same time you must be firm. It is hoped that force will not be needed but you must be prepared to meet resistance.
While our parties are boarding, the remainder of the ship's company will be at action stations. NO NOISE before they go on board.
Avoid provocation and excitement.
Dress for all hands, Night Clothing and boots or shoes.
You will now fall in by platoons and parties for equipment and orders.

Rifles, bayonets, cutlasses, steel helmets and revolvers were handed out. We were not at war with the French but we had been told to attack them and that was that.

The gunnery staff had been hard at it producing orders and

equipment in the few hours' notice they had been given. There was a list of the platoons and the executive officers and midshipmen who would lead them. I decided that it was the moment to call in a debt.

I found the second G in the starboard 6-in battery surrounded by his minions. He was an approachable and popular officer who was killed in *Penelope* at Malta the following year. I reminded him that I played the games at his spotting table and he put me on the list as First Lieutenant's doggy. A 'doggy' was a junior officer attached to a superior to run errands and be useful.

The First Lieutenant had the forecastle party detailed to clear the forward end of *Paris*. He was a tall, spare officer with a red face and a taciturn manner. At sea he stumped around the upper deck in leather seaboots, and as a non-specialist nearing his last shot for promotion, seemed a real sailor, misjudged in a navy run by the Staff.

The platoon practised their French while we waited; some added a few words of their own, reducing the proceedings to a parody of the enterprise upon which we were engaged. At 0330 we were told to shut up, go forward and fall in. We went quietly over the side like thieves in the night doing our best not to bump the next ahead. As each sailor reached the top of the brow the scabbard of his fixed bayonet was collected from him. Those ordered to carry loaded rifles filled their magazines in the battery below; ammunition for revolvers was handed out in packets at the gangway.

Jimmy led off, with me at his heels and the platoon in crocodile astern in hush-hush progression through the dockyard. I was entitled to be there, although it had meant wangling it. Precedent was with me. There are references in the records to paymasters volunteering 'for this service' when ships were called upon for boarding and cutting out and the like. We were allowed some of the fun provided we asked nicely. At Jutland the first aircraft to take part in a naval battle had an assistant paymaster as observer.

I strode through the night like Wyatt Earp on the way to the OK Corral until I remembered that, unlike the marshal, I had an empty six-gun. I was unarmed. I fumbled with my packet. There was a stage whisper from ahead.

'What are you doing?'

'Loading my revolver.'

'Don't. I am not going to get shot up the bum by a bloody Mid.'

The platoon snaked past a coal dump, a black shadow in the night sky between us and *Paris*. It held a section of Royal Marines with Bren guns in case the French tried to keep us out with their anti-aircraft mitrailleuse, screened by sandbags on the upper deck of the battleship. We had not been told about the marines; had they opened fire from the darkness above us the confusion would have been substantial.

We reached the end of the coal, twenty yards from the forward brow of *Paris*, just out of sight. Jimmy stopped and the platoon shuffled to a halt. We had with us a party under the Navigating Officer to disarm the sailors in the forward air defence positions and secure the bridge. It was now getting light. We could not communicate with the after parties, hidden from us by the coal. Nothing was said and we waited for Jimmy.

The Navigating Officer abruptly led off without a word and went for the brow at the rush with his small party behind him. I saw them run across the upper deck and up the bridge ladders towards the sandbags, which showed no signs of life (the matelots there were asleep). Jimmy followed on with the platoon in support. At the bottom of the brow he stopped dead and I went into him. He stepped to one side and waved the first few seamen on and then he and I went after them. There were no Frenchmen in sight and we ran for the nearest hatch.

Down below she stank of Gauloise and sweat; the platoon set to work on the hammocks. She was grubby between decks and the crew of 1,800 needed for her six 12-in turrets slept where they could. We found men slinging in the heads. They were slow to catch on and at first seemed unwilling to turn out and go aft. The platoon warmed to their work and were tickled to find that their French had some effect; if they yelled loudly enough, the matelots knew what *levez* meant even when delivered in accents from every part of the British Isles. Few were dressed and they were given little time to reflect. As soon as their feet touched the deck they saw a bayonet waved at them and lost no time in joining the queue aft. The plan was to get them over the quarter deck brow and out of the ship before they became abreast of events.

In short time the forward messdecks were cleared, and a crowd of French sailors in assorted rigs became jammed on and below the main midships ladders leading to the upper deck. These ladders resembled a staircase in a liner, being much wider than anything in our ships; there were a lot of Frenchmen there. More were being herded into the press, muttering. Jimmy told me to find out what was happening and why they were not filing on to the upper deck and ashore. I found a leading seaman near the front of the mob and asked him the same question. I got a straight answer.

'Them stupid fucking bullocks won't let them up, sir.'

I struggled back forward and reported to Jimmy that the Royal Marines were blocking the hatches. He told me to find the Major of Marines and give him the First Lieutenant's compliments and ask him to allow the Frenchmen out while they were still in hand.

I went back the way we had come and found the Major at the top of the ladders, surrounded by his detachment, exercising military control on the upper deck, as had been the task of the Corps for generations. The Major was an amiable officer who had been a pilot. He had a long scar on his cheek and walked with a measured tread. He was known as Lightning and had no intention of allowing the war, or anything else, alter the agreeable pace he had set himself. By now *Paris*'s crew were near the waiting bayonets of the marines, being pushed there willy nilly from below. The Major intended to do his historic duty; *ils ne passeront pas* while he was there.

I gave him the message which caused him surprise. He said that his orders were not to let anyone up until the ship had been secured. It was unarguable that a battleship was not secure until there were sentries on the magazines and shell rooms and the guns had been rendered inoperable. That would take some time and meanwhile the half dressed Frenchmen ran the risk of being kebabbed by the Royals. I could see by the Major's furrowed brow that he was wrestling with the problem and there was no senior officer to help him. The Commander was still in *Revenge* and the Captain had boarded *Paris* with us. At that moment he was talking to the French admiral. The Major had no choice; he barked an order and the mob surged out and on to the jetty.

It had begun to drizzle and the French sailors lined up in front of the coal heap, intimidated by armed men, facing their ship from which they were now barred by their friends, with a Hobson's choice for the future; either fighting alongside the ally who had duped them, or returning to their own country, overrun by a hated enemy.

I made my way forward by the underground route and got lost somewhere on the lower deck. No one from *Revenge* was about. I crossed a flat and saw two petty officers collecting gear. I was able to get the gist of their conversation. It was *mieux comme ci*; they seemed glad that their immediate future had been decided for them. The flat was deserted except for the three of us. They looked at me and went on talking and packing their kit as if I had not been there. I got the message and have it still. I reported to Jimmy who told me to fall out and follow the platoon back to the ship.

I joined two Mids and a Royal Marine subaltern on the quarter deck of *Paris*. We stood about, reluctant to go home, partygoers in the dawn after a summer ball. A grim faced lieutenant from *Thames* came from the French submarine and went to the jetty, where our Surgeon Commander had appeared, with pyjamas under his uniform and a scarf round his neck. He had walked from *Revenge* in slippers. We heard his Irish brogue in loud complaint that no one had told him what was going on and he had just been shaken and asked for medical help. He disappeared into *Surcouf* with the *Thames* officer and we realized that the confrontation there between the French and British had been for real.

One of our surgeon lieutenants followed him and an ambulance arrived. A party gathered round the submarine conning tower and manoeuvred a stretcher on to the casing, across *Paris* and into the ambulance. I saw the grey-faced and unconcious figure of the Captain of *Thames*, his commander's reefer loosely round his shoulders and a large piece of cotton wool over a bloody wound in his right chest. Another stretcher followed the same route with an RN lieutenant on it and the cotton wool lower down on his right side. He was concious and twisted with pain. This was the reality described in the books, Hardy's 'rattling good history'. All

I knew, as the stretchers passed, was that the night's lark had laid low two men for whom I had an instinctive respect, for no useful purpose that I could understand. Both officers died later, one that day and one the day after. A French officer had been killed and another wounded. There were two casualties from *Revenge*. Leading Seaman Webb had been killed and Able Seaman Heath wounded.

The junior officers who had been in the boarding parties gathered in the gunroom. The adrenalin went down and the casualties, the first the ship had suffered, reduced our exuberance. If the crew of *Paris* had showed some of the fight put up by *Surcouf* it could have been a bloody shambles. We did not discuss the whys and wherefores; if the assault had been planned to keep the French on our side it was a failure.

We had taken two ships which were liabilities rather than assets and given away the lives of two experienced officers, one the Captain of an operational submarine, and a long service leading seaman. We had attacked an ally without warning and would have to pay the price for that long after the ships and the dead were forgotten.

The assault is described in Churchill's *Their Finest Hour* as follows:

> In the early morning of July 3 all the French vessels at Portsmouth and Plymouth were taken under British control. The action was sudden and necessarily a surprise. Overwhelming force was employed, and the whole transaction showed how easily the Germans could have taken possession of any French warships lying in ports which they controlled. In Britain the transfer, except in the *Surcouf*, was amicable, and the crews came willingly ashore. In the *Surcouf* two British officers were wounded, one leading seaman killed, and an able seaman wounded. One Frenchman was killed in the scuffle, but the utmost endeavours were made with success to reassure and comfort the French sailors. Many hundreds volunteered to join us. The *Surcouf*, after rendering distinguished service, perished on February 19 1942, with all her gallant French crew.

The French had given their word not to let their ships get into German hands. We found it easy to take them because they thought we were their friends. So much for the author's argument; he is equally weak on the facts.

The predominant part of operation GSF at Plymouth involved the seizure of *Paris* and *Surcouf* by parties from *Revenge* and *Thames* and the seizure of the Fleet destroyers *Le Triomphant* and *Mistral* by parties from the cruisers *Galatea* and *Newcastle*. Shortly before *Paris* was boarded the Commander-in-Chief Plymouth, Admiral Sir Martin Dunbar-Nasmith VC, with the Captain of *Revenge* and two staff officers preceded us and asked to see the French Admiral Cayol urgently. He was handed a letter and asked to haul down his flag and clear his ships. He was distressed and is reported to have said, 'So, you make us come alongside to make it easier for you, eh?'

To which the C-in-C replied, 'Ah, frankly, yes.'

Admiral Cayol repeatedly stated that he could not leave without the approval of his government. It was necessary for the C-in-C to give him a direct order to go ashore. Before he left he told the C-in-C that he had previously considered scuttling his ships but had not done so because it would have obstructed the harbour and been an inconvenience to the Royal Navy.

The Captain of *Le Triomphant* point blank refused to surrender his ship and reminded the boarding officer that he would not have brought her to England if he had not been loyal to the Allied cause. While this discourse went on the boarding party took her over. The French captain was refused permission to speak to his crew.

In *Mistral* both the Captain and the Captain (D) refused to leave unless they and their men were allowed to have their belongings. This was at first refused but when it was seen that trouble was likely, the order was changed and they were allowed to take their gear. The ship then began to take a list to port; the forward and after magazines had been flooded. The Captain denied all knowledge of the flooding. He was sent below to the wardroom with several of his officers, whereupon all flooding stopped.

When interviewed by the Flag Captain from *Newcastle*, who had been sent over to provide gravitas, the French senior officers made their feelings plain. They began a tirade about being attacked by thieves and robbers whom they held in contempt for the treacherous and underhand methods we had used. The Captain of *Mistral* said the British were not taking their fair share of the war and were spending their time playing football and tennis instead of mobilizing. He was ordered into a boat at the point of a revolver. As he went over the side he shouted out that the British would be finished in ten months. The French ratings took events more philosophically and looted their canteen before they left.

In *Surcouf* the boarding party were carried in *Revenge*'s launch with one of our midshipmen in charge of the boat. As they neared the French submarine a quartermaster on her upper deck ran along the casing hammering on the hull. He went down the forward hatch, which was shut after him; we were expected. The other quartermaster was disarmed by the boarding party. All the hatches were found shut and there was no way into the submarine save though the conning tower hatch, which could be opened from outside. An intrepid lieutenant from *Thames*, although it was apparent that they were ready for us, opened the hatch and went down to the control room. He was met by the French Captain and First Lieutenant, both fully dressed. They were told to leave but refused to do so until they had seen their Admiral in *Paris*. They left under escort for that purpose. The fore ends and after ends of the submarine were then evacuated with difficulty. Some of the technical ratings refused to leave. A French officer was seen to pass a piece of paper to an electrical rating who went to the main switchboard, followed by an electrical rating from *Thames*. The Frenchman put out all the lights and was hit over the head with a mallet by his shadow. There was a short fight which was won by *Thames* and the lights were put on.

The officers of the *Surcouf* assembled in the wardroom with the Captain of *Thames* and another submarine officer, the First Lieutenant of *Rorqual*. The French officers refused to leave their ship until their Captain had returned from *Paris* to give them permission. The Chief Petty Officer Coxswain of the *Thames* was on duty in the control room above the wardroom, in attendance upon his Captain, and noticed each officer go to the heads in turn. It was likely that they armed themselves while there. The Captain of *Thames* called out for two hands from the guard in the Control Room to come to him, having no doubt become suspicious of the French behaviour.

The first one down was Leading Seaman Webb followed by

Able Seaman Heath. Shortly afterwards the French officers opened fire. Leading Seaman Webb received two bullets in the heart. Able Seaman Heath had seven bullet wounds in his face, arms and neck. Both British officers were wounded. There was no reply from the British, who had been attacked without warning.

The coxswain of the *Thames* lay on his stomach and opened fire with his revolver through the hatch on the French officers below, killing one and wounding another. Fire was returned at the coxswain and then all firing ceased. An officer from *Thames* arrived in the control room and ordered the French to come up. Four came up saying '*Finis*'. They refused to say whether any more remained below and would not leave the ship without their Captain's permission. Eventually, one more wounded officer emerged. It was probable that he had remained below to shoot again if anyone came down. One of them was sent over to *Paris* to see their Captain who gave them permission to go. They all left except for the wounded officer, the pilot of their aircraft, who had been shot in the chest and arm. The coxswain and three other ratings from the guard then went below.

They found a French officer dying in his cabin leading from the wardroom. The Captain of the *Thames* had collapsed by the door of the Captain's cabin. Leading Seaman Webb was nearly dead in the entrance to the French officer's cabin. Able Seaman Heath was inside the cabin shot in the face. The First Lieutenant of *Rorqual* was holding on to the ladder in a collapsed state. Five out of the six pistols on the table had been fired. The casualties were given first aid and medical help sent for. Dr. Nistour of the *Surcouf* attended to the wounded Frenchman; his help was not sought for the British wounded.

The French officer walked to the ambulance despite his chest wound. Able Seaman Heath tramped back to *Revenge* with his seven French bullets onboard and went to hospital after treatment. He made a full recovery.

It cannot be said with certainty that the failure to attach medical support to the boarding parties cost the lives of the two submarine officers. This was before plasma on immediate call; it might have been that neither could have survived the shock and loss of blood before their wounds could be attended to, and the bleeding stopped. The facts are that neither received injuries that were obviously fatal, judging by Able Seaman Heath's experience the weapons were of small calibre, and they did not get skilled help for nearly an hour after they were hit. The absence of medical support in the assault deprived them of any chance they may have had.

The attacks on the French ships were repugnant to admirals of the calibre of Cunningham and Somerville. They were not supported by the First Sea Lord and politics prevailed. Churchill justified a dishonourable act for which he was responsible by the following hyperbole.

> The elimination of the French Navy as an important factor almost at a single stroke by violent action produced a profound effect in every country. Here was this Britain which so many had counted down and out, which strangers had supposed to be quivering on the brink of surrender to the mighty power arrayed against her, striking ruthlessly at her dearest friends of yesterday and securing for a while to herself the undisputed command of the sea. It was made plain that the British War Cabinet feared nothing and would stop at nothing. This was true.

Others were required to clear up the mess in *Paris* and *Surcouf.* We had not taken the French ships to encourage them to remain pro-Ally, as the commander of *Revenge* had been told; nor to prevent the Germans having them, because they were already under our control. The assaults were political acts of gesture militarism, one of many in the record of their instigator; they had no effect on the war, save to antagonize the French. Their junior ratings had largely gone along with the seizures and allowed their anxiety to go home to overcome their pride. It was not so with the officers and senior ratings. The doctor of the *Surcouf* told one of our midshipmen that he and his brother officers were amazed at the methods we had used. Their sympathies had all been with us and exactly the same results would have been achieved had we come without arms in daylight.

Later that forenoon a tug went through the basin loaded with French sailors from *Mistral* and *Le Triomphant.* They cheered as they passed *Paris* and sang the Marseillaise. The French ensign was hoisted slowly to the gaff of the tug and a small group of

French officers stood to attention with their caps off. They had lost their ships but kept their dignity. We had done the dirty work and were glad to leave next day for Canada.

As was the custom the kit of Leading Seaman Webb, a widower with a daughter, was auctioned among his shipmates. It was my duty to record the bids; trivial items of a seaman's kit were bought and handed back again and again to be re-sold by those who wanted to help his family, while maintaining the fierce pride of the Lower Deck by not asking them to accept charity. I remember Webb as a tall, quiet three badge leading seaman, old for his rate, and probably nearing his pension after twenty-two years' service. The word was that he had never had much luck.

Thames carried on with a new captain to take the place of the one killed in *Surcouf.* She was lost with all hands on her next patrol exactly a month later, probably mined, off Stavanger. The submarine spare CO, who had taken her over at short notice, was the Officer of the Watch I had been sent to shake on my third night in the Navy. It will never be known whether the abrupt change in command contributed to her loss. If there is a Churchill Club in Valhalla for those he sent there it will take a long time to get a drink round the crowded bar.

Some fifty years after these events I attended a ceremony in Portsmouth. The French naval attaché from their London embassy was there to represent his country. I asked a serving admiral I knew whether they had now forgotten it.

'Not really,' he said.

CHAPTER 6

INVASION DUTY

Revenge joined a convoy off the Mull of Kintyre, bound for the North American haven with refugees, German prisoners of war and schoolchildren embarked in the liner *Monarch of Bermuda* and two Polish ships, *Batory* and *Sobieski*. With them was the new Dido class cruiser *Bonaventure*, whose lithe beauty was coarsened by the absence of her fifth 5.25-in turret forward. The builders had left a gap, to be filled when the guns and armour were ready. A nymph with two front teeth missing, she flitted from scouting ahead in daylight to fine on our starboard quarter at night. I wondered what it would be like to serve in such a butterfly. She was sunk by a German submarine south of Crete in March 1941; her short life lasted ten months.

The turn round in Halifax lasted eleven days and we left again on 23 July with TC 7, a large troop convoy of six liners.

The passage was enlivened by a test firing of blank 15-in charges to repel aircraft. The guns were loaded with cordite only and fired at maximum elevation in four sectors. There was a prolonged roar and a gout of red flame at least eighty feet long from each gun, followed by a pillar of smoke from the air blast. The Americans had demonstrated what happened when heavy ships were subjected to bombing in the Mitchell trials, almost twenty years before, but gunnery orthodoxy won the day, the carriers and aircraft were not built, and we were reduced, in the middle of this war, to practising air defence by firing cordite into the sky. It was hoped that the heat and blast would throw attacking aircraft off course, an outcome which would have been a long shot in Orville Wright's time, and a non-runner now. The advances in military aviation between 1918 and 1939 had tip-toed past the Naval Staff.

Few of the escorts had air or surface radar which had only

begun to come into service. All depended upon the eyeball. I remember one Able Seaman Black, a Newfoundlander, reporting that he had seen a mast at red forty-five degrees. The visibility was perfect. Everyone on the bridge trained their glasses on the bearing but there was nothing there. I asked him to confirm it. He did. I asked him to make sure that his glasses were clear. He did. The Principal Control Officer, two officers of the watch, the Yeoman of Signals and two midshipmen tried again but there was nothing to be seen. This took about three minutes. Lookouts were my responsibility that day and I was wondering what should be done about Able Seaman Black when there was a shout from the Yeoman. Shortly afterwards a neutral merchantman sailing alone gradually appeared. It was a demonstration of an acuity of vision approaching the supernatural. Black had his name put into Daily Orders and was given ten shillings from the Gunnery Improvement Fund, to encourage the others.

In the gunroom, the authority of the Sub-lieutenant dwindled under the constant challenge it received from the Young Gentlemen, forever on the edge of riot. He left suddenly, without ceremony. The next Sub was a man of the world, sophisticated for his years, who diverted us with tales of his adventures, but was enough of a naval officer to slap us down when required.

He was a keen bridge player at sea and insisted we played with him when he was not on the afternoon watch. Winnings and losses were recorded in the mess Card Book and the Sub believed that too many losses against his name were bad for discipline. Thus when he was winning the gunroom table was not laid for tea until the rubber had finished. If he was losing he was liable to sweep the cards off the table and announce that the game must not be allowed to delay tea for those going on watch. He ignored protests.

He believed our education was lacking because he suspected, with some cause, that most of us had little experience of women beyond mothers, sisters and nannies. In warm weather, when the Gunroom off watch sunned themselves on X gun deck, the Sub reminisced upon the pleasures of the chase. For his time he was a fast worker and his exploits, at the age of 21, were wide ranging. London was his headquarters; I remember him coming back from leave, pale but determined, tall, dark and good-looking with his top reefer button undone and a battered suitcase at his side aiming a determined course through the dockyard towards the ship. We gathered round the gunroom square port cheering him on to the brow while he was still on his feet. When he came into the mess he received a roar of welcome and demands for a full de-briefing.

He had one yarn which, knowing him, could have been true. During his Mid's time his ship visited New York. It was shortly after the war started and he went ashore in uniform to an official cocktail party. Inevitably he succeeded in taking some young woman to bed, and found he had minutes to spare before getting back onboard for the morning watch. The ship was alongside and he threw on his uniform and greatcoat, found a taxi and just made it. It was only after he had taken over, and begun walking the quarter deck with the Officer of the Watch, his telescope under his arm, that he remembered that in the rush he had not had time for everything. He swore that he kept the whole of the morning watch wearing a condom.

He died later in the war, like he had lived, at full throttle. After Sunday lunch at his air station he took off on some wild impulse, because he loved flying, lost it, and went in. He was that most attractive of men, the happy warrior. Nowadays the talk is of pensions, marriage allowance and university degrees and I do not think the Sub would have prospered.

Beneath the general good manners and public school voices the Gunroom had the instincts of a pack of dog hounds. Occasionally, they got out of hand and challenged the unwary visitor, usually with no worse result than the removal of his trousers. It happened to the two Royal Marine subalterns and a Belfast RNVR we disliked; we tried it on the new gunnery lieutenant and were repulsed, yelping, by his power of command. He straightened his tie and stayed for a drink as if nothing had happened; thereafter he had our respect. Such events happened in a flash, with no preliminaries.

Occasionally, at sea, there would be sudden trials of strength, always good-tempered, between two midshipmen who would wrestle on the deck for as long as was needed for a winner to emerge. The rest went on writing up their logs or letters home, indifferent to the struggle.

Guest nights were often violent, and, when it looked like a lively party, the messman invited his cronies into the pantry, where they took it in turns to look through the hatch. I remember talking to a guest, a lieutenant from *Repulse*, when a bottle of Drambuie hurtled between us and broke on the fan trunking. Conversation was maintained and, except for telling the thrower to put it on his mess bill, the Sub made no comment.

The thread that bound us together and made us what we were lead back to Mr Midshipman Easy. We no longer fought duels but might have done had it been legal; our lives were softer, but we came from the same stock and our habits and the rules under which we chose to live were, like his, unique in the profession of arms among the British, or anyone else.

Midshipmen received occasional invitations to lunch in the wardroom. In harbour pre-lunch drinks were always the same. A marine wardroom attendant offered a tray containing claret glasses with one half tots of gin in them and two shakers, one of Angostura bitters and one of lime. It was assumed that the guest would have gin, everybody did, and any other drink had to be specially asked for. In his disengaged hand he carried a jug of water. Bitters or lime, if required, had to be shaken by the officer into the gin before the marine added the water. Nothing was said and the system had the merit of speed. The gin cost one's host threepence a time.

Officers under 20 were not allowed spirits so that it was agreable to be offered them rather than have to persuade a messmate over 20 to treat you. The consumption of gin in the wardrooms of HM ships then would be considered heroic by modern standards. On one occasion I was getting up from lunch with my host when a dead beat lieutenant-commander, who had probably been drinking gin for two hours, sat down to eat and poured his last gin over his salad. He told the attendant that he was in a hurry as he had to work the Big Stick. The Big Stick was slang for the main derrick, used for hoisting boats and stores and designed to be worked with circumspection if no one was to get hurt. He was sober and his behaviour, though perhaps eccentric, was not remarkable.

All officers, of all three messes, were careful to ensure that they did not go over their daily spirit allowance of three full tots without putting a 'G' (for 'Guest') alongside their names in the officers' wine book. The wine book was signed monthly by the Captain and many captains not only signed it but examined it to ensure that the rules were not broken. Drink played a significant role in the social life of the Navy, forward and aft, and an officer drinking more than nine gins a day might be called to account. There was a limit to the number of 'Gs' that could be used, particularly if the ship had been at sea for most of the month.

On 31 July 1940 we approached the UK with TC 7; 8 Fleet Destroyers and 2 Sunderland flying boats met us. There were many submarine contact reports and a Sunderland sighted and attacked one thirty miles ahead of the convoy. Nine German submarines were stationed west of Northern Ireland at this time. The first U-Boat had entered Lorient on 7 July and by August Brest and La Pallice were also in commission. The Battle of the Atlantic was about to start in earnest. By the end of the year forty-nine merchant ships were sunk in submarine attacks on convoys on passage through this area.

Revenge reached the Clyde on 1 August and found the anchorage full of shipping, while the country waited for the German invasion. All hands set about camouflaging the ship. Our ram was a Victorian give-away which identified us at once as an old battleship. It was painted out in the hope that our bows would look like a battle cruiser and encourage the enemy to overestimate our speed. Our upperworks were dazzle painted in light grey, dark grey, green and brown. It was effective and blurred the ship's hard silhouette.

I was able to assess this art work while crewing for the Young Doctor in a dinghy race. I thought it fitting to draw his attention to a T-class submarine which was coming up harbour at a good lick and across our course to the next mark. The Young Doc did not welcome advice from the Gunroom and pointed out that steam gave way to sail. I had no time to remind him about the small print and he put the helm up too late, filling her with the wash and putting us out of the race.

We left for Halifax again on 11 August with more bullion, and escorting five liners. On Tuesday 20 August 1940, the ship completed 50,000 miles of steaming and 200 days at sea in the 351 days the war had lasted.

We were 3,000 miles from our homes, which were threatened by invasion, while we waited about in a Canadian seaport. This might have affected morale had we not been a good ship with good men. Nevertheless the Captain cleared lower deck. The situation in Europe was so bad that there was no good news to tell. The Captain was not to be put off by trifles of that kind. He told us that Germany was suffering from the RAF raids and it was not all one way by any means. Anyone believing that in August 1940 would believe anything, but that is to miss the point. By talking to the ship's company about the war he reminded them that he knew how they felt. They knew that there was nothing that he could do about it. It hardly mattered what he said, he was with them and they were with him.

On 27 August, we left Halifax with another troop convoy made up of the liners *Empress of Australia, Pasteur, Scythia, Georgic* and *Oronsay*. The phoney war was over and their send-off was ominously prolonged. Although the first ship did not leave until midday cars in large numbers began to collect early in the forenoon along the sides of the estuary to see off 7,000 Canadian men-at-arms for another European war.

The hands fell in for leaving harbour as usual, and the Royal Marine band, as usual, played 'Roll Out The Barrel' as loud as they could make it. The cars sounded their horns and the crowds waved and cheered, the soldiers in the troopships cheered back and everyone there got the torn banner flying in the wind feeling and Dieppe was only a seaside place in Normandy. This time the RCN destroyer *Ottawa* came all the way across.

As we neared twenty degrees west the weather closed down and a convoy routed on opposite course cut straight through us, miraculously without incident. A 12,000 ton ship, the *Afric Star*, appeared right ahead, a cable's length away. *Revenge* went hard a starboard and she passed us within shouting distance. The Captain yelled at her through a megaphone to watch out for our next astern and her Master waved an acknowledgement as she disappeared in the murk. Although she survived this episode, the *Afric Star* was sunk in mid-Atlantic by a raider the following January.

The Sailmaker died of a heart attack and we buried him at 12 knots. It would have been reckless in the service in which we were engaged to have slowed down for the sacrament, as custom and decency demanded. The top guard rails were slipped. The quarter deck was washing down and the voice of the Chaplain could be heard only in fragments on the wind. The bright colours of the Union Flag provided life and colour against the green and white of the sea the other side of the hammock and the slide. The handful of officers saluted. The noise of the wind and the sea, the throbbing of the screws and the briskness of the ceremony was far removed from the slow ritual in a country churchyard.

Twelve submarines were operating in this area and a convoy was attacked with the loss of five ships between 2 and 5 September. Flotsam was seen from time to time and an empty lifeboat. We arrived at the Clyde on 4 September and set about bringing the ship's degaussing equipment up to specification to complete our defence to magnetic mines.

The anchorage was full and the shipping increased by the hour. One of the RNVR Mids had a brother in the RAF and he arrived onboard with a pal. The brother wore a golden caterpillar in his lapel which he had earned in Norway, when he was shot down by one of our AA cruisers and saved his life by parachute. The friend had the DSO. We were impressed and gave up the jokes about Brylcreem boys. They offered to give us a flight. The Hudson bomber was parked at Abbots Inch with an air gunner standing by it like a groom with a second horse. Our pilot put on a pair of spectacles and we hurtled round Glasgow, all that could be done in the time they had. The DSO made a very low pass over the aerodrome for our benefit and then it was all over and we made our way back, feeling ordinary.

The next day we went down harbour and anchored just inside the boom. After dinner the Captain assembled all the officers in his harbour cabin. It had never happened before.

He told us that we were leaving for Plymouth during the middle watch. Our North Atlantic escort duty had been cancelled because the intelligence appreciation was that the Germans intended to invade England; the most likely date was the following Sunday,

15 September 1940. Our job in the South was to deal with any heavy ships the enemy might bring into it.

He sat on the club fender. The midshipmen sat on the deck and thirty or so others crowded in where they could. I have little doubt that everyone there felt the same. The country faced invasion and we had some idea of the opposition the enemy would find if they got ashore in force. The Army were short of equipment and morale after Dunkirk. The RAF lacked numbers. We believed that if the Navy did not stop them they would land and it would be all over. Fighting them on the beaches and the landing grounds sounded all right on the wireless and in the press, but militarily it was a forlorn hope. The country was on her own against the best equipped and trained army in history.

The first *Revenge* was in Plymouth 352 years before, when the Armada was in the Channel; in the ninth *Revenge* it was our turn. We went through the boom at 0145 and entered the Irish Sea.

Our escorts were four 20-year-old destroyers, *Mackay*, *Westcott*, *Scimitar* and *Skate*. The cruiser *Emerald*, another member of the Halifax Escort Force, formed up astern, and the ships went south at 17 knots, while we watched the land go by and hoped that some might see us in the distance and take heart that we were there. Our countrymen did not know it, but luck was on their side in that the Naval Staff had been told to scrap the five R-class battleships in 1939; the German threat had kept them going.

Mr Churchill had decreed that forty escorts were to be sent to the Channel, whatever the effect on the submarine war. The Admiralty obeyed, but hedged their bets by sending some of the oldest ones, in the reasonable assumption that it might be a one way trip and the newest ships would be needed to continue the war from other places.

It should be remembered now that the Naval Staff and the politicians had so prepared us between the wars that no ship in our force hurrying to Plymouth on that summer day had been laid down less than twenty years before, our air defence was provided by obsolescent twin-engined Ansons and a strange machine known as a Fokker T8W, while the Gunnery Officer planned the layout of sandbags on the upper deck to protect us from near misses.

The Squadron entered Plymouth Sound at 0900 on 14 September as the Cruiser Flag, indicating an air raid Red Warning, was run up from the signal tower on the Breakwater Fort. The warnings continued all day while more sandbags and splinter mats were embarked. The ship went to four hour's notice by day and a half hour's notice by night.

We shared the Sound with the modern 6-in cruiser *Newcastle*, the minelayer *Adventure* and a collection of destroyers, including those manned by the Free French and Poles. The battle plan had the advantage of simplicity. Every ship there would get to sea as soon as possible, independently, and go for the enemy pell-mell without waiting to form up. This meant that the MTBs and light forces would be first, the destroyers next, then the cruisers, and ourselves, the only capital ship, last. It would be a bloody mêlée, particulary if the battle was at night, and the unsupported small ships would have to do the best they could until the others got there.

We settled into a routine amid the constant alerts from reconnaisance aircraft. The 15 September came and went. On 19 September *Revenge* fired her first shot in anger since 1916, at a single aircraft. On the next day we fired seventeen rounds at an aircraft on a photographic flight. There was no sign of the enemy invasion fleet and enthusiasm for our historic mission began to fade.

Two of us decided that the Gunroom needed a good Nazi song. We visited the music shops in Devonport and Plymouth but did not find the record of the Horst Wessel we were looking for. It would have been remarkable if we had. This was not a joke. So far our side had not been winning. We were conscious of the difference between our poorly equipped services, forced already on to the defensive, and that of the enemy, bulging with weapons and enthusiasm. We envied and admired them. The highest form of morale, according to Erwin Rommel is achieved by a superlative state of training. Our inter-war period had been spent in a routine nearer to the Victorian past than the air and submarine present. Like the French we had been complacent, hoping to get by. Militarily speaking, the German political system delivered the goods and we were in the military business. This did not mean that any of us were National Socialists; we thought their music would set the mood.

There was another invasion scare on 26 September and the force in the Sound went to one hour's notice for steam. The Squadron was joined by *Paris*, moored with her beam facing to seaward to provide a floating battery for engaging an enemy going for Plymouth.

The ships opened fire on some aircraft near the harbour, mercifully without successs, as they were all on our side, and included a humble 90 knot Walrus. The next day we went into Cawsand Bay to carry out degaussing trials. While there six Heinkels were engaged before being driven off by Spitfires without getting close enough to bomb. We went back to our buoy in the Sound and four hours' notice for steam.

The Captain went ashore. Before he left most of the Gunroom disappeared into the forecastle of the brass funnelled picket boat to hitch a ride. She went away towards the dockyard, smoke curling out of her shiny stack while the Captain looked back at the ship. The Sub and I adjourned to the mess to console our presence onboard on duty with tea. The alarm rattlers went for about the fifth or sixth time that day and we got to our feet to put on tin hats and go to action stations. A 4-in gun went off on the boat deck above our heads and it occurred to me that we ought to move a bit quicker. The next bang shook the cups, brought lining down from the deckhead and the ship quivered. 'That,' said the Sub, 'was not a bloody gun.'

We went to X gun deck and saw that *Revenge* had been near-missed on the port side. It was easy to see the centre of the explosion; the sea was covered with mud and stunned fish. Some of the quarter deck guard rails had been shredded by splinters, one of which had gone through the trouser leg of a hand in a dockyard boat alongside. No one was hurt. The aircraft was alone and long gone; the bomb was probably a 250-pounder. As well as hoards of mackerel the catch included a conger eel like a boa-constrictor. We kept the mackerel and gave the conger to the warrant officers' mess, who claimed they had eaten it for breakfast. I doubt whether that was true; the creature was a disgusting sight.

The picket boat had turned round and was discharging black

smoke in a frenzy to get an anxious captain back to his ship. He had seen the cloud of spray when the bomb landed when, through no fault of his, he was two miles away in the officers' afternoon boat.

The attacks continued. The next was a further up the scale. A large formation of Heinkels dropped bombs around *Newcastle*, *Adventure* and ourselves without getting near enough to do damage. *Paris* was the first to open fire and the force put up a good barrage which compared well with the shore batteries. Fighters turned up and chased the enemy away. When the excitement ended we shifted berth back to the Hamoaze and found that we had been reinforced by two ex-American four-funnelled destroyers, and, more to the point, four modern 'J' and 'K' class destroyers of Lord Mountbatten's 5th Flotilla. Our first radar set arrived. We were getting into it.

The last episode in this exciting week was hard to interpret. We landed 160 rounds of armour piercing 15-in shell and embarked 160 rounds of high explosive, used for shore bombardment, in their place.

On Wednesday 9 October we went back to the Sound and came to a single anchor. The 5th Destroyer Flotilla were in the Sound too and their Captains came onboard during the afternoon for a briefing. For the second time the Captain addressed all officers off watch in his day cabin. He told us that our force would shell Cherbourg harbour the following night in co-operation with the RAF, while other ships created diversions to the west and east to keep enemy light forces out of the way.

The next day was spent waiting in the Sound. The turrets crews closed up and exercised loading runs for the umpteenth time. The practice had a new dimension. The high explosive CPC (Common Piercing Cap) shells were inches longer than the usual Armour Piercing Cap projectiles, and heavier. This made them more awkward to handle and in the service we had in prospect each turret would be ordered to get off as many rounds as possible during the firing run. Everyone knew that the result would mean winners and losers in the rivalry between the four turrets and a poor performance would be remembered.

An hour before sailing the Captain talked to all hands through the SRE. He said that it was not his intention to risk the ship unnecessarily. The firing run would last for about a quarter of an hour, during which he hoped we would succeed in getting off over 100 tons of high explosive into the German installations and invasion craft known to be at Cherbourg. The news was received quietly. He finished by saying that at the end of the operation we would go to Portsmouth. This brought an almighty cheer. Portsmouth was the ship's home port and she had not been there since re-commisssioning in June 1939.

The Gunroom spent the waiting time on X gun deck, sunbathing and arguing about the chances of landing the shells in the right place after a dead reckoning night approach. It seemed that the French had a good chance of a bad night as well as the enemy. The Sub got bored and decided to show off. He put on swimming trunks and walked along one of Y turret guns, trained on the beam, and dived in. The recognition he got was modest; the water was probably colder than it looked. He gave up and went below.

I bathed and changed into clean underwear, the routine before an engagement, received Holy Communion at one of the special services held by the Chaplain, and was relieved to find that I was looking forward to it; truth to tell, such was my ingenuousness, I might have been Henry the Fifth the night before Agincourt.

The destroyer escort of *Javelin* (Captain (D) 5) *Jupiter*, *Kelvin*, *Kashmir*, *Jaguar* and *Kipling* left harbour before us and the whole force formed up in screening positions on *Revenge* shortly after 8 pm. There was a *frisson* when the 6-in magazine keys could not be found. They had been drawn by the Commissioned Gunner who was missing from all the usual places. He was run to earth, the keys recovered and the cordite made ready.

Revenge headed south in full career at 18 knots. To the sentimental, who believe that the best ships have lives of their own, her vibration at 276 revolutions showed her excitement at the prospect of renewing the battle she had begun nearly a quarter a century before at Jutland.

CHAPTER 7

CHANNEL NIGHTS

The Main Force, led by *Revenge*, with five destroyers of the 5th Destroyer Flotilla and seven motor gunboats, had the job of landing the punch; the Western Covering Force of two cruisers and five destroyers kept the ring clear down Channel. The Eastern Covering Force of one cruiser and two destroyers watched the other side. The RAF were to bomb the target two hours before we arrived, and assist with navigation by illuminating Cap de la Hague light at precisely 0320, when the Main Force would start its final approach.

The night was moonless and still. The plan demanded that no signals be made after forming up; accurate navigation and timing were essential. We depended on the gyro compass and log to keep us there or thereabouts. The Main Force needed a good departure fix from Portland Bill but the light was out because of enemy aircraft in the area. We turned south off the Bill and steered 151 degrees for the Alderney Race, a well worn track for yachtsmen heading for the Channel Islands. It was not a yachting occasion for the new navigating officer, who joined the ship that day, his predecessor having fallen down the bridge ladder and ended in hospital.

At 0200 we assumed first degree of readiness. The MGBs had been detached with orders to search for E boats to the west and stay clear of us for the rest of the night. The sky was bright with star shells in their direction; the Western Covering Force was doing its best to distract the enemy. On the port bow gun flashes on the horizon showed that the RAF had started on Cherbourg.

At about 0315 the noise of aircraft overhead was followed by a clutch of flares. The light at Cap de la Hague and the green fields around it sprang out of the night; the RAF were making it easy.

69

The navigating officer wrote to me over fifty years afterwards to put the record straight.

> I see that the reports on Cherbourg refer to the assistance given by the R.A.F. flares and their fire in the port. Actually it was a distraction rather than a help and I relied entirely upon dead reckoning which the aerial photographs of the port subsequently justified.
> The night was calm, a battleship is easy to steer accurately and the Channel Tidal Flow Charts seemed to be spot on.

Navigation was the key. If we were too far out the shells would drop into the sea; too close and they would land in the town on the French. The officer who had the responsibility for walking this tightrope had hardly been in the ship long enough to find his way to the bridge. He wore a tweed jacket and a hunting stock for the operation. Whether his uniform had not arrived or he felt more comfortable in those clothes I do not know.

While Cap de la Hague was lit by the flares *Revenge* altered to 096 degrees for the remaining nine miles to the target, and increased to 18 knots. I watched the fireworks over the town through the slits in the armoured tower. Every sort of anti-aircraft weapon, including flaming onions, were on view and it was evident that the enemy believed that they had only aircraft to deal with; the longer they thought that the better for us.

The noise of the wind and sea was broken by the firebell in B turret. No more of the silent approach and sneaking up. With a thunder that was heard in Brighton *Revenge* engaged the enemy with her main armament for the first time since she fought it out with *von der Tann* and the First Scouting Group twenty-four years before. Eight tons of high explosive left us for the land with each broadside and above B turret we were on the platform's edge when the Flyer went through. A 15-in gun is all blast and flash and vibration, rather than noise, and the ship shook from truck to keel while the four turrets crews loaded and fired in a controlled tumult at the target eight miles away. The enemy was static and we were on a fixed course, so that there was no delay for spotting or course corrections. The guns were spread for line and laddered for range between salvoes to ensure that the target area was covered. The firebell in B turret was in continuous song, tolling

Cherbourg, 11 October 1940. 15-in. salvo from Revenge.
Taken from escorting destroyer.

(we hoped) for the *Wehrmacht*. The muzzle flashes turned night into day and when the noise stopped the darkness was a welcome cloak from retribution.

In eighteen minutes 120 15-in shells with 104 tons of high explosive were fired into Cherbourg. The Royal Marines in X turret got off thirty-four rounds, one more than the next best gun's crew. The seven destroyers with their 4.7-in fired 801 rounds in three minutes forty seconds. We had plastered them with 126.16 tons of high explosive. A large fire could be seen forty miles away and it seemed from the glare that we had hit the target hard. The smoke reached several hundred feet into the air.

The Force turned north and increased speed, trying to hide. Five minutes after altering course the shore batteries engaged us, beginning with low angled 88s and then bringing in heavy guns from a coastal defence battery. They kept it going for forty minutes until the range opened to eighteen miles. They were good and their accuracy must have been radar assisted. *Revenge* was their mark, being the biggest target. The shells came in salvoes of six guns per minute with a spread of 400 to 600 yards and fell in the area of the Force, some as near as 50 yards, but no ship was hit, except by splinters, and there were no casualties. At extreme range the noise of the guns seemed to have no connection with the flash, the scream of the projectiles and the explosions. It was the same thunder and lightning effect experienced during a throw-off shoot. What gave the kick was that these guns were not throwing-off.

The Force made smoke when the splashes got near to *Revenge*. It showed black against the night sky, inviting the enemy to make spotting corrections and the tactic was abandoned. In the race to get out of range the battleship worked up to 21.5 knots, only a half a knot below her speed on builder's trials in 1916. Nothing broke, but when the she made smoke her speed dropped a knot. Slowly the flashes died away behind us.

We passed through the Nab entrance in time for breakfast, with twenty Hurricanes weaving about at 10,000 feet above, and the destroyers in line astern. At midday I was sent to *Javelin* to enquire when Captain (D) would have his report of proceedings ready, as the Captain wished to brief the C-in-C that day. The Officer of the Watch told me that Lord Mountbatten had gone to London.

Nevertheless his report is dated 11 October so that the logistical problem must have been solved. *Javelin* and *Kelvin* were the only ships of the seven modern destroyers of the 5th Flotilla which survived the war.

The operation was a sideshow which took place in the early days and hardly appears in the history books. The word 'Cherbourg' is not in Bomber Command diary for that night. A good degree of inter-service co-operation was achieved, without communications, in confined waters and without radar. The written orders were few and the briefings minimal. Bearing in mind the chaos that often came later, when combined operations got going, the raid on Cherbourg was a matrix. Its success had much to do with the date. At that time the Navy and the RAF were still being run by professionals. Recognition for the leading participants was minimal; mentions in despatches were given to the Captain, gunnery and navigating officers of *Revenge*, and to Captain (D) 5 and his second in command.

The results of the bombardment have been hard to trace. On a visit to Cherbourg in my sloop *Breeze* in 1983 we were gale bound and I made it the excuse to persuade my two companions to trudge up the hill to the Citadel. The museum was open and given over to large photographs of American jeeps and officers in tin hats and well cut uniforms taking the surrender after the siege in 1944.

I asked the curator where he kept the material about the combined naval and air bombardment of October 1940. He said he was a schoolboy then and remembered little. Although he had been in the job for some years, and was well acquainted with local history, he had never heard of the 1940 attack. I pointed out that at least 150 tons of high explosive had hit the harbour and the town in a short period and it seemed unlikely that it was unrecorded. The museum was about to close and the curator told me shortly that he was aware of no such attack and if I wanted information I should enquire at the Town Hall. I gave up and we took a taxi down the hill to a rotten dinner in a restaurant with a roof which let in the rain. It was not a good day and the trip back the day after helped to put the quest out of my mind until I took up this task, when I tried again.

I wrote to the Mayor of Cherbourg and his archivist sent to me a copy of a diary kept in secrecy by one of the town's inhabitants. It describes the night of 10/11 October 1940 as the worst of the war. The centre of the Simon factory, making agricultural machinery, was destroyed. The damage was especially severe on the east side of the town in the Val de Saire area. He lists eight streets which suffered in particular. In the Bilan district twenty-seven were killed and thirty wounded, some severely. The western area of the town did not suffer so much. In Octeville five people were killed. The town's undertaker placed an order for fifty coffins. One of our unexploded 15-in shells was found fifty metres from the Boulevard Maritime, another on the southern breakwater and a third stuck upright in a field four kilometres south of Rouges Terres. The diarist was intrigued by the word 'Sheffield' he found on it. Perhaps we had been using some of the Jutland outfit of ammunition and this accounted for the duds.

The Military Attaché at the German Embassy gave me two addresses in Germany and one replied. We had been engaged by Batterie Hamburg of four 24-cm guns with a range of 26,750 metres. The diary of this battery did not survive the war but the German naval war diary reports the attack and no damage. This was confirmed by a further letter from a member of Batterie Hamburg. The French bore the brunt, but the secret had been kept. M. René Salle was the name of the Cherbourg diarist. His simple record of the deaths of the townspeople bore witness to George Orwell's belief; all wars are rackets.

The ship spent five days in Portsmouth, her home port. The sailors went home and the Gunroom to Southsea. A run ashore started at the Stable Club and then on via the Nirvana Night Club, ending at the Queens Hotel. The mess travelled as a pack bent on squeezing the evening dry. For an overture we lifted the rear wheels of an Austin Seven as the Sub Lieutenant RNR who was driving it let in the clutch. We chatted to him and his girl friend as the wheels spun round. We dropped the wheels and he shot off into the blackout.

The air raids were frequent. During a lull in the noise the Canadian Mid started his own raid. He found a tin tray which he threw high into the air before it landed with a crash in the street. He tried it once or twice but overplayed his hand and a young policeman arrived. David created a diversion by climbing a lampost and engaging the officer in repartee. Our behaviour was inexcusable and not improved when we both, together with a captain's daughter in her new Wren uniform, broke off the action by leaping a fence and running across a field helpless with laughter.

The Wren was returned to the sanctuary of her Wrennery and by the time we reached the dockyard, the raid had got going. *Victory* was bathed in light from the flares and we felt drawn to her, once more in the line, 135 years after Trafalgar. The gap between the edge of the dry dock and her ancient timber cried out to be bridged, if only as a gesture from the new navy to the old. Her hull was beyond reach and despite an eye-popping joint effort we failed to pee on her.

The ship went back to Plymouth on 16 October after a night passage hugging the coast on a zig-zag course of such complexity that only 70% of the distance run was made good. The empty cordite cases from the bombardment were landed and fresh ammunition embarked. There were many air raids and boat traffic was stopped in the Hamoaze because of air dropped magnetic mines. One of the minesweeping trawlers exploded a mine but was herself sunk by the explosion. We beat *Newcastle* 28–4 at rugby and the Captain told the ship's company over the Sound Reproduction Equipment that the tide had turned in our favour in the war. Leave was granted to 120 men from each watch in turn.

My leave lasted forty-eight hours before I was recalled and told to rejoin at Glasgow. The ship had been sailed from Plymouth in a hurry and I found her again at the Tail of the Bank. On 13 November we left for Halifax and during the two day turn round the Wardroom gave a cocktail party for the American officers who had delivered ten World War One four-funnelled destroyers to their RN crews. They were a part of the deal to exchange fifty of these old ships for bases in the West Indies and Bermuda. The stories about them were critical. In one ship a welding torch applied to the iron deck resulted in a fire; the deck had been repaired with wood. Several of them were so unseaworthy that they had to give up the attempt to cross to Europe. They were unsuited to defending convoys against the submarine storm that was about to break in the North Atlantic. If we were supposed to get anti-submarine escorts we were swindled by the Americans, but it may have been that in 1940 the British government was in no position to argue.

The Gunroom were not invited to the party but met the guests on the jetty and escorted them to the foot of the brow. As naval officers of a foreign navy they were then honoured by being piped over the side, although it was after sunset. I met the last one in the shed and took him through the rain to the ship. I checked that he was really the last and went onboard. I was wearing a burberry showing no marks of rank and was received by a pipe from the side party and salutes from the Officer of the Watch and Midshipman of the Watch who mistook me in the gloom for another American. I thanked them civilly and ignored the insults.

Revenge left two days later in a temperature of eight degrees below. The weather reached hurricane conditions. The launch and first cutter were stove in and the steel boat deck pushed two feet into the air. The two starbooard paravanes went over the side from their stowage brackets on the forecastle. The steel ladder from the boat deck to the forecastle carried away and went on an unlikely journey over the upper deck until it was held by the ensign staff on the stern. We had to heave to to avoid more damage, carry out emergency repairs and allow the pumps to catch up. The sea cascaded through the 6-in casemates, flooding the batteries and messdecks and flattening any kit lockers in the way.

On Christmas Eve we were in sight of the Newfoundland coast. The upper deck, guns and rigging were covered with ice and snow, reindeer country lay only thirty miles or so on our starboard beam and the weather moderated, but despite these opportune events we were unable to get back to Halifax in time to avoid spending our second Christmas Day of the war at sea.

The ship was not in harbour so that the drinking was muted. The Irish Mid sipped too much rum somewhere and revolted everyone by vomiting quietly into his soup at lunch.

The five days in Halifax were spent in clearing up the mess and repairing the damaged rudderhead. The shipwight's party tried once more to find a way to keep the Atlantic out of the 6-in

HMS Revenge, *1941.*

casemates, but the batteries were too close to the water, and if the guns were to be trained and elevated, the flooding in heavy weather was a price that had to be paid. The 6-in were there to repel destroyer attacks from the High Seas Fleet, gone long ago, and we would have been better off without them. The Dreadnoughts of the Grand Fleet were similarly afflicted. In *Iron Duke* the two after guns were removed to the upper deck.

These were the days when Kretschmer in U 99 and Prien in U 47 were at the height of their careers, but the defence of the Halifax convoys was less arduous than might have been expected between November 1940 and January 1941, because there were few U boats in the Atlantic. All that was to change in the following year and meanwhile lack of numbers did not save HX 90 losing eleven ships in a pack attack on 1/2 December. The German heavy ships were beginning to come forward again; *Admiral Scheer* passed safely into the Atlantic at the end of October 1940 followed by her sister pocket battleship *Admiral Hipper* in December 1940. *Gneisenau* and *Scharnhorst* did not begin their famous cruise until February. These raiders were under orders not to engage the ocean escorts, such as *Revenge*, in case they suffered damage which might interfere with their main aim of destroying Allied shipping.

The submarine threat was reduced by maintaining a zig-zag course, altered at irregular intervals in accordance with patterns set out in a book held by the merchantmen. *Revenge* initiated the changes, in daylight by a flag signal. Alterations were timed with a zig-zag clock, equipped with a felt-ended spring and a metal contact. When the circuit made an electic bell went off and the convoy was ordered to assume the new course together. The system relied upon a trigger mechanism like that in an infernal machine, as I found out.

We were about two days short of the dispersal point when I relieved the Irish Mid for the morning watch. He told me that the zig-zag was being changed at 0415. I heard his steps down the bridge ladder. He stopped and I heard him coming back. He said that he had not had time to re-set the clock. I told him he would have to do it as I did not know its tricks. The Irish Mid was the Navigating Officer's assistant (or 'tanky') and played with it every day. The chart house door shut for the second time and he rattled down the ladder without reply. It was then about 0408. I heard the Captain order the Yeoman to hoist the flag signal; when it was lowered the convoy would all alter course together on the new zig-zag. That moment would come when the bell sounded.

I looked at the brass case of the clock with its old-fashioned dial and the dreaded felt-covered arm ticking away towards the metal peg. I could tell the Officer of the Watch that the clock had not been set; this would have been bad for the Irish Mid. Or I could re-set it myself; it was only a clock after all. While the Midshipman of the Watch in the ocean escort was thus engaged the outcome was awaited by the Masters and Officers of the Watch in forty merchant ships, not to mention the Commodore and the signal staffs, the quartermasters on the wheel and most important of all, my Captain standing on the compass platform a few feet away confident that his officers knew what they were doing.

Provided the bell went off at precisely 0415 the problem was solved. All I had to do was jockey the felt tipped arm into position. I moved it down the dial and the arm began to bend on the contact. So far so good. It seemed to be held up so I gave it a tweak to free it. The circuit made and before the clamour stopped I heard the Captain shout 'Executive! Downhaul!' and the new course to steer. The flag hoist came down and the battleship began to turn to starboard about four minutes before the allotted time. The merchant ships had to decide whether to ignore the signal and risk collision or do what they had been told and hope for the best.

I doubled out of the chart house to the compass platform and pushed past the Yeoman, Officer of the Watch and Princpal Control Officer. It did not seem to be an occasion for protocol.

'The zig-zag clock went off too soon sir, I was setting it and made a mistake.'

By this time the ship had begun to swing towards the starboard column, which had not altered. As the gap between *Revenge* and the line of ships closed I had no doubt that I was about to become responsible for a disaster. For the Captain however it was a bagatelle. He brought the ship back to the original course, cancelled the flag signal and turned to the Officer of the Watch.

'What is going on?'

'I have no idea, sir.'

That left me. The Captain did not waste time with questions.

'You are the Midshipman of the Watch.'

'Sir.'

'You are a bloody fool.'

'Sir.'

That was it. It is a mistake to fiddle with alarms.

We joined up with the old carrier *Argus* and the cruiser *Kenya*. This was the first time we had had a carrier with us on convoy duty and an optimist might have concluded that the message was registering. It was not until mid–1943 however, when the USN and RAF provided air support in the numbers needed, that the submarine war turned our way.

The ship rounded the Lizard by night and then went up Channel at 18 knots to Portsmouth for refit, in which our first radar, an air defence set, would be fitted. *Revenge* de-ammunitioned and locked into a dry dock for work on the hull to begin. Enemy air activity was modest, although Portsmouth had been heavily attacked shortly before our arrival. The streets were avenues cleared through heaps of smouldering and stinking rubble and, judging by the dockyard workmen, morale had suffered. The manifest idleness they displayed was too much for one RNVR sub-lieutenant with the middle watch. He turned out all the sleeping workmen of the night shift, together with those found smoking in forbidden places, lined them up on the quarter deck and told them that he had placed them under arrest. He took the view that these people, upon whose proper work the efficiency of the ship in war depended, must be guilty of some crime, probably treason if nothing worse. Needless to say there were no charges and the matter was hushed up quickly. The Sub had not appreciated that part of the deal in the coalition government ensured that trade unionists were not harassed by naval officers for having a rest when they should have been working.

I returned from leave on 10 March 1941, glad to get out of London and away from the bombing. The ship was at South Railway Jetty, re-embarking ammunition before sailing. Astern lay our sister ship *Resolution*, about to begin her refit. The usual German

Royal Clarence Yard, Gosport, 11 March 1941. Taken from HMS Revenge.

reconnaissance aircraft came over during the afternoon and the fun started an hour after sunset: 238 bombers crossed the Channel.

It began with incendiaries and parachute flares. I had no air defence station and for want of something to do I went to the GCT. Able Seaman Smith, the communication number, was there and together we watched the bright stars drifting over the dock-yard. An incendiary lodged in the funnel casing. Smith found a broom from B gun deck locker and we climbed over the back of the bridge, hoping to push it off. At the first try the broom head went up in flames. Smith announced that he intended to piss on it. He hooked one leg round the bridge ladder, gave one hand to me to hold him there and undid the flaps of his bell bottoms with the other. He did his manly best but it was useless. The incendiary gave off a green light for a moment and then burnt away as merrily as ever. We gave up and went down to report.

On the quarter deck two Free French officers, recently joined, walked up and down in determined unconcern. The flares became thicker and the noise of aircraft loud. A Vickers gun on the stern mounted on a metal post was doing nothing and the RNVR Officer of the Watch and I used it to engage the flares. We had never fired a machine-gun, but working it was not the problem; we could not hit anything with it. We sprayed the nearest flares, dangling brilliantly from their parachutes, firing the gun in turns; some were very close and it seemed impossible to miss. The ammunition rattled away until it was nearly all gone and the gun overheated but the illuminations still turned the dark March sky into midsummer. I gave it up after I followed a flare too far and sent a burst into Gosport, the other side of the harbour.

The incendiaries started fires everywhere. The Commander arrived alongside on a bicycle, snatched by the call of duty from his honeymoon bed in Southsea. The 4-in were firing but with no radar or searchlights it signified little. Those without air defence stations were ordered to take shelter from the coming storm in the 6-in batteries. I stayed on the quarter deck, I cannot now remember why, unless it was because nothing much had happened there so far.

The main stream arrived thirty minutes after the last incendar-ies, and the bombing went on for six hours. It began with high level aircraft laying sticks across the dockyard, the two battleships at South Railway Jetty providing the icing on the cake and the reason for the major raid.

The RNVR and I stood by Y turret to see the show, brave as could be. We saw the dockyard turn gradually into flaming ruin. A bomb landed between the bow of the *Victory* and the dockside. Her masts and yards became crimson from the glare and we prayed that she would survive. A Royal Marine guard saved her. The enemy seemed to be flying lower and the bombs got closer to South Railway Jetty. One stick began the other side of the signal tower and marched towards the ship, the last bomb bursting on the jetty a 100 yards away. The RNVR, marine sentry, quartermaster and I dived under the turret. We came out, feeling sheepish. When another stick came near we bolted again, and spent the rest of the night darting in and out like rabbits when the whistling seemed close. After a short while I decided I did not give a damn what anybody thought about my moral fibre. One of our own 4-in shells exploded in the harbour near by and caught us unawares because there was no warning.

The squadrons in the last wave just before dawn belonged to the first eleven. They dived on the target rather than bombing from a straight and level run. Although the ship was not hit they deserved full marks for effort. The last aircraft of all went into a dive but no bombs fell. He was not satisfied and went back up for another go. The second time the bombs landed in the centre of a fire in the Royal Clarence Yard at Gosport. After the explosions a large ball of flame lifted into the sky and it was over.

Dawn found the ship blackened by the incendiaries and flares, with her upper deck littered with lumps of concrete from near misses, but that was all. An unexploded bomb was found at the end of our brow a few feet from Y turret. Had it gone off our bolt hole would not have saved us. We lost one seaman from a fire party ashore. His cap was found but nothing else. The dockyard was a shambles with fires still burning and the roads covered with debris. There were no workmen to be seen and we sent sailors ashore to help with the mess. The survivors from the old destroyer *Witherington*, in dry dock and on her beam ends from a near miss, came onboard for breakfast and a bath. In the chest flat one of the

Mids examined a hole in his reefer; his shirt sleeve had been cut off and his arm was bare except for a dressing where a small splinter had punctured it. In answer to his enquiry we hastened to tell him that it was not worth a Hurt Certificate let alone a wound stripe; small holes did not count unless they were in your head.

I went to the Pay Office, ten minutes late and unstirred by the prospect of a day's arithmetic after the night's examination.

'You are an idle bugger,' said the Chief Writer, 'sir.'

He was quite right. I was not paid my five shillings a day to play heave-ho my lads on deck all day, or all night. The Chief was a good departmental man and took little interest in much onboard beyond his job. This seemed to be a habit of the genre. I went round the world with one who did not go ashore until we were back in Portsmouth.

Someone up there must have realized that it was not a good idea to have two battleships in the dockyard, within a cable of each other, at an easily identified jetty near the entrance to the harbour, and we went outside to an anchor and then to the Clyde. On 16 March 1941 we set out once more for Canada, arriving at Halifax seventeen days later.

We took with us on his way to America General Sikorski, the leader of the Polish Government in exile. He was invited to the gunroom and the Sub did his best to pitch the conversation at a level appropriate to our important guest.

'How long do you think, General, it would take the Germans to reach Moscow if they attacked Russia?'

'Three weeks,' said the great man.

That seemed to take care of that. He left us upon his secret affairs while we got ready for more of the never ending convoys.

CHAPTER 8

EASTERN DEPARTURE

Revenge provided the ocean escort for HX 119, 121 and 125 between 7 April and 17 May 1941. HX 112 lost 5 ships in a pack attack, HX 121 3 ships and HX 133 6 ships, but the merchantmen continued safe and sound while we were with them. The Halli-wagon ploughed on peacefully after nearly two years of war, ignored by the enemy. In the first six months of 1941 the U-Boat strength in the Atlantic rose from 80 to nearly 160; the great convoy battles were about to begin but it seemed to be no concern of ours.

The decision was made to provoke the Almighty in a modest way by holding a concert party ashore for the Queen's Air Raid Distress Fund. The show was held in the gymnasium of Dalhousie University, Halifax.

The old jokes can be relied upon and the artistes took no risks with new material. For the Burlesque Follies of 1941 the dancers came on in ballet tights and skirts, tiaras, flaxen wigs and silver wings, 52-in busts and painted faces. Boots and hairy legs completed the ensemble while the stage thundered under the weight of the twelve biggest Royal Marines in the detachment. A sub-lieutenant with a tenor voice sang 'Sweet Mystery of Life'. The ship's plumber gave impersonations, recognized at once as ship's officers and bringing the house down, although our guests could not share the jokes.

The last act but one stole the show. A physical training instructor appeared, naked to the waist, bearing a bright pair of cutlasses. He was announced as 'Chief Petty Officer Jones, late of HMS *Ajax*'. *Ajax* was a household word then. She was one of the three cruisers in the *Graf Spee* action off Montevideo. The announcer did not say that the Chief left *Ajax* three years before the battle.

85

The audience were enthralled by a display of club swinging with cutlasses to the rhythm of the band. The Chief was the Navy's Sergeant Troy, macho and dangerous, and the young women there squeaked with excitement, bewitched by the shining weapons and his muscular torso, lucent with hair oil. He was a knight fresh from the triumph in South America and the hero of the evening.

The applause delayed the finale. The company came on to sing 'There'll Always be an England', while the band waited for the Captain to finish a conversation with an officer who had just arrived and was standing before him in the front row. The Captain left. The Commander announced, with apologies to the civilian guests, that the show was over and all *Revenges* were required on board at once. On the other side of the ocean in the Arctic gloom *Norfolk* had sighted *Bismarck* and *Prinz Eugen* outward bound through the Denmark Strait.

We were a long way from any likely scene of action. *Ramillies* was escorting a convoy. Both ships were ordered to stop whatever they were doing and steer north-east. *Revenge* had two obstacles between her and the glory in prospect; we had not re-fuelled and were at four hours' notice for steam. We oiled at once and sailed independently when ready. Thereafter we obeyed the rules and fuelled as soon as we returned to harbour.

The Admiralty broadcast the general situation in the North Atlantic after the breakout. I remember two sentences, '*Hood* blown up by an unlucky hit.' '*Revenge* closing from the west.'

We were closing like mad in an effort to bridge the gap and make up for the amateur performance which had delayed our start. There was no hope of getting into it unless the German squadron broke clear and began its mission to attack North Atlantic shipping.

The story has been told a thousand times. *Hood* was sunk after a brief action taking with her Vice-Admiral Holland, our old Admiral, and all 1,200 of her crew except three. *Bismarck* was slowed down by a Swordfish strike and *Prinz Eugen* detached to act independently. *Bismarck* was sunk on 27 May 100 miles from Brest, three days after we left Halifax. We were ordered to look for *Prinz Eugen* and then join up with HX 128; we were back in Halifax on 6 June, deflated.

Junior League Dance, Lord Nelson Hotel, Halifax, Easter Monday, 1941.

If the Germans had got out the odds would have been against us in a single ship action. *Bismarck* could outrange and outrun us and her firecontrol equipment belonged to a different age. Had she reached the convoys her orders were to engage the ocean escorts and leave the pedestrian work of sinking and capturing the merchant ships to *Prinz Eugen*. *Scharnhorst* and *Gneisenau* had been told to keep clear of us and the new orders reflected the ability of *Bismarck* to sink capital ships.

In the signals that deluged the cypher office while the chase was on I remember one which ordered another battle cruiser, *Repulse*, to keep clear of *Bismarck*. Like *Hood* she was lightly armoured for a capital ship battle. *Prince of Wales* was recently out of the builder's yard and unready to take her place in the line. The German squadron could have finished her off had they chosen to delay to do so. The enemy never sent a new ship to fight until she had properly worked up and the armament and crew were ready. Despite the obsession with gunnery between the wars the Germans again seemed better at it and again this seemed to surprise the gunnery world. A friend of mine was duty cypher officer in *King George V* and took the signal to the Chief of Staff, an ex-gunnery officer, reporting the loss of *Hood*. The Chief of Staff did not believe it and told him to de-cypher the signal again to double check before he reported it to the Commander-in-Chief.

The end of the search for *Bismarck* verged on farce. The Admiralty failed to pass her position from radio intercepts to the Commander-in-Chief but sent him the bearings. The staff in *King George V* plotted them incorrectly and fixed *Bismarck* ninety miles from her true position. The hunters all set out in the wrong direction. When the error was found the quarry had gained a 150 mile lead towards her haven at St Nazaire and the pursuers were running out of fuel. Not to be outdone the Admiralty told the flagship to stay on the scene even if it meant she had to be towed home, thus ensuring the loss of a second capital ship. This was a contribution of the Prime Minister to the tactical debate, although the signal was sent under the authority of the First Sea Lord. A United States Navy ensign in a Catalina spotted her and it was a famous victory in the end.

The *Bismarck* survivors were picked up by *Dorsetshire* and *Maori*.

The first ship was a county class cruiser with an exceptional freeboard and ill-equipped for the task unless she lowered her boats. The second was a Fleet destroyer and well suited but she was called off before the job was properly started, and a thousand brave men were left to drown.

The lesson to be learned was that our staff system was second rate, and in an emergency which was foreseeable from the day that *Bismarck*'s keel was laid, we had to rely on chance for success. The lesson for the Germans was the old rule of war that forces should be concentrated. Had they delayed the cruise of *Scharhorst* and *Gneisenau* until *Bismarck* was ready, and let all the big ships loose together, with their supporting heavy cruisers, it would have needed more than luck to get us out of it.

The turn round in Halifax lasted four days and on 10 June we got ready to leave as ocean escort for HX 132, 134 and SC 34. We had an unwelcome duty to carry out before we could go. The battleship *Rodney*, which had been caught up in the *Bismarck* operation and helped to sink her, had onboard the relief for our Captain. We saw *Rodney* enter harbour and one of our boats followed her, returning with the relief. It took less than an hour for the handover and when it was done the Heads of Departments gathered at the gangway while a whaler was brought alongside. It was their time honoured duty to pull the outgoing Captain ashore. There was no time for more ceremony and all that anyone knew about it was a line in daily orders that the Captain would leave the ship shortly before sailing.

The upper deck gradually filled until it seemed unlikely that anyone not on watch was below. The Gunroom stood in a group on X gun deck, watching silently like the rest. The Captain shook hands with the Heads of Departments, who then manned the whaler, the Commander last. The Commander took his place in the stern, his hand on the tiller and the crew tossed oars. The Captain glanced forward at the crowd before walking quickly over the side while the pipes sounded for him for the last time. The whaler cast off and the senior officers did their best to look fit enough to pull 200 yards to the Yacht Club steps without making too much of a mess of it.

The boat left the gangway and gradually cleared the ship's side.

The noise began forward and increased to a roar of cheering, the sort that comes from a First Division football crowd. It lasted until the whaler reached the shore, a tribute from a thousand men who were there to say goodbye because they wanted to be.

When he had left the boat and was about to get into the car the Captain looked back at the ship for the first time. He waved once and was gone. By the time the whaler was shackled on special sea dutymen had sounded. We were through the boom and on our way to catch up twenty minutes later.

The Gunroom dispersed in reflective silence leaving the eulogy to the Sub.

'The Rammer was a decent old sod.'

There was a one day turn round after that trip before we left again with HX 134. We were back only four days later. Something was in the wind. July 1941 was a bad month for the enemy and only one convoy was attacked. Preparations were being made by the politicians for the Roosevelt-Churchill meeting in Newfoundland in August 1941, meanwhile we were to be kept out of the way; large ocean escorts were wasting assets. *Bismarck* had gone, the two battle cruisers were penned in Brest, and the submarine threat was not reduced by offering the enemy a battleship target.

Our new Captain decided to sharpen us up and we went alone to Bermuda for some gunnery. The harbour was empty. A Walrus flying boat made fast to the Admiral's sternwalk while the pilot lunched with a pal in the wardroom.

Six gunroom officers had tea with the Commander-in-Chief's wife. We put our swimming towels on the gravestone of a midshipman, taken long ago by yellow fever. Our hostess fed the fish from the end of the jetty and told us *sotto voce* that the Flag Lieutnant was a survivor from the sloop *Penzance* sunk in the North Atlantic by a submarine nearly a year before. Thus reassured we acknowledged his claim to dwell in the Eden we found about us. There were American bulldozers at work on their new base, bartered for the old escorts, but otherwise it was the 'remote Bermudas' paradise described by Marvell in Cromwell's time.

The dockyard provided a Battle Practice Target for our 15-in shoots. The Sub was Officer of Quarters of A turret and invited me to to watch a firing run. After the racket of the loading drill the noise was unremarkable when the guns fired, and except for the leap of the recoil and change in air pressure the signs that a ton of shell had been slung for twelve miles were modest.

Years afterwards I attended a Yemini prince, a visitor to the Coronation, who was shown the practice firing drill in a 6-in turret in my ship. While he was being shown something else, he asked to go back to the turret. The crew were brought back quickly and we took him inside for another run. He ignored the crew and went to the light switch. We went from darkness to light for the next five minutes until he had had enough. He had a refreshing approach to artillery; sadly, a loving uncle killed him shortly afterwards.

The Sub was a man of action and decided that his hands-off role as the Officer of Quarters demeaned his military splendour, particularly in the presence of a guest. He announced to the Gunner's Mate that he would work the rammer in the right gun the next time it was loaded and fired.

The Gunner's Mate was Captain of the Turret and as highly qualified in gunnery as Whale Island could make him. Officers of Quarters came and went but the Gunner's Mate was the top man in the turret and there was nothing in the book about young officers working the machinery. That was the job of selected gunnery rates. He said so. The Sub, thus thwarted, turned on the charm. He climbed behind the gun and rammed in the practice shell. When the cage rattled up with the cordite charge he loaded the gun correctly. It was too easy. The cage came up with the second cordite charge and the Sub rammed it in with the dexterity of an old hand. The gunhouse was sprayed with fragments of cordite waiting for a spark to blow us all to Kingdom Come. He had forgotten to check the setting and the ram had gone through the bag. The Gunner's Mate screamed 'Check Check Check', the run stopped and the crew broke the circuits and awaited events.

The Sub was full of contrition because he had made life difficult for the Gunner's Mate. This worried him more than the carnage he might have caused. He dealt with that by pointing out that if the Turret Officer was not allowed a say he might as well not be there. In peacetime there would have been a Board of Enquiry and probably a court martial. Happily it was all dealt with without either and we got on with the war.

It was not my week for gunnery. One shoot began early and I was asleep on a gunroom bench when the noise started. The steel deadlight screwed over the scuttle above my head shot across the mess. The next salvo brought a tongue of flame through the opening where the scuttle had been blasted away. Everything moveable was scattered and the air became thick with dust and smoke. It was apparent that the Marines in X turret next door had gone mad. When we heard the cease fire bell we went on to X gun deck to investigate. The whaler usually stowed there had been pulverized and was swept over the side later with a broom. The paint on the screen was scorched and bubbled by blast from the right gun which had been fired within a few feet of us.

We got the story from one of the subalterns. The turret had followed the director and reached the limit of its 'A' arcs, the safe training bearing in peacetime. This was reported to the Officer of Quarters. The turret continued to follow the director and reached the limit of the War Arcs, used when the enemy was in sight. This was also reported to the Turret Officer but no action was taken to confirm the bearing with the director. There was a fault in the system and when the director fired the right gun it fragmented the whaler and blasted the gunroom. When it comes to obeying the last order Cardigan at Balaclava had nothing on a Major of Royal Marines.

Back in Halifax we lay alongside for a month while the Admiralty thought of something to do with the four surviving 'R' class battleships. The summer seemed to last for ever and for the first time in nearly two years we were in harbour long enough to get to know some people.

The new Captain was an ex-flag lieutenant with immaculate uniforms, a monocle and an Edwardian approach. He entertained the locals and left the ship to the Heads of Departments.

I was ordered to show a Canadian colonel and his family round and give them tea in the gunroom. The eldest daughter was a green eyed beauty of nineteen and there were moments thereafter when it seemed a reasonable plan if the ship stayed in Canada for the rest of the war. Week followed week while we were immobile alongside Pier 40.

I asked for two days' leave to go fishing. On the evening of the first day we were floating in a canoe on the warm waters of Lake Micmac with music coming from Dorothy's family home and the veranda lights shining on the lake. We heard the telephone and a shout through the darkness. I was back onboard within the hour and we left the next morning. The sisters drove along the estuary road and waved the ship through the Halifax boom for the last time. Two days later we were back in Bermuda.

This time we had an American heavy cruiser and her oiler for company. We met them at a cinema show in the support ship but conversation did not flow. They showed no interest in the war at sea and we were unable to achieve a rapport. Their talk was of a cruise to Pearl Harbour and their next leave period. They were playing with a soft ball and we found them lightweight, and in a way, irritating.

On 22 August 1941, *Revenge* left for Africa and entered the tropics for the first time in her life. The Government had decided that the 'Rs' should go East, the Atlantic having become too hot for them. In white uniform we saw the dolphins play and the paravanes at night cut phosphorescent lines through the warm water, while St Elmo's Fire ran down the mast and yards.

At Freetown we waited for troop convoy WS 10 X *en route* to the Western Desert. The soldiers arrived in thousands; after two days we left with them for the South, on their long journey to the war. Our luck had held in our unescorted journey to Freetown and continued to hold in West Africa. We left Freetown on 1 September; on 21 September four U-Boats attacked SL 87 south of St Paul's Rocks and sank seven ships. On 24 November U 124 sank the light cruiser *Dunedin* with all hands in these waters, using her last torpedo at maximum range. Seven submarines were stationed off Freetown from time to time until mid-December.

The Freetown convoy was the first that *Revenge* had escorted which carried British troops. The prefix 'WS' stood for 'Winston's Special', presumably because the Prime Minister had taken the decision to send the first one. Three liners, *Strathnaver*, *Strathmore* and *Orion* had over 10,000 soldiers onboard while three 8,000–10,000 ton merchantmen carried their stores. The ships were tactically loaded so that the formation, sometimes of up to divisional strength, had all it required ready for discharge in the right order.

An anti-submarine escort was provided by four Flower class corvettes for the first two days. *Revenge* took station between the Commodore's ship *Strathmore* and the Orient liner *Orion* on the port side of the starboard column, led by the Commodore's ship. The convoy maintained a zig-zag course and the speed of advance was 13½ knots. These details set the scene for what happened next.

We were finishing dinner on the evening of the second day when the gunroom lockers, about eight feet high and ten feet long, collapsed inboard, missing two Mids sitting at the table by a whisker. The ship shuddered. The exodus was total and quick. We ran to the starboard side and found the bow of *Orion* soaring above us, stuck into our upper deck on the after end of the armour belt. The rest of her was at right angles to *Revenge*. The liner drifted aft and as she went the swell lifted her jagged bows, removing our guard rails and splintering the teak. When she reached the quarter deck the rotund figure of the Commander (E) appeared, leaning over the ship's side and following the crunching aft, to see whether the screws were at risk. He was alone in this endeavour and seemed not to notice the liner rising up and down a few feet from his head. *Orion* drifted clear leaving untidy knitting where our guard rails had been.

On the way aft her bows came down on the left gun of 'Y' turret, trained on the beam for night defence stations. The gun was run back and stayed there. It was evident, as the distance between the ships widened, that *Orion*'s bow was crushed and twisted to starboard from twelve feet above to twelve feet below the water line, with a rat bite in her stem about eight feet into her. She had been going full astern when she struck us but it was for her an argument with the Rock of Gibraltar.

The damage to *Revenge* was trivial. The second Gunnery Officer's cabin was wrecked, some guard rails and teak deck churned up and the ship's side scraped. Every check the ordnance department could think of was tried on the 'Y' turret gun and in the absence of any better idea it was given the ultimate test and fired. It worked perfectly with no sign of the 20,000 ton thump that had landed on the muzzle. The Mark I 15-in gun was designed and built in the great days.

The collision was our fault and did us no credit. The engine room had asked permission to exercise a break down in steering and the Officer of the Watch had given it, although the ship was zig-zagging at over 13 knots, surrounded by six large merchant ships. Something went wrong in the engine room drill and the ship went out of control, steering rapidly to starboard between *Strathmore* and *Orion*. *Orion* took avoiding action by turning away using full starboard helm and sounding one short blast. When collision was inevitable she went full astern on both engines. Had she not kept out of the way, and we had hit her amidships, she would have been sunk and 2,000 soldiers introduced to the surface of the South Atlantic.

Our Officer of the Watch was court-martialled and convicted of negligently hazarding *Revenge* and suffering her to be hazarded. He was dismissed his ship and severely reprimanded. The sentence was annulled by the Admiralty on the grounds that the evidence was insufficient to support the charges. He was later given his own command and retired as a commander.

Court martial records are not released for 100 years so that the reason for the annulment is hidden. The Captain gave no orders, and in their absence the Navigating Officer took over at the last moment when the collision was inevitable. This probably saved the skin of the Officer of the Watch. The Navigating Officer, who was outstanding in all he did, retired as a lieutenant-commander.

The record of the Navy for collisions was not good. Some were major disasters, such as the sinking of the destroyer *Duchess* by the battleship *Barham* in 1939 and the running down of the cruiser *Curacoa* by the liner *Queen Mary* in 1942. As a service we prided ourselves upon the ship-handling abilities of our commanding officers and compared them favourably with those of other navies. I am not sure the record supports this claim although I may be partial in this, having been in four major collisions.

The convoy formed up again after the excitement but from now on *Revenge* took station one and a half miles ahead by day and three cables astern by night. This formation was assumed, according to our report of proceedings, 'after clearing the coast'. A more likely reason was that the Commodore suggested it. The soldiers had had a nasty shock.

At Capetown the Captain marched across to *Orion* as soon as both ships were secured. His intention was to apologize to the

Master but the word came back that the meeting was not affable. The Master is alleged to have said that whoever was on the bridge of *Revenge* when the collision took place was not a seaman, a remark on the scale of insults equivalent to telling the Prince of Wales at Tranby Croft that he had cheated at baccarat.

The soldiers descended on Capetown from the WSC convoys in strengths unknown since the Boer War and the locals were hard pressed to show the hospitality most of them wished. After three days we all sailed again for the North; *Revenge* took her place on her new station ready to counter Japanese 8-in gun cruisers acting as raiders. If the Japanese chose instead to send fast modern battleships for the job the 'Rs' would be in difficulty. It was unarguable however that our new role gave us something to do. We could not stay in the North Atlantic where the threat was submarine; we could not go to the Mediterranean because our air defence and speed were inadequate. The decision to keep the 'Rs' in commmission seemed to have sprung more from sentiment than strategy; their large crews floated around the Indian Ocean instead of manning the new escorts for the Atlantic battle or the landing craft for the assault on Europe. Big ships remained the hard core of the Navy; the Army had similiar difficulties in replacing horses.

We arrived at Kilindini on 22 September, having turned our escort duties over to the old 6-in cruiser *Ceres*, who took the convoy on to Aden. On the same day I was put ashore and left the ship which had been my home for two years.

In her officers and men and the excellence of the standards that were sought in her she showed the best of the regular navy, diluted now with war time drafts. I was lucky to have been there at the end of the story that began with the 74s and would never return. The days of the line-of-battle ships were nearly over. In her unmodernized and vulnerable state, unprepared for a war that had been foreseeable for years, she was a memorial to the failure of the Naval Staff and the dishonesty of politicians. For those of us lucky enough to have served in her none of that mattered. She had been born under a lucky star and from first to last she was known to the Navy as a happy and successful ship. Lack of the right ironmongery in a world war did not change that. She inspired affection, particularly among the many who had changed from boys to men while they were in her.

My tin box and suitcase were brought up and I waited for a boat to take me ashore, on passage to join the cruiser *Emerald* as Captain's Secretary. *Emerald*, was now back on the East Indies station where she had spent most of her life.

The quarter deck division were painting Y turret, and while I waited, a seaman boy slipped on the top of the gunhouse and a tin of paint spread a grey film over the teak. I heard the voice of the Captain of the Quarter Deck behind the turret. It was quiet and thoughtful.

'My son.'

'Yes, Chief.'

'Do you know what ought to happen to you?'

'No, Chief.'

'You ought to be put back and fucked for again. Is that clear?'

'Yes, Chief.'

I left her for the last time with the music of this exchange in my ears and reported to the Navy Office. It was manned by Kenyan reservists who told me that I should wait for *Hermes* to arrive and take passage in her for Ceylon or Singapore where *Emerald* was likely to be. I was sent to an Army camp meanwhile.

I found myself in a banda hut surrounded by askaris of the King's African Rifles, the air awash with Swahili. I managed enough of this to ask for hot water and similiar basics but the strange routine was not going to be fun. I transferred myself to a hotel to await *Hermes*. She arrived a day or so later but showed no inclination to leave so I stayed where I was. The heavy cruiser *Exeter* arrived, fresh from her refit after the *Graf Spee* action.

I shared a room with an air engineer officer and through him met 814 Swordfish Squadron, the only one that *Hermes* had, being a very small carrier with a complement of fifteen aircraft. The aeroplanes had been disembarked to Port Reitz airfield and I was able to enjoy the view at 90 knots and 5,000 feet over the harbour. On one of the flights the pilot developed an attack of malaria, to which he was suddenly prone, and landed in a hurry, sweating and shaking. As we helped him out he tried to apologize for the uncomfortable ride but I could hardly hear him. The attack went as quickly as it arrived and in a day or so he was OK.

I joined *Hermes* and we sailed with *Repulse* in company for the Seychelles Islands, where I hoped to find *Emerald*. *Hermes* was a toy when compared with the Fleet carriers now coming forward. Her design was rudimentary and the arrangements for the aircraft were basic. The only way on to the flight deck was by one narrow iron ladder. The wardroom was next to a boiler room and equally hard to reach. Her flight deck was small and demanded skill from the pilots, who could not land from astern because of funnel gas. The technique demanded a right angle approach and a final steep turn to line up and land on. This was the first carrier sent to the East to be ready for the Zeros and fleet carriers of the Japanese. In order to give the enemy a further advantage, which they most certainly did not need, the Admiralty had chosen that moment to relieve most of the aircrew in 814 Squadron and replace them with freshly trained reserve officers.

After clearing Kilindini the departing aircrew said goodbye to their friends and took off for Port Reitz to hand over their aircraft to the new boys. While we waited for them to arrive the flag deck below the bridge filled up with morbid spectators, confident that they would get their money's worth.

One Swordfish went into the island, scattering the onlookers; another came in too fast and just caught the wire before stopping with her wheels sticking through the mainplane. The rest got down in one way or another, making dummy runs before attempting the deck landing. The Squadron Commander, a major of Royal Marines, did not look pleased. In the middle of it all *Repulse*, the Senior Officer, reminded *Hermes* that gunnery still ruled; if a German raider was found, *Hermes* would not be needed and *Repulse* would take care of her. The aeroplanes could stay in their carrier.

It took ten days to reach the Seychelles because we carried out a sweep for raiders. By the time *Hermes* got there the number of her undamaged aircraft had been much reduced. Another had gone into the island. Another landed heavily and skidded down the flight deck, with her wheels sticking out of the mainplane and two A/S bombs rolling ahead. The bombs bounced like tennis balls and came to rest a few feet short of the bows from whence they were heaved on tiptoe over the side.

Another Swordfish circled the ship repeatedly as the light went, and eventually ditched. Her crew were picked up by the RNR lieutenant in a cutter under oars. They stepped from the sinking aircraft into their dinghy, automatically released from the main-plane, and arrived onboard with dry feet. The pilot and observer were treated to a drink by the squadron C.O. and, as was the custom, to ensure that there was no loss of nerve, he told them that they would be flying next day. 'Not me,' said the RNVR sub-lieutenant observer. The wardroom was silent for a fraction of a second and then conversation broke out louder than ever. I was the youngest and most junior officer there, and a passenger, and this was none of my business; I crept quietly out. The observer had lost his best friend shortly before. He had walked into a propeller and the observer had seen it all. I noticed that he was in the air again a day or so later.

The day before the ship reached the Seychelles one of the damaged Swordfish had its repairs completed and the Major took it up for an air test. He would normally have flown alone but the Senior Pilot agreed that I could go with him. I fixed myself to the cockpit floor with the wire provided but there were no other preparations and the Major did not acknowledge my presence. I thought it prudent to take off my cap in case it went over the side. There was no need for flying overalls or goggles and we swooped over *Repulse* with hardly more sensation of speed than that from a motorcycle. The pilot did his right angled turn and we crossed the stern. I thought we had missed the wires and stood up to look at the island as we passed it on the way round for a second go. The aircraft caught the last wire and I was thrown into a heap at the bottom of the cockpit. By the time I had sorted myself out I was alone in the hangar with the wings folded back. The pilot had jumped from the lift on to the flight deck and was gone before I was able to say thank you.

On 26 October the squadron arrived at Mahe and *Emerald* was there. I joined her the same day and found myself the senior midshipman in the gunroom, having only two months to go before my first stripe.

HMS Emerald *(pre-war photograph).*

CHAPTER 9

SINGAPORE TWILIGHT

Emerald took a long time to build, even by the leisurely standards of a Royal Dockyard. Laid down two months before the end of the Great War with a designed speed of 33 knots, she was towed after the Armistice from Wallsend to Chatham to be finished. Commissioned seven years later she spent her working life with her sister, *Enterprise*, on the East Indies station, where her three funnels enhanced her authority in Arabia. She had seven 6-in guns in open mountings but her main armament was torpedoes, an unlikely weapon for responding to a challenge from a nation on the Indian Ocean rim. There were eight above water tubes each side and in a night action she would have been a formidable opponent if able to get close. She had a collection of dated anti-aircraft weapons and a seaplane for reconnaissance. The war complement of 600 to keep her going included a Gunroom of eleven officers. Between the funnels there was a Krooman's hut for local labour, now empty.

When I joined she had just finished a refit at Singapore, making good the damage after a collision in the Malacca Straits with another cruiser, *Dauntless*, steering an opposite course on a black night. Both ships were darkened and unaware of each other's presence. *Dauntless* altered to port, incorrectly, and struck *Emerald* in three places on her port side, killing sixteen men asleep on the upper deck and reducing eight loaded torpedo tubes, half her main armament, to flaming ruin. Neither warship made the challenge, and *Dauntless*, having shaken herself free asked, 'What ship?' manifesting her readiness for war.

The Board of Enquiry found that her lookouts did not have binoculars and, despite the navigational hazards in the Straits, her Officer of the Watch was alone on the bridge. *Emerald*'s Instructor

Lieutenant, asleep on the quarter deck, awoke to see a wall of flame bearing down upon him, and jumped over the side, only to recall when in the water that he could not swim. *Dauntless* lowered a whaler and picked him up at the last useful moment. *Emerald* was able to bury eleven of her dead the next day but had to wait another two days, after the dockyard had removed the wreckage, before the last five were recovered.

This avoidable tragedy illustrates some of the defects in the system in those days; the incompetent staff sailing two darkened ships on opposite courses in pilotage waters without warning them of each other's presence; the unreadiness for war in both ships; the willingness to deal softly with the Command ashore and afloat when they fell into fatal error, and the inadequate communications. The RNR lieutenant on the bridge of the *Dauntless* was court-martialled and punished, the only officer to be blamed.

I was not required to serve as the Captain's Secretary; the Captain already had one and vetoed a change. I was put in charge of cyphering.

The gunroom was small and home to six Dartmouth midshipmen, two sub-lieutenants and me. The Sub of the Gunroom was the Air Branch Officer observer who sat behind the Chief Petty Officer pilot in the Sea Fox aeroplane.

As a new boy I was bidden to accompany the Captain and Paymaster Commander to lunch with the Governor, alone in Government House, save for a section of Punjabis sent there to protect him. Another remote island like this was visited by a German cruiser in August 1914. She was received with a gun salute, which was returned, the officers were dined by the Governor, stores and fuel embarked and an agreeable visit concluded before she sailed away. Some days later when the mail boat arrived the Governor learned that the Empire was at war with Germany and he had entertained an enemy raider. That is the story and I have heard it more than once; I am confident that it did not happen in the Seychelles. Perhaps it was somewhere else.

The Governor was Sir Arthur Grimble, remembered now for his book *A Pattern of Islands* about colonial rule in the Pacific. I found him an educated and charming man who expressed an enthusiasm for Keats which, in a lapse I immediately regretted, I told him I shared. I knew well that poetry was not a requirement and it was best to shut up about it. Thereafter Sir Arthur directed his remarks to me and seemed not to notice my embarrassment when the two senior officers were at one point left talking to each other. He was obstinately disinclined to change the conversation to the war, or the Navy, or the Seychelles economy and went happily on about La Belle Dame and floating about the summer waters as if the others had not been there. The jolly conversation between the Governor and a Pay Mid was not received with approbation by the others, who put on the expressions of grown ups in the presence of precocious young. It was not a good start.

Repulse and *Hermes* disappeared and we shared the delights of the island for the next two weeks with a Catalina reconnaissance squadron of the RAF. The Gunroom discovered that a local beauty with red hair was walking out with one of the pilots, but sought consolation when his aeroplane took him to Colombo. The trick was to memorize the number on his Catalina and hope that it would not come back early.

Our routine was idyllic, with swimming, sailing and practice on the 6-in loader to keep fit, and the island to explore. The population varied from white to black. The leading families with the whitest skins had French names and spoke French to each other; we took the place from France in some old campaign.

The good luck continued. The ship was employed during the few weeks left before Japan came into the war in showing the Flag to the East African colonies. The cruise began at Lindi where there were some anxious moments because our chart was out of date. At Dar-es-Salaam, in former German East Africa, then Tanganyika, the mooring was tricky and involved lying stern-to with a line from aft to palm trees ashore. We entertained the locals on the quarter deck, to the delight of the insects who swarmed up the manilla rope from the trees towards the lights, negotiating the rat guards as if they were not there before devouring the hosts. They seemed not to bother the guests, either male or female, being no doubt tired of their usual diet.

Our departure the next day was awkward because of a current which pushed us towards the south side of the narrow entrance. In the hubbub on the upper deck the Second Lieutenant missed his cue and the Important People, including the Commissioner, assembled near by to see us go, heard the Commander in overdrive.

'Blenkinsop', he yelled, 'you are wetter than a nun's nunkey!'

The Commander was tall, thin and red faced with many years of submarine service. He carried a hankerchief at all times which he gnawed repeatedly. He exuded suppressed fury, perhaps because he was away from the action, or because he disliked the climate, or not being in command of his own ship; no one knew. The executive officers, with one exception, were wary of him. The odd one out was Hank, an American from California who had talked his way into the RCNVR to get into the war, and found himself watchkeeping in an old cruiser, further from the clash of arms than he would have been had he stayed in Los Angeles.

He was Officer of the Watch in harbour one day, engaged in sorting out a mix up in the boats, while the Commander watched from the gangway, gnawing away. He could bear it no longer and told Hank what to do.

'Right,' said Hank, 'you seem to know all about it. You better do it.'

He pushed his telescope under the Commander's arm and went below. He was genuinely indifferent to rank.

He talked his way into submarines later and survived the war only to end up in prison for smuggling liqueurs across the Channel. Unfortunately for him he overdid it and smuggled with a landing craft, loaded with the contraband. No less than three trips were made said the judge who sentenced him.

'Three, hell,' said Hank, *sotto voce*, 'thirteen.'

When he was alongside the depot ship in his submarine, a famous American general came to a wardroom guest night. It is said that Hank made love to the general's FANY driver between the soup and the Loyal Toast. He probably went to the dinner too.

You can smell the cloves at Zanzibar before you see the island; our wake was a white curve on a still blue sea for miles astern when we turned for the harbour. The English colony in this Arab stronghold were heartened to see us and held a dance at the Club, with waltz music delivered fortissimo by an African military brass band.

Tanga was our last call and the most enjoyable. The English colony was particulary friendly; at the Club dance, the husbands, following a plan, spent the evening in the bar, leaving their wives to entertain the visitors. This arrangement was agreeable to hosts and visitors alike and may even have been endurable by the wives.

The Captain put up a notice in the gunroom and wardroom when we got back to Mombasa and surprised everybody. 'I congratulate you all. Like the Italians we may not be much good at fighting but we are magnificent lovers.'

We left Mombasa at 18 knots for Durban and exercised the Sea Fox on passage. The aeroplane was made ready and the crew embarked. The torpedo party loaded the catapult and prepared to fire it while the ship turned into the wind and increased speed. The pilot started the engine and the order came from the bridge to launch aircraft when ready. The torpedo officer waited for the signal from the pilot. The pilot opened the throttle, the little machine vibrated and the catapult crew ducked in the slipstream but nothing happened.

A message came from the bridge. 'Report cause of delay in launching aircraft.'

The answer was that the aircraft was not ready for launch. This reply was unacceptable.

The Captain was a gunnery officer by specialization and an ex-commander of Whale Island. He regarded the aeroplane as a weapon under his control, like any other. He had given the order to fire and wanted to know why he had not been obeyed. He drew no great distinction between firing the aeroplane and firing a gun. The Sea Fox revved up to its puny crescendo and once more nothing happened. The engine was switched off and the Sub-Lieutenant observer made his way to the bridge while the ship resumed her original course. The Sub reported that his pilot was not prepared to fly the aircraft because the engine had not developed enough revolutions. He explained with difficulty that in the flying world the pilot had the last say, and it mattered not that he was a chief petty officer and junior to the officer observer. The engine needed new plugs and until they were fitted it was unlikely that it would be able to drag the Sea Fox safely into the air. It was no good giving direct orders to the pilot because the decision was his alone. Thwarted, the Captain turned on the Paymaster Commander, the stores officer, and asked where the spark plugs were. They had been awaited for six months and could not be got from *Enterprise*, who needed them for her own aircraft. There was nowhere else to try.

Durban was throbbing with wartime business of every kind. The harbour held the transports on the way to Aden and the Western Desert, together with their warship escorts and, increasingly, the ships being collected to form an Eastern Fleet when the expected war with Japan started.

The ship was called upon to provide a landing party of seventy men to back up the local Naval Liaison Officer who had a mutiny of sorts on his hands. A naval draft taking passage in a Belgian merchantman broke out of their ship and refused to leave a dockside warehouse until persuaded by the show of force from our sailors. The draft had been embarked in an unconverted cattle and convict ship without shore leave since leaving UK, and had something to complain about.

The Durban air was not good for discipline; 30% of the ship's company broke their leave on the night before we left to escort the auxiliary *Derwentdale* back to Mombasa. The Captain cleared lower deck and told the hands what he thought of their behaviour and that their leave would be restricted in future. It was not a great matter but illustrates how the rules were enforced then. No enquiry was made to determine why one third of the sailors had defied authority; welfare and man management and the other abstractions did not come into it. The ship's company were bound by the Naval Discipline Act and the Captain was there to see that he was obeyed without question. In his ship, as he was once heard to say to the Chaplain, he was like God; he no longer had the power to flog but the Act enabled him to make life unpleasant for the recalcitrant and he intended to use it if he had to. He had no interest in popularity and would have despised behaviour aimed at seeking it.

The stay in Mombasa lasted twenty-four hours and while we were there the war with Japan began. We went back to Durban at 20 knots and the Young Gentlemen enjoyed the bustle and the knowledge that they had, by the attack on Pearl Harbour, been translated overnight to the front line. Our main base was Singapore and it was our duty to protect India, Burma, Malaya and Africa from the Navy of the enemy. The War Plans of 1939 required us to defend Anzac too, but the Mediterranenan adventure had put paid to that.

The general view onboard was that the Japanese should not be taken too seriously. They copied our ships and weapons but had little technology of their own. They wore glasses and could not fight at night. It should not take long to deal with them, particularly as the station had now been reinforced with heavy ships and the Fleet carriers were expected. This euphoria was not shared by the Captain of Marines, who had been an Assistant Military Attaché in Tokio, or the Paymaster Commander who had spent years there learning Japanese. Although in a position to say much, they said nothing.

Half way through the passage back to Durban we heard about the loss of the *Prince of Wales* and *Repulse* at Kuantan. I was leaving the gunroom and Donald was in the flat outside and told me. It was the second event in the war, after the German breakthrough to Boulogne, that will stay forever in my memory. Boulogne questioned the future of the Empire; Kuantan answered it.

We derived what encouragement we could from the statement of the Prime Minister to the House of Commons that he was sorry, and would send aircraft to Malaya as soon as possible. He had much to be sorry about, the ships having been sent there because he insisted on it, contrary to the advice of those among the Naval Staff who, on this occasion, had the guts to oppose him.

Strategy was none of our business; all that concerned *Emerald* was the immediate change in routine. The party was over and from now on we would be expected to earn our keep. We suffered our first casualty in the new war when a stoker fell off a hotel balcony and fractured his skull. We had no time to bury him and the battleship *Royal Sovereign*, just arrived, agreed to hold the funeral for us. We passed *Dauntless* on our way out of harbour and the terrible deaths of sixteen of *Emerald*'s crew in the collision was recalled by the following signals.

From *Dauntless*: 'Sorry to have missed you'.

From *Emerald*: 'Hope we shall meet again soon'.

Thus mourning her dead *Emerald* sailed for the war with half her torpedo armament, a stranded aeroplane and an unsettled crew.

Kilindini harbour was dominated by the American troopship *Mount Vernon* with 3,000 British soldiers embarked. I was handed a secret signal to be passed to her concerning the voyage we were about to start together. The only cypher we had which we believed to be held by the Americans was a diplomatic one. It seemed unnecessary to encypher a message for a ship a few hundred yards away; I delivered it personally to the Signal Officer in *Mount Vernon* and asked him if he held the diplomatic cypher. He had not heard of it. I pointed out that we did not appear to have any means of secret communication by radio. This seemed to present no problem to him. He announced that he intended to report the omission at once to the Admiralty and his Navy Office in plain language, using his initiative, and without reference to his Captain. They were very green. I begged him to forget it as there was nothing to be done at this stage and now that the RN and USN were operating jointly, it seemed certain that the Signal Branch would have to get its act together and ensure that the navies could talk secretly to each other, without having to enter harbour and send an officer in a boat. He calmed down and I went back onboard to report, but there was no interest and it went no further.

The conditions between decks in *Mount Vernon* were not good. The men were in tier bunks jammed together and fed in watches. The Brigadier shared a small cabin with three colonels. The ship had been six weeks on passage and the troops had had no opportunity to keep fit by marching ashore; onboard there was not enough deck space to exercise. These soldiers were destined for the Malayan jungle to fight the Japanese.

We saw little evidence that the short time in harbour was being used to get the men into trim. They wandered up and down the jetty, pale and glum in ill-fitting shorts, eating oranges given to them by our sailors, who felt sorry for them. Their officers turned out in strength to a dance in Government House on Christmas evening, resplendent in service dress, Sam Browne belts and shiny shoes and buttons. They outnumbered the handful of females by about twenty to one and spent the evening talking to each other round the bar. A drunken sailor joined the party and staggered about until he was removed by the patrol. The Army treated this trivial episode with shrill disfavour and it was apparent that something was wrong. It was easy enough for us, of course, we did not have to advance under fire on foot, but it did not look good.

Emerald left with *Mount Vernon* on 29 December 1941 on her first task in the new war, escorting four 13 knot ships to Singapore, where the need for them had become desperate. Among the stores were fifty-one Hurricane fighters in the motor vessel *Sussex*, together with their ground and air crews. It was common knowledge by then that Singapore had little chance without fighter defence.

On New Year's Day I shipped a stripe and assumed the acting rank of Paymaster Sub-Lieutenant, being unable to attain the substantive rank until I had passed the qualifying examination. Unlike executive and engineer officers, paymasters were not sent ashore to take courses for their sub-lieutenant's examinations and were required to prepare on the job.

One of my entry was Captain's Secretary of *Penelope* on passage from Malta to Gibraltar, when she was bombed continuously. He sat down to answer his questions on Naval Law, History, French and the professional subjects, knowing that each moment might be his last, while the racket went on and the ship was riddled with bomb splinters from the near misses. Although this was good eighteenth-century stuff, all in the day's work, his Captain decided to report it, either to get the system changed, or, more likely, because it made an amusing yarn. Thereafter captains were invited to send the papers in with a covering letter indicating the opportunities the examinee had had to prepare and the actual conditions under which the examination had been taken. My moment was postponed because the papers had not caught up with the ship, having been sent to *Revenge*.

The convoy gathered at Addu Atoll, then a secret anchorage in the Indian Ocean known as Port T. The escort was reinforced by *Exeter* and the Indian Navy escort *Jumna*. *Exeter* was anchored near the entrance and made the challenge, to which *Emerald* gave the wrong reply, not having changed the signal on the first day of the month. This episode could have brought disaster at night and there was an urgent enquiry. The cypher making the change had been received corruptly so that it could neither be de-cyphered or even identified as a message with which we were concerned. I was the Cypher Officer with overall responsibility. The Captain of Marines was Confidential Books Officer and had failed to notice that the usual amendment was missing. The Signal Officer should have checked the relevance of the corrupt message at the first opportunity. All three of us dropped the ball. The whole rigmarole should have been the responsibility of a signal officer, as in other navies, but we had none, the job being given to the Navigating Officer who had plenty to do without it. Spe-cialist signal officers were not drawn into the drudgery of cypher-ing being more concerned with the intricacies of manouvering by flags and preparing seating plans for lunch and dinner parties.

Addu Atoll was manned by Royal Marines surrounded by rotten palm tree stumps, crawling with insects, said to breed the typhus bug. Its defences were primitive; the Japanese had not heard that we were using it. No one went ashore and we left the next morning for Singapore. *Emerald* was Senior Officer of the Escort, her readiness for war up a notch or two after the disaster at Kuantan. The aeroplane now developed the required revolu-tions and shared dawn and dusk patrols with *Exeter*'s Walrus.

The first alarm came when a ship reported a shadowing aircraft. We flew to action stations, engrossed by the silver dot high above the centre of the convoy. It had to be from a carrier, ominous for the soldiers, sent there without fighter cover. We awaited the first attack. The spell was broken by a merchantman who reported by light signal that he had been navigating on the Japanese aircraft for the past two days. Being a wag he did not add any clues. The Navigating Officer took a sextant bearing of the aeroplane and, after a look at the star globe, reported that the threat was Venus and unlikely to cause trouble while we were at sea.

Exeter's Walrus and our Sea Fox were hard at it scouting ahead. They brought in reports of merchant ships but nothing sinister. We were approaching the Sunda Strait between Java and Sumatra when the masts of an unidentifed ship appeared on the port bow and the ship prepared for action. As 6-in rate officer I had a good view from the spotting top. Through the binoculars something appeared where the bows should have been and then sank in the swell to be followed by a second object rising from the stern. We agreed that it was unlike an ordinary ship and the objects rising and falling could have been aircraft flying off. When her hull came up she was identified from the bridge as the Dutch cruiser *De Ruyter*, who had been expected to join the escort in two days time. She had a heavy tower bridge and gunnery control position and it had been this superstructure, together with the big funnel, rising and falling, which had fooled us.

Having thus wandered into the convoy without mishap her Admiral came by motor boat to call on the Captain. We remained underway and the barge followed astern while he was with us. The crew wore Victorian sennet hats and their bare chests were burnt mahogany by the sun. The Admiral was onboard for about a half an hour and when he left the cruiser disappeared as silently as she had come. The strange ship, the old-fashioned uniforms, the careless grace of her arrival and departure, belonged to another time and brought elegance to our tedium. Six weeks later she was blown apart by a Japanese torpedo in a night attack and took her Admiral and all hands down with her.

The destroyers *Jupiter*, *Encounter* and *Vampire* joined the escort; the Sea Fox returned from a long patrol to report that they had flown over land and been jumped by Buffalo fighters of the Dutch Air Force. Although there was little co-operation between the two countries the Dutch pilots had recognized a friend, while for his part the Sub had taken his finger off the Lewis gun just in time, before doing his best to take one of them with him. We passed through the Sunda Strait with two Dutch destroyers on the screen and a Dutch Catalina and Fokker carrying out A/S patrols, all new arrivals that had appeared without warning. Thus supported we turned north for Singapore and the passage through the Banka Straits between the Islands of Banka and Java.

In the channel, the convoy formed into a column six miles long with the warships split up to give the best A/A protection through the narrowest part, where there was insufficient sea room to manoeuvre to avoid bombs. *Vampire* led, followed by *Emerald*, and the two Dutch destroyers brought up the rear. The crocodile was well into the straits when Singapore radio broadcast that a formation of Japanese bombers was heading south. At the same time *Exeter* reported a large group of aircraft approaching from the north. We got ready for them. All depended upon whether the enemy would sweep over the straits or over the open sea to the east of Banka Island, being unlikely to have fuel for both. If they went east they would miss us. Westward, they would find our long column locked in the narrow strait in the worst formation to repel aircraft, an attack from ahead or astern being equivalent to crossing the 'T' of the enemy in a surface action. A bomb would have a chance of sinking the next astern or ahead if it missed the primary target. Ships sunk or damaged would impede the passage of those behind as they tried to get out of the trap and reach open water.

I shared the spotting top with the Gunnery Officer, a chief petty officer and a communication number. Guns was a fat and cheerful peacetime RNVR who compounded his physical disadvantages in the tropical heat by chain smoking from a tin of fifty Players, which were always in his hand. It was said that he took up a fresh tin about lunch time. He was a solicitor in private life, with an analytical turn of mind; no doubt he had reached a conclusion about our gunnery, which may not have enthused him. The ship had little to offer against aircraft, and everyone knew it.

We awaited the outcome of the even bet whether they would go east over the empty sea, or west, to a dream target. The Chief pointed out that if things did not turn out to our advantage any bombs near us would explode underneath, showering the splinters upwards through the spotting top floor. This was urgent and cogent intelligence and each of us took off his tin hat and sat on it in the hope of surviving with vital parts preserved. It was meant to be funny and the repartee was still being exchanged when the word came from the bridge that *Exeter* had reported that they had gone east of the island and had turned for home. We fell out, thankful.

There were mines in the approaches to Singapore and *Vampire* managed to explode one on the surface. Most of the convoy entered Keppel Harbour while the warships and *Mount Vernon* were sent to the Naval Base on the north side of the Island. We went alongside our oiler, secured to the jetty on the south east corner of the Johore Causeway. The Causeway was solid with traffic, trucks, guns and ambulances going north and ambulances coming south in unbroken streams. In the pouring monsoon rain a party of coolies were digging trenches in the ground by the end of the jetty. The depth of the works showed that they had not been there long. No one seemed to be in charge of them and they stopped digging to look at us and the Causeway traffic.

Our orders were to leave that night and we laboured to embark stores from the dockyard, which were ours for the taking. After dark the last boat came alongside with its load scattered in the water inside her. Both watches were called to clear the boat at the rush. We had to shine a cluster light to enable us to separate the mixture of provisions and naval stores, which were then thrown onboard by the shortest route. For once the dockyard forgot about signatures. Before the job was done the Commander decided that the seamen needed a rest. He fell them out although he knew that the work would have to be done by a handful of men in the Supply Division who could not do it in the time.

The Paymaster Commander, making a point, stood in the bottom of the boat in tropical rig with the rain streaming over him, collecting potatoes with a bucket. The rest of the Supply Division, officers included, formed some sort of a chain from the boat across the upper deck, fired up, not about the stores, but because they were determined not to be seen off by the Executive Department. This happened at Singapore Island four weeks before its fall raised the curtain on the last run of the British Empire.

I lugged a carcass across the crowded seamen's messdeck to find the hatch to the storeroom below shut. I wrestled with the tackle to lift the cover; two hands gave up eating their supper and silently raised it and struck the load below, unwilling to see an officer make a fool of himself. The Paymaster Commander called us off shortly afterwards and told the boat to take what was left back to the Yard.

The ship was unable to creep away through the blackness of the monsoon night because the dockyard pilot failed to turn up. The weather and absence of navigation aids in the channel made it impossible to attempt the transit without him and we left at first light, entering the Rhio Strait, unchallenged, at 26 knots with *Exeter* and the destroyers *Electra* and *Stronghold* in company. The hospital ship *Talamba* appeared, steering north alone and we warned her about the floating mines. The squadron worked up to over 30 knots and the bow waves got higher as our sterns sank into the water and the paint on the funnels scorched. Aft, the cutlery danced about in a frenzy among the fiddles on the gun-room table. We crossed a sandbank, with enough water over it according to the chart. At that speed the stern was right down and we felt a tremor as we passed over. *Exeter* also touched. In dry dock later we found the hull burnished by the sand.

In Batavia the Dutch were trying to forget the tidal wave gathering in the north. The local paper carried the headline 'Velkom General' and a picture of Lord Wavell, sent there, like *Prince of Wales* and *Repulse*, to save the day.

In the largest hotel I found a wedding reception was in full swing while the guests raised their glasses to a Dutch army officer and his blonde bride. Shops, taxis, restaurants and night clubs did business as usual and the pony carts and their passengers ran everywhere. Either they had thought about their future and de-cided to eat, drink and be merry, or they had deceived themselves that help was at hand. Their dream world had lasted so long, and seemed so changeless, that they could not believe it might be swept away. General Wavell was the British Empire in person, and even if he had been sent there without troops or aircraft, he would be able to defend them from any Asian threat. The Admiralty took a more realistic view.

The Commander-in-Chief of the newly formed Eastern Fleet, Admiral Sir Geoffrey Layton, was in Batavia, earmarked to be the first Flag Officer Ceylon as soon as Admiral Somerville arrived on the station to take over from him. Admiral Layton had to get to Ceylon to be by the right chair when the music stopped. *Emerald* was big enough and fast enough to take him and his staff to Colombo with the briskness required so we got the job, thus missing a place of honour when the Battle of the Java Sea was fought a month later.

The Chief and Petty Officers' Recreation Space was taken up

with filing cabinets, and the port waist, where the destroyed torpedo tubes had been, became a tarpaulin covered mound. The Staff came on board in twos and threes and shared our cabins, sleeping on deck like the rest of us.

We left with a vice-admiral's flag at our foremast and went on to 22 knots. The First Lieutenant was seen on the forecastle shouting and pointing to our wake which had taken the shape of the Severn Bore. Speed was reduced and the pilot asked how much water we were in. He hoisted seven fingers and laughed a good deal before reassuring the Captain by pointing out that it would soon be eight metres. Meanwhile the ship had been steaming at 22 knots with three feet of water under her.

In the Sunda Straits four darkened ships appeared on opposite course and refused either to answer the challenge or to give way. *Emerald* switched on navigation lights and altered away; it was assumed that they were Dutch patrol boats. Once again neither side knew the other was there. The staff officers sleeping quietly on our upper deck had some responsibility, but it had been a busy day for them and they slumbered on while we passed Krakatan and its smoking volcano.

The following morning I collected my blanket and staggered off the upper deck to dawn action stations, leaving the Admiral's Flag Lieutenant out to the world in the billet he had taken next to me. I remember that he had blue sheets, a domestic detail that was relished by the Gunroom, who made the predictable ribald comments, not having encountered such refinement before.

On 21 January 1942 the Admiral was landed at Colombo and transferred his flag to the Hong Kong and Shanghai Bank the same day, while we went into dry dock to look for damage to our four screws after the scrape over the sandbanks. I was also landed, to enable shore treatment to be given to an eye infection which had defeated the medicaments available to the PMO.

CHAPTER 10

EASTERN FLEET

The Grand Oriental Hotel filled a corner site close to the harbour and was both Grand, with solid, albeit faded, accommodation, and Oriental, providing rest for the traveller at the gateway to India and the Far East. I stayed there to be near the eye hospital in Colombo; there was no convenient naval mess.

The fall of Singapore was three weeks away but the city seemed unaffected by the apocalypse in prospect. The struggle between the white and coloured races for domination of the Far East was of concern to those with power; it meant little to the indigenous millions of India and Ceylon.

The hotel ran a peacetime routine. There were families without fathers who spent the day in the public rooms, reading newspapers and exchanging the latest news from Malaya, but otherwise it was business as usual. The staff were long serving and numerous and the dining room offered a dozen choices of curry. This was abundance after the thin gruel of the gunroom messman.

I was told by the local ophthalmologist, incorrectly, that I had trachoma, a tropical condition with which he was very familiar. He was a busy man and he added one more to his long list of patients with that disease without the discipline of an accurate diagnosis. In Tahiti, Gauguin wrote to his friends in Paris, '*Ici, nous sommes tous un peu syphyllitique.*' In Ceylon the locals were all a little trachomatous.

My red optics lent encouragement to the diagnosis; they looked nasty and trachoma was a nasty disease. At the hospital the out-patients were divided into 'contagious' and 'non-contagious'. Whether this distinction was social or medical I never found out, being grateful for the invitation to join the non-contagious section.

The treatment was daily cauterisation of the inner eyelids,

116

performed by one of a twittering band of little nurses, who seemed amused by my visits and were kind to me. They exchanged sallies in their own language and bubbled with laughter before setting about my affliction. After the first session a Sikh gharry driver was good enough to see me back to my room where I waited for sight to return. Thereafter I persuaded the songbirds to use less mixture on the brush. I was told when I got home that no permanent damage had been done, save for a little scarring.

The hotel had its quota of Somerset Maugham characters. I remember a blonde woman of about forty, approaching the bottle by a fairly direct route, who told me her story. She had gone to India at the age of 18 as the wife of a much older man she did not love. He agreed that the marriage would not be consummated until she said so. He was the colonel of an Indian cavalry regiment and spoiled her utterly. She had a photograph album of pennoned horsemen and polo occasions which was always near her. She was carried off by an officer from the regiment of her own age, who had to resign his commission after the divorce. Later on he left her in India without money or friends. She seemed to have no plans and drifted to Colombo to see what was going to happen next. If Maugham had written it she would have been forsaken again, this time by a man half her age; in fact she became friendly with a planter who was older so that it may have turned out well for her.

The music at dinner was played by a Hungarian orchestra who had been on tour when the war broke out and were now completing the second year of an engagement intended to last three weeks.

Among others in transit was a warrant officer from *Repulse* who had been slow in getting out of the wireless office when she turned over. The experience left him with an impulse to talk, and like the Ancient Mariner, he was hard to discourage.

Cheered one evening by a captive audience he got on to his early service in submarines. He was painting the side of his boat in Wei-hai-Wei with his best friend on the stage beside him. His friend groaned and fell towards the hull but managed to hold on. The Ancient Mariner asked him the matter and was told that he had had a chancre removed by a Chinese quack. He was twisted with pain but dared not report sick with venereal disease because it would have meant discharge from submarines and loss of pay. There was blood on the stage and the AM begged him to give up but he would not and shortly afterwards went on with his work. In his contempt for adversity the long service naval rating of those days could have had few equals.

After six weeks there it occurred to me that if I did not get away I would be caught up in one of the shore staffs proliferating in Ceylon. I persuaded a naval doctor to pass me fit, subject to further treatment on board, but it was difficult to get a passage back. The staff were uncertain of *Emerald*'s whereabouts, and knew only that she was running convoys in the Bay of Bengal and had been to Rangoon and Calcutta. I visited the office daily, anxious that if I had to wait for them to do something I might get becalmed there, another wedding guest at the mercy of the Ancient Mariner.

Mount Vernon appeared, this time heavily laden with Australians and New Zealanders, on the way home from the Western Desert to defend Anzac from the Japanese. She was joined by a second transport with large drafts of Americans. Both ships gave leave at the same time and few of these birds of passage failed to alight at the GOH, the first licensed establishment they saw on the way from the harbour.

The hotel foyer, the size of a skating rink, filled immediately and the waiters rushed from table to table to keep up. The customers found the service slow and placed multiple orders. After a half an hour the first glasses were broken; twenty minutes later came the first burst of song, followed shortly by the first fight. The staff ran for cover. The tables were swept away and from the landing, where the prudent had retreated, we looked down on a sea of roaring, shouting and singing drunks, engaged in rucks and mauls with swinging fists and no referee. Chairs went on to the street in clouds of glass and it was only the press of bodies which prevented the contestants from getting down to some grievous bodily harm.

The hotel receptionist was a middle aged Scotswoman who had no doubt seen a lot before, and did not intend to be overawed by childish behaviour from a collection of quasi-colonials. She took station behind her counter and every time a drunken arm came near she struck with an ebony ruler. She was magnificent and had more effect on the mob than a sergeant and ten sepoys, who were pushed out of the door. Order was restored by the Naval Patrol; the noise died down to the sobs of the maudlin and retching of the legless. It was a great night; the receptionist showed how the Scots deal with barbarians in drink.

The Naval Staff collected twelve canvas bags of confidential mail for *Emerald*; it had come from England, sealed, so they were not sure of its importance and decided that it ought to be delivered, or at least got out of the office, in case they were held responsible for holding on to it. I was told to rejoin my ship at Madras if she was there, and if not, to follow her with the bags until I found her. Accompanied by a Canadian engineer on passage I headed for the night train to India. The bags guaranteed comfort as their secrecy demanded that we had a compartment reserved.

The platform was solid with Tamils on the way home, squatting in groups and chattering in anticipation. The train came in and they rushed it, disappearing at speed with their luggage, children, old people and brass pots into the carriages. The station-master and one of his staff fought a way through the corridor. We found our compartment full to the brim with a family who had stowed themselves and their gear on the seats, floor and luggage racks and did not flinch at the gold lace at the door. The station-master showed anger and they left neatly and silently without a word, being used to the routine. One day a passenger with a reserved compartment would miss the train and they would be on their way. We settled in the sleeper with the bags about us, feeling no guilt.

It took about thirty-six hours to get there. We left the train once to take the ferry across the Palk Strait to India. The bags were piled amidships and we sat on them in case one of the throng of dhoti clad passengers should be an enemy agent looking for re-cyphering tables.

The sea was a flat calm and there was no movement onboard during the short voyage. A man sitting by the ship's side looked about him to collect attention before being seasick on the deck about a foot inboard from the guardrail.

Oh, East is East and West is West,
and never the twain shall meet,
Till Earth and Sky stand presently
at God's great Judgement Seat.

We arrived at Pondicherry at midnight with flares lighting the
brass everywhere and the dark sandstone walls brooding over the
swarm. This was where Clive had opened his account as an ensign
in the Company's service. The French were pushed out and the
great days began. They lasted in India for 200 years. The train
took us over the battlefields of the Coromandel Coast to Madras,
through places redolent with the history of the Empire. Singapore
Island had just surrendered after an undistinguished campaign
against inferior numbers. It was a good moment to be passing the
fields of Trichinopoli and Wandewash, where inspired victories
were won by a handful of my countrymen. Whatever moral
questions are raised now, the getting of the Empire in India was
done by men who could have held their places in Alexander's
Companion Cavalry.

I found *Emerald* at Madras alongside a wall in the harbour. She
seemed beautiful to me with her three raked funnels and skinny
hull despite the detritus of the East about her. If she had been a
dredger it would not have lessened the pleasure of walking onboard among friends.

The Captain sent for me to enquire whether I had heard
anything of *Exeter* while in Colombo. By then she had been sunk
in the Java Sea battles but I knew nothing. The Commander-in-
Chief did not send out situation reports and private ships continued to be unaware of the whereabouts of others on the station.
The outcome of chance encounters between darkened ships at
night remained a lottery.

Madras showed no signs of the new war, and the advance of
the enemy into Burma on the other side of the Bay of Bengal.
We were entertained in an Indian Army mess, built with a
colonnade around a dining room like Paddington Station. It was
put there in the Company days to enable the officers to watch
the regiment's elephants parade after dinner. There was lunch
and tennis with the Chief Justice and drinks with the Worcester

Regiment. One company of that battlion with no armour or heavy weapons was responsible for defending many miles of coast. They had been in India for years and the officers had their families with them. The Major and his charming lady were anxious to hear news of Malaya and the new war, which was about to change their lives.

We were challenged to cricket by Madras University and took the field in an arena bigger than any I had played on, with a pavilion like the one in St John's Wood. Our opponents were good and made no concessions to our lack of practice, or the war, in which we detected a pointed absence of interest. We were British and they were there to beat us.

We faced defeat at the end with the skipper and two tail-enders having to last out the final half hour. The captain was a tall, thin seaman lieutenant with a Scottish name which concealed a Yorkshire approach. He had batted through most of the innings and with twenty minutes to go tried to sweep the ball, deflected it on to his head and knocked himself silly. He was helped off to be stitched. Our last man came out and was bowled with five minutes left. The stumps were drawn, the students whooped with pleasure and began the long walk back to the pavilion, only to be met by the gangling figure of the skipper, on his way to resume his innings and force a draw, with a hankerchief round his head and a bloody shirt.

> I am hurt but I am not slain;
> Ile lay mee downe and bleed awhile
> And then Ile rise and fight againe.

The ship covered the evacuation of the Andaman Islands and returned to Madras with 1,800 men and women, mostly soldiers, in the liner *Neuralia*. On the way to the rendezvous we picked up nine Indians clinging to two boards, which kept their heads above water, but not much else. They were survivors from a dhow on passage from Akyab to Chittagong which had been swept out by a strong current and sunk by gunfire from a Japanese submarine. Six salvoes had been fired from about 200 yards. The first sank the dhow and the rest were fired at the survivors, most of whom had shrapnel wounds. Although the attack had taken place three and a half days before, they were all alive except two who had died earlier on the day we picked them up. They had immersion feet and could hardly stand on limbs bloated by sea water, but after two days with us they walked ashore at Madras, tender but convalescent. It showed endurance which few Europeans could have matched under the tropical sun.

This footnote to the war was quickly forgotten. On Saturday 21 March 1942, *Emerald* arrived at Trincomalee to join the newly formed Eastern Fleet.

The big ships there were *Warspite* and *Ramillies*, both of Great War vintage, although *Warspite* had had sufficient refits to bring her nearer to the standard of the enemy battleships. Among the cruisers was *Dorsetshire*, commanded by *Emerald*'s last captain with his VC won at Kronstadt in 1919. Air power was provided by *Hermes*, looking up-to-date with a newly fitted homing beacon.

We exchanged practice shells with *Dorsetshire* in a throw-off shoot at 27 knots and 26,000 yards using full calibre and full charge ammunition. At that range *Dorsetshire* was hull down and had it been for real she would not have hit us. When it was *Emerald*'s turn the Sea Fox acted as spotter for passing enemy alterations of course. Our shooting was abysmal and the gunnery department were cast into gloom until the reason was found. The Sea Fox had been transmitting spotting corrections for practice and these had been picked up and applied in *Emerald* although they had no relevance to the shoot. The result was chaos. As a penance the aircraft was ordered to carry out more communication exercises. The spinner fell off the propeller, breaking it, and she had to forced land. It seemed that we were not to be an aviation ship.

Bigger things were in the wind. On 30 March we left Trincomalee and rendezvoused the next day with the rest of the Eastern Fleet, under the Commander-in-Chief, Admiral Sir James Somerville, in *Warspite*. A Japanese task force was expected in the Indian Ocean.

Admiral Somerville had taken over from Admiral Layton on 26 March. As Commander-in-Chief Ceylon Admiral Layton had orders to assume command over all services on the island and prepare its defence. It was believed that the enemy would attack Ceylon, a key centre for the maritime defence of the Indian Ocean. The Admiralty suggested the Island be defended by keeping the two old 'R' class battleships, *Ramillies* and *Royal Sovereign* at Colombo, as if the *Prince of Wales* and *Repulse* disaster had not happened. The proposal was ignored. The Americans could not help; the seaborne defence of India, Burma, East Africa and Ceylon fell upon the ships that could be scraped together until better days arrived. There was one modern carrier, *Formidable*, equipped with Albacores for strike, and American Martlets and Fairey Fulmars for fighter cover, a flotilla of modern destroyers and *Warspite*; the rest would not have been out of place at a Reserve Fleet Review. Their age did not matter so much as their lack of air defence.

The Fleet was a tremendous sight and the big ships trumpeted military splendour. The fast division, Force A, was *Warspite*, *Formidable*, the 8-in cruisers *Dorsetshire* and *Cornwall*, ourselves, *Enterprise* and the modern 7th Destroyer Flotilla. The slow division, Force B, was *Resolution*, *Royal Sovereign*, *Ramillies* and *Revenge* of the 3rd Battle Squadron, *Hermes*, the old 6-in cruisers *Dragon* and *Caledon* and ten old destroyers.

The C-in-C had been told to expect the Japanese on All Fools' Day and from 31 March to 2 April we steamed in a rough circle off the south-east corner of Ceylon. We were no match for the enemy we expected and the C-in-C's first aim was to avoid battle and keep the Fleet intact, at the same time making a night torpedo attack if the opportunity offered. We sought neither to find nor lose the enemy, only to place ourselves in his likely path. As a plan it is hard to understand and seemed to disregard the reality of carrier borne air power. If we were sighted there was no question of declining a fleet action as if making a 1916 North Sea sweep. As soon as our presence was known we would be in a defence battle against repeated air attacks. This is not to display the wisdom of hindsight; the tactical and strategical position determined that there was no plan that offered success, however limited, and we steamed about waiting for the enemy and hoping for the best. The inevitable decision to retire to East Africa until reinforcements arrived was taken later.

It was the last time that the R-class formed a line of battle together. Each ship watched the rudder indicators on the main-mast halyards of the next ahead and on each compass platform the Battenburg Station Keeper gave the course to steer in a fleet underway. Down below, the turret, shell room and magazine crews made ready for a fleet action between ships of the line. The old enemy had long gone, and the drills had the same relevance to modern war that the evolutions of the Household Cavalry would have brought to Alamein. The reality was that each man was limited to one bucket of fresh water a day from the old condensers for all his needs, while the main engines laboured to thrash 20 knots out of each aging hull.

That evening, with the sun behind them, the battleships were the Grand Fleet resurgent, a reminder of the years of na-tional decline which had brought them near to a fleet action where they risked defeat in the face of superior warship technology, a skill in which we had led the world for generations. The ships steamed in majestic line off Dendra Head, each with her fighting top and four turrets in silhouette while the sun set on the old Navy and the Empire.

The Catalinas had not found the enemy by the evening of 2 April and from that the Admiral deduced that they were not coming, or had heard about us and were keeping away. The third possibility, which became fact, was that they were coming but had not yet been spotted.

The Fleet arrived at Addu Atoll on 4 April to re-fuel. *Hermes*, *Cornwall* and *Dorsetshire* were sent back to Ceylon, and the Fleet deprived of their support, despite the imperative to concentrate its resources until it was certain that the Japanese threat had passed. It seems to have been accepted that sending these ships inde-pendently to the place where the Japanese would attack, would invite their destruction. It was an operational decision which ensured the worst of all worlds, a mistake which would not have been expected from a Staff College student writing his first appre-ciation.

Force A were still fuelling on the afteroon of 4 April when a Catalina from Ceylon sighted the main Japanese battle group. The aircraft was shot down but managed to get off her enemy report.

Happily the airmen were picked up and joined *Exeter*'s crew in the prisoner of war camp.

There were 5 fleet carriers, 4 battleships, 3 cruisers and 8 destroyers under the command of Admiral Nagumo, who had sailed from Sumatra with orders to attack Ceylon. A separate task force left Mergui under the command of Admiral Ozawa to sweep through the Bay of Bengal and sink or destroy. This force had 1 light carrier, 6 cruisers and 4 destroyers. Admiral Nagumo's ships were modern and the carriers were able to put 91 bombers and 36 fighters into the air. The fighters were Zeros, outclassing as well as outnumbering our Air Group in *Formidable*.

Force A finished fuelling by midnight and sailed north east. The plan was to avoid the enemy by day and catch them with a night torpedo attack as they retired. There was no hope now of preventing the attack on Ceylon. The scene was set for a disaster.

Dorsetshire and *Cornwall* were ordered to rejoin the Fleet with all despatch; they left Ceylon twelve hours before it was attacked by the Sumatra force. The Naval Staff in Colombo had to give the cruisers a course to steer which would avoid the aircraft of the approaching enemy and yet bring them back to the Fleet as soon as possible. The task seems to have been beyond them.

> One point which had escaped the notice of everyone, including the C-in-C himself, was the range and performance of the Japanese naval aircraft. In the Operations Room and also in our ships' plotting rooms we gave them the same performance as our own, but it later transpired that we had sadly underrated them. Actually they had nearly double our performance.

Footprints in the Sea by Captain Augustus Agar, VC, RN, p. 304

Thus the pencil line on the chart was drawn on a bearing a few degrees too low. A small mistake, but 424 men paid in full for it the next day, when the Sumatra force attacked Colombo with some 120 carrier aircraft.

In *Emerald*, the officers sunbathing watched a Martlet from the carrier in an exuberant show of aerobatics. It stopped abruptly, to our disappointment, and we intercepted the reason why. The signal read, '*Formidable* aircraft from *Formidable*: We are not amused.'

I lay on the quarterdeck with an old copy of *Reader's Digest* and contemplated the hereafter.

> I saw Eternity the other night,
> Like a great ring of pure and endless light,
> All calm, as it was bright.

Violent death at 20 did not bring such lyrical pictures to my mind, seeming to be no more than a step into oblivion, a short step if modern technology was kind, but no big deal.

I opened the magazine at random and found an article about Trafalgar. The author had included Nelson's prayer before the battle and I read again the sad, innocent words written at the supreme moment in the history of my country.

> May the Great God, whom I worship, grant to my Country and for the benefit of Europe in general a great and glorious victory, and may no misconduct in anyone tarnish it, and may humanity after victory be the predominant feature in the British Fleet. For myself individually, I commit my life to Him who made me and may his blessing light upon my endeavours for serving my Country faithfully. To Him I resign myself and the just cause which is entrusted me to defend. Amen, amen, amen.

It seemed unlikely that we would have to fret about our humanity after a victory; the likely end for us would bear no comparison with Trafalgar. That battle marked the beginning of the *Pax Britannica*; this one would end it.

These morbid reflections were interrupted by a shout. We gathered by the ship's side to look at a thin pillar of smoke in the far distance to the north west; *Cornwall* and *Dorsetshire* would be late. Two hours afterwards, when nothing had been heard from them, the Commander-in-Chief signalled that our fleet mates had probably been sunk.

The Admiral's night intentions were to locate and attack the enemy with aircraft and to engage him with ships the following day, after we had rendezvoused with Force B. The true tactical position was that the Fleet was steering north west, on an opposite course to the Japanese who were retreating to the south east after the strike on Colombo.

Formidable flew off search aircraft and it was rumoured that one of them had sighted the Sumatra force; we heard the engine of an Albacore over us and watched her go straight on to attempt a night deck landing. She hit the flight deck and crashed. The flames leapt into the night sky and it seemed that the enemy must have seen the blaze. In fact they were now at least eighty miles away and increasing the gap.

Force B rejoined at dawn but it was not until about 1500 that our sister ship *Enterprise*, with two destroyers, left at 28 knots to search for survivors, who had then been in the water for over twenty-five hours. They picked up some 1,100 but over 400 were lost. Later I asked my opposite number in *Dorsetshire* how many bombs had hit her. He told me that he saw one miss and then he found himself in the water.

At 6 pm on the 6th the Commander-in-Chief made the obvious decision to get out of it while the going was good and the Fleet reversed course and steered north west for the Maldive Islands. Admiral Nagumo prepared for an attack on Trincomalee, arriving off the east coast of Ceylon in the position to fly off aircraft am on the 9th. The harbour was cleared but *Hermes* and her destroyer *Vampire* were spotted and sunk in ten minutes. Six of her aircraft, of 814 Swordfish Squadron, had already been shot down over the jungle on the day of the attack on Colombo. They dropped their torpedoes into the trees but were unable to avoid annihilation.

In the Bay of Bengal Admiral Ozawa destroyed over 100,000 tons of defenceless merchant shipping. We picked up a message from one of them which was to the point; 'Am being followed by a battleship.'

These melancholy events were taking place a long way from the Eastern Fleet, which arrived at Addu Atoll on the 8th to refuel. While we awaited our turn for the oiler I saw a skimming dish approach out of the night. The boat was hailed and the reply was 'Dorsetshire'. A figure in tropical rig wearing captain's shoulder straps and with an arm in a sling came over the side of his old ship and disappeared into the Captain's cabin. The word was that he had stayed on the bridge as she heeled over with the intention of going with her. He was seen by a marine and two sailors who yelled out to him not to be so bloody daft and to jump as they had a float to cling to. Their Captain took no notice, whereupon two of them pulled him into the Carley float just before she went. That was how they thought of him.

Force B oiled ahead of us and left; within twenty-four hours we followed, *en route* for Bombay. The plan was to retreat to East Africa until the odds were more even. The Japanese returned to the Pacific to complete their unfinished business at Pearl Harbour, when they had missed the American carriers. Thus, with both sides out of the arena India and Ceylon were open to attack from the sea. The enemy carriers were sunk at Midway and the Coral Sea a month or two later and there were no more sorties in strength by the enemy into the Indian Ocean. For this deliverance we had to thank the United States Navy.

The Eastern Fleet had achieved nothing in the recent operations, save survival; in Bombay the urgent work on morale began. The ship's company were addressed by Rear-Admiral Tennant, our new admiral, lately Captain of *Repulse* and just back on the station as Rear-Admiral 4th Cruiser Squadron, with his flag in *Newcastle*. He told us that there would be no mail, no leave and plenty of blood, sweat, toil and tears together with endless sea time. There were no jokes, but the Admiral was liked and respected, and the sailors attributed his speech to the hard time he had had in *Repulse*, and bore him no ill will.

The next visitor came unannounced, having pulled himself to our gangway from *Warspite* in a dinghy. The hands were mustered on the forecastle at the double to hear their Commander-in-Chief. Admiral Somerville stood on the capstan and gave a short lesson in how to do it. He talked about having another crack at them when reinforcements arrived and explained that we had been looking for the Japanese rather than the other way round. He then reminded us that we did not have the ships we needed yet but it would be different next time. He ended by saying that he had really come onboard to look at the *Emeralds* and give them a chance of looking at him. It was virtuoso stuff and when he left we were sure that we had looked at the scramble round Ceylon in the wrong way. We were the heroes, not them.

Bombay was full of HM ships and the facilities for the Fleet ashore were stretched. We gave up sending boats to the Gateway of India steps because of the crush there and landed our people in the dockyard, which was further and hard to find from shore. The first time three of us tried it the gharry took ages to get there. I asked the driver how much and turned to the two Mids I was with for a share but found myself alone, the others having slipped away quietly before negotiations were opened. Having a solitary stripe I was fair game.

We wandered round the splendour of the Willingdon Club but felt like fish out of water. We decided to get away from the marble and palms to see life in the raw and told the gharry driver to take us to Grant Road. The address was immaterial because every house there was engaged in the same trade. The gharry driver, an expert in fornication and the ways of young sahibs both, correctly deduced that he would not be put to much inconvenience and said he would wait.

The three of us tramped up the stairs in determined unconcern while we thrashed our self-confidence off its knees. Business was quiet. We were shown into a large room where about thirty girls were sitting round the walls. They were dressed in bright satin colours and beads and looked embarrassed. Most of them were younger than us. We had expected whores of Babylonian appeal and these were our friends' schoolgirl sisters.

We stood in the middle of the room with Madame at our elbow, waiting, while the dancing class sat on their chairs like swallows on a telephone wire, waiting too. It was hopeless. Whatever it was that Hank and the Sub were enthralled about we had not found it here. The problem was how to get out of the shop without buying anything.

I told Madame that we were there upon a social visit only and hoped to have an opportunity of meeting her again on another occasion. One of the girls giggled and there seemed a sudden, distant, prospect that the ice would be broken, when we were interrupted by footsteps outside. Through the open door we saw the landing filled with sailors from one of the carriers. There were more on the stairs. Discipline came before sex and we waved goodbye to the little sisters and got back into the gharry. We made

it clear to the driver that if he said anything at all we would reverse
the roles between him and his horse. It was apparent that original
sin required more preparation than we had given to it.

The fleet left Bombay. *Emerald* weighed anchor and went ahead
only to stop engines and anchor again, leaving the others to go
without her. A seaman had fallen from the starboard .5-in mount-
ing to the iron deck and fractured his skull. Our motor boat was
called away at the rush to land him and we chased after the fleet
at 25 knots five hours later. On passage, *Emerald* and the other
ships of the 4th Cruiser Squadron obeyed their new admiral's
order to improve our defence to air strikes. Having survived the
action at Kuantan he knew what the priorities were. On Thursday,
23 April 1942, my 21st birthday, Force A entered Colombo to oil.

The harbour showed evidence of the attack. Two armed merchant cruisers were wrecks and the old destroyer *Tenedos* sat on
the bottom with her upper deck awash, a victim of her own
torpedoes, exploded by a near miss. A merchantman had her bows
blown in by a torpedo hit. The rain cascaded down.

I invited my messmates to birthday drinks at midday and went
ashore to bring the cypher log up to date. I was delayed and found
my party had been held without me. I received thanks all round,
but no lunch. No one wanted to go ashore that evening because
of the rain. I found myself alone in an empty officers' boat
determined to do something about the anniversary.

The GOH was crammed, but because the staff had run away
after the raid those who wanted food had to serve themselves. I
joined the queue, which was menaced by two drunken Australian
private soldiers, loudly expressing their views on being barred from
the dining room. They told each other and everyone else what
they had done to the Eyties in the Desert and what they would
like to do to the Poms. The queue looped widely round them and
hoped they would go away. They had other ideas and advanced
on the only waiter at the dining room door, who showed signs of
despair. A small man in civilian dress invited them in an educated
voice to be his guests at dinner. With an idle swipe one of the
giants knocked him down with a bloody mouth and the two of
them walked unopposed into the dining room where they complained in loud aggressive voices about everything and everybody

Bombay, April 1942. Donald, Author, Hugh.

in sight. They gave the impression that they would be disagreable
when sober.

I collected some cold expensive food, ate it alone, and decided
to celebrate what was left of my birthday with a drink on board.

During dinner my burberry was stolen. I flogged through the monsoon to the jetty to find that our boats had stopped running. I hitched a lift and arrived back, sodden. The bar was closed and everybody had turned in. It was the only day we spent in harbour for six weeks and we left next day for Madagascar. Each of my four sons has elected to have a cheque rather than a twenty-first party, influenced perhaps by hearing this dismal story, which preceded the offers.

We refuelled in the Seychelles on 30 April. While we were oiling the hands were fallen in to witness punishment, when a warrant was read on a telegraphist for seven days' cells. *Emerald* had no cells but that was no bar to the Articles of War and he was put into a boat and sent to *Warspite* to complete his sentence.

At sea the next day a Martlet fighter crashed and sank in ten seconds. The pilot got out and a general tally-ho took place to pick him up. The destroyer *Foxhound*, not unnaturally, was first off and altered hard-a-port across our bows making it neccessary for us to go hard-a-starboard to avoid her. Another destroyer, the Australian *Nestor*, also hauled out to make for the crash. While these two were manoeuvring *Newcastle*, the nearest ship, lowered her sea boat and picked up the pilot.

Later that day the 4th Cruiser Squadron was detached and the second in command of each ship ordered to take control during ship manoeuvres. Our real need was to work up air defence to increase our chances against aircraft. Giving the right engine and wheel orders was a fetish and may well have come from the boarding days when sails and rudder were vital in laying a warship alongside the enemy. This was no longer the problem but the old ways persisted and a commanding officer who was known as a good ship handler, albeit with moderate ability otherwise, was ahead of his betters who had been seen to bump a jetty or keep poor station.

On 4 May we joined up with *Resolution, Caledon, Dragon, Hotspur* and *Griffin*. We were to provide a covering force to the east of Madagascar to head off any interference from the Japanese while a task force under Admiral Syfret secured the island. The operation was code named Ironclad and was a complete success; meanwhile reinforements for the Eastern Fleet had begun to arrive.

The Commander-in-Chief's office was set up in a girls' school in Mombasa and the Fleet settled down in Africa until it became safe to go back to Ceylon. Having a base meant that the comforts of life caught up and the administrative gears could engage again. We had outrun our supplies after leaving Trincomalee at the end of March and welcomed the change from rice to tinned potato powder.

The Captain was appointed President of a court martial in the fleet carrier *Illustrious* to try a flight deck sentry for manslaughter. The prisoner was an able seaman of limited intelligence who had obeyed an order of the leading hand of his mess to shoot him in the leg so that he could get out of the ship and home. The leading seaman was a strong character and the ship's best boxer. The shooting took place on the flight deck at night after he had been drinking ashore. The shock of the wound killed him. There were witnesses who said that the accused had repeatedly refused the order but in the end pulled the trigger in frightened confusion.

It was an incredible trial. The sentry was represented by a chaplain and pleaded not guilty. There was no cross-examination of the prosecution witnesses and the submission on behalf of the accused, who was not called to give evidence on his own behalf, consisted of a résumé of his family history and the effect on him of the loss of a brother at Dunkirk. He was sentenced to eight years' imprisonment.

We were all subject to the Naval Discipline Act and its rigorous provisions. Historically, it had become accepted that not only did the Act take away the common law and statutory rights of the individual but the rules of natural justice might be by-passed. The President and Members of a Naval Court Martial knew that they would not be there if there was not something in it and as a result corners were cut. This was all improved after the war, meanwhile the flight deck sentry had not been properly heard in his trial on a serious charge. I have to say that the result would almost certainly have been the same had he been defended by Marshall Hall; the Eastern Fleet could not afford any tremor in its discipline at that stage in the war. The rule of natural justice that an accused should be properly heard was a disposable luxury.

The papers arrived for my Paymaster Sub-Lieutenant's examination and I addressed them during a full calibre 6-in shoot. Nearly a year later I read in an Admiralty Fleet Order that I had been given a first class and the extra seniority that went with it. I am sure that either my papers were mixed up with someone else's, or the Captain's covering letter was misread in the Admiralty, and the examiner thought that I had taken the papers while the guns were being fired in action.

The sailing at Kilindini was good. I remember a reach in a whaler with the warm wind bowling her along and the sun on my bare back and legs, and my feet on the mainsail. For a moment everything stopped; I remember thinking that this was about the best that life could provide.

We escorted another Winston Special for part of the way to Aden and returned to Durban. Here we lost a charming RNR sub-lieutenant, the victim of a love disease. He was the most languid and laid back officer I ever met, having been indoctrinated into the ways of the East during his years with the P&O. He had married just before leaving home but never wrote letters. He reasoned that he had gone to war and could not be expected to return. If he did it would be a bonus, if not letter writing was an unnecessary distraction. Later on I met his sister who told me that no one in his family had heard from him for nearly a year.

Durban seemed full of young wives whose husbands were locked up by the Germans in Tobruk. The favourite place was a night club with wide plush seats and a glimmer of light. There was a tragedy there when, in a stupid row over a woman, a major on his way to the desert hit a friend on the head with a soda water syphon and killed him. He went back to his transport and shot himself.

We took another WS convoy up the East African coast with the 8-in cruiser *Shropshire* sharing the ocean escort duty. About three days out of Durban I was in the wireless office at dawn action stations when the ship heeled over to starboard, throwing those standing sideways. We increased to full ahead. A signal came down the tube from the bridge prefixed EMERGENCY, reporting that the enemy was in sight, consisting of two heavy ships and three carriers. The convoy was ordered to scatter.

The Chief Telegraphist looked sombre while the signal was

being rattled off. Within minutes it had been repeated world wide by the Admiralty and everybody knew that there was about to be a shambles off Madagascar. It was evidently the Captain's intention by the use of full speed to lay a smoke screen between the enemy and the convoy, to give them a chance to get away while the escorts engaged with guns and torpedoes and tried to dodge the air strikes.

I was on the ladder on the way back to my action station when I heard a second signal come down. The wording was short, there being not much to be said. 'Cancel my so-and-so. Clouds.'

The Chief Telegraphist smiled, something he had never been known to do before, and the battle was over. The cancellation was repeated world wide and two post captains were obliged to reflect upon the damage done to their hopes of flag rank.

On 1 June 1942 we entered Kilindini harbour and found it fuller than ever with warships and merchantmen. The Captain cleared lower deck and told us that the ship had been ordered back to Portsmouth for a long refit.

As was the custom we were sailed the next morning to avoid becoming a source of envy to the rest of the Eastern Fleet, who had to soldier on. We wore no paying off pennant and went down harbour as usual. The word had been passed however; we were given a ragged cheer here and there and some rude gestures from *Enterprise*.

At Durban the orders to go to the UK seemed too good to be true when we were sent north again with another WS convoy for Diego Suarez. The harbour had been attacked by Japanese midget submarines launched from their parent boats I 16 and I 20. *Ramillies* had been substantially damaged and a tanker sunk by torpedo hits. A Japanese reconnaissance aircraft flew over the harbour the day before the attack. This must have come from a submarine and it brought *Surcouf* and her aircraft to mind.

The ship left Diego Suarez on 24 June for Simonstown and thereafter it was downhill all the way. An albatross kept us company 100 yards astern for days, swaying regularly from one quarter to another and so far as we could see never touching the sea, let alone landing on it. It was not apparent how the bird kept itself alive.

We refuelled in the Belgian Congo from an oiler hidden in the jungle at Pointe Noire, and again at Freetown. The Chaplain asked a shore side colleague to lunch and was so engrossed in theological discourse over the gin that he forgot to put his guest ashore. The bretheren arrived on the bridge in distress and stood before the Captain in penance. The prospect of two clergymen on board for the next five days brought a quick reaction. One of the local escorts was ordered to close and send a boat and our man was told to give thanks.

After fuelling again at Gibraltar the Bay of Biscay was crossed at 25 knots on a zig-zag course giving the transit boats from the French coast no chance to bring us down. On 23 July 1942 we anchored in Plymouth Sound.

A motor boat brought out the mail and fresh bread and as she got closer we were astonished to see that the bowman, in bell-bottomed trousers, was a woman. The Wrens were given bananas and their boat made fast. When it had unloaded the crew could not be found, delaying the return journey to the dockyard, and demonstrating a degree of inefficiency with heterosexual undertones which drove the Commander into a gnawing frenzy. He yelled at the Officer of the Watch to get those bloody women out of the ship. The Chief Boatswain's Mate and a midshipman were sent to carry out an immediate search while there was time. The girls were mustered and their boat left with cheers from the hands on the upper deck, overwhelmed by the presence of nubile white women. They had no time to see how green was the grass on the cliff tops after the dust of Africa and India.

The ship was swept up Channel by three minesweepers and we secured alongside in Portsmouth Dockyard on 24 July 1942. We were luckier than most of the Eastern Fleet who had operated against the Japanese so far. *Prince of Wales*, *Repulse*, *Hermes*, *Cornwall*, *Dorsetshire*, *Exeter*, *Thanet*, *Electra*, *Encounter*, *Stronghold*, *Tenedos*, *Vampire*, *Hector*, *Hollyhock* and about fifty smaller ships stayed forever on the station.

CHAPTER 11

LONG WORK UP

Emerald paid off and we gave her to the dockyard. Her speed alone had put her in the front line. The Sea Fox was a gesture to the new world; otherwise she was the stuff of 1916. She could have dealt with a German raider but in an air war the odds were long against her. Her luck had held and she had brought us home, ready for another go somewhere else.

While we waited for the dockyard to take her over two of us decided go to London. The Portsmouth station was out of action; Henry and I caught the train at Havant within the hour and found ourselves with rooms in the Normandie Hotel, walking with the throng from Piccadilly to the Strand.

The crowd made progress difficult; everyone seemed congenial and walking for the fun of it. There were other changes; Americans sitting on the steps of the Strand Palace Hotel, drinking from bottles with their disengaged arms around a bevy of whores. We were obvious newcomers in the concourse with sunburnt faces and up from the country expressions.

In the bar of the Savoy we found a seaman lieutenant from Henry's term with a medal we did not recognize. He responded to the predictable cracks about not knowing that he had attended the last coronation at Monaco by pointing out that it was the Virtuti Militari, a Polish decoration for valour. He said it meant nothing to ignorant peasants like us, but any Pole he met insisted on buying the drinks.

He had been liaison officer in one of their submarines which got stuck on the bottom and depth charged. There seemed to be no way out. The crew were dashing in all directions and shouting things in Polish he could not understand so he sat in the wardroom

137

and read a book until it was over. They told him they had never met such bravery and gave him the medal.

We stopped near Charing Cross to make a plan for the evening and were engaged in conversation by two agreeable young women. We were flattered by their attentions and stood by to answer questions about our adventures ashore and afloat. One of them interrupted the conversation. 'We've got a place in Victoria,' she said, 'you can come back if you like.' This was not what we expected but it settled our programme. They were sporting amateurs who went to the West End to collect two men in uniform from the throng when they were short of funds. They believed they were helping the war effort by this arrangement which was generally satisfactory to all parties; for all I know they may have been two from a band of women in mid–1942 prostrating themselves for Britannia and pin money.

Portsmouth was an armed camp, alive with uniforms and sand bags, barrage balloons and the thump of practice gunfire. Southsea had lost its appeal. My turn came to go and I heaved my kit out of Waterloo Station with orders to report to the rear-admiral at the head of my specialization, with an address in St. James's. He liked to interview officers in from sea.

I could not find a taxi and was invited to share one by a pretty girl and her mother. The girl was doing what passed for a London season and rattled on about the people she had met and the parties she had been to. They kindly tried to bring me in but it was hopeless. I knew nobody and must have seemed nothing like the image in blue and gold that may have been their idea of a naval officer.

My interview with the Head Man did not go well. I reported that I had not been employed in *Emerald* in the job to which I had been appointed. He asked me why the Paymaster Commander had not intervened, but did nothing himself to question the system. The senior officers of the Paymaster Branch then were paper tigers. He asked me if I had a preference for my next ship and I remembered the beautiful *Bonaventure*. I told him I would like to go to one of the new *Dido* class cruisers.

My mother was now the only member of the family in the house and relieved that I was there. My father had been in India since 1941. When *Cornwall* and *Dorsetshire* were lost the Japanese saw the three funnels and announced that they had sunk two ships of the Emerald class. It was several days before the Admiralty corrected the mistake, which by then had appeared in the newspapers. My mother was unable to get information and had feared the worst. I had nearly one month at home but it was not a great success. No one was about and the petrol coupons were soon gone.

The landing at Dieppe made some think for a moment that the second front had started, while the censored press took time to explain the limited scope of the operation. I had a feeling that I did not know what was going on. I was relieved to get a letter at last, appointing me Captain's Secretary of HMS *Carlisle*, and ordering me to join at Devonport on 20 September 1942. She shared a role of the *Dido* class in repelling aircraft but there the similarity ended; I was not to be appointed to a new cruiser but one completed on Armistice Day 1918.

I found her alongside the wall without guns or funnels, her topsides littered with air hoses, stores and dockyard rubbish. I stood on her upper deck amidst the jumble, delighted to be there. This ship would be different from the rest in which I had served. Here the endless prologue of training would end and I could expect to be a full member of the side.

She displaced 4,200 tons and was built with five 6-in guns. These had been taken out before the war and replaced with four twin 4-in mountings to engage aircraft. Where No 2 gun had been she had a Chicago Piano multiple pom-pom. She had to make do with Oerlikon rather than Bofors for close range. In the current refit her radar was being updated and an improved fire control system fitted for the 4-in. There would be 20 officers and 380 men.

Her record was second to none. She had been in the front line from the start and likely to go back, the only survivor of the six 'C' Class cruisers converted to the anti-aircraft role. She began in Norway and moved permanently to the Mediterranean for the Malta convoy battles, Sirte, Greece, the Tobruk-Alexandria run and the Crete battles. At Crete a German bomber sprayed her bridge and killed her Captain with a bullet through the head. She

HMS Carlisle. *Plymouth Sound, November 1942.*

was not known to the newspapers because she did not sink the enemy but did the dirty work of repelling aircraft. She had a reputation in the Mediterranean for survival.

I learnt most of this from the Officer of the Day, an RN lieutenant, who was sitting in a hut among the debris in his shirtsleeves, whittling a piece of wood with a knife. His manner was strange. He thought she would probably return to the Med after her refit. He talked about enemy aircraft, Ju 87s and 88s and He 111s and SM 79s with a sinister familiarity, seemingly anxious to ensure that I realized how lucky he was to be alive.

> The snares of death compassed me round about: and the pains of
> hell got hold of me.

He made that clear. 'Thank Christ,' he said, 'that I am not going back for some more.' It was just a fraction overdone; perhaps he needed a rest. Anyway, the odds would be more in our favour next time.

The other officers gradually arrived and we went onboard each day to do what we could to produce order out of the chaos, meeting at gin time to discuss progress.

Water had to be brought from shore when the temporary supply was disconnected. The second engineer officer, known in the Navy as the 'Senior Engineer' or 'Senior', found one day that there was no water for his gin. He sent a stoker into the dockyard at the double and held forth about the cruelty of fate, like a man dying for lack of a blood transfusion. The stoker came back, breathless, with a large jug which he held over Senior's glass. With great delicacy, under the close supervision of his slightest movement, he was allowed to put a thimbleful of water on top of the gin. 'The inefficiency of this dockyard is a subject for a question in Parliament,' said Senior.

As the Wardroom collected it became apparent that we were to be manned almost entirely by reserve officers. The Captain, Engineer Officer and me were the only ones who had had any cadet training or served in a gunroom. This excluded two RN seamen lieutenants who were with us for work up only and would leave as soon as we became operational.

Three officers left in short time. The first was the Young

Doctor, the assistant to the Principal Medical Officer. He hardly fitted the description, being a police surgeon in middle age, who was honest enough to admit that this was not his scene. Next was a paymaster lieutenant who seemed highly strung and showed it one evening after dinner by felling a senior officer with a rugby tackle. The last to go was the First Lieutenant, a dead beat observer who seemed to know what he was about until it was suspected that his difficulty in seeing eye-to-eye with the Captain might be aggravated by Drambuie. The PMO produced a psychiatrist and he was landed without fuss. Later in the war he won a DSO in a landing craft.

The next First Lieutenant was a splendid officer who had begun his naval career as a seaman boy. He said one day that the best moment in his life was when he read his name in the *Daily Telegraph* appointing him to his first ship with commissioned rank. He had three brothers on the lower deck and there was nothing he did not know about sailors. He used his knowledge to earn their respect and he was liked and trusted forward and aft.

The Captain was a gunnery officer of the Old Guard. He had commanded a monitor and knew that he had little chance of further promotion. He had a distrust for 'the office', by which he meant the staff ashore, and advised his officers to keep away from them at all costs. This was counsel he followed to the letter so that the ship was often without information unless one of us had ferreted it out. He had a belief in the capacity of the RN to do anything, which made itself felt. He was probably better suited to the unhurried pace of a monitor than the desperate urgency of a flak-ship.

He had a favourite story. A sailor got into a first class carriage by mistake in a train without a corridor. He found a pretty well-dressed girl in one corner and a grey-haired old man in a morning coat in the other. 'Excuse me,' he said to the girl, 'forgive a common sailorman speaking to you like this, but I wonder if you might find it more agreeable if I shut the window?'

'That is very kind,' said the girl, 'I think I would like it shut, but what about this gentleman?'

'Oh, fuck 'im,' said Jack.

One of my first jobs was to answer a letter from a sailor's

mother. He had been killed in 1941 and she enquired about his funeral. I sought out the Chief Gunner's Mate who had been there and remembered the occasion and the man. He was in No 2 gun's crew and killed when a bomb near missed amidships. I asked him about the funeral. He said there had not been one. Like a fool I asked why. It was a hose and squeegee job he said. I told the mother that her son had been buried at sunset off Crete with full naval honours, because I could not think what else to do. The Chief Gunner's Mate was killed the following year by a near miss while standing by the same gun.

The Engineer Sub-Lieutenant and I got fed up with the barracks and took a flat on Plymouth Hoe. He smuggled gin ashore for a party by putting the bottle in his greatcoat pocket, which he carried over his arm to prevent the bulge of the bottle being seen. He was a South African and wore a thin serge uniform suited to his country. He walked up to the police and customs on the dockyard gate in a snowstorm, doing his best not to shiver while he thought of an answer if he was asked why he was carrying his greatcoat in a blizzard.

The bombing had removed the Royal Hotel, killing Helen. The Duchess was still there but showing more grey hairs. I met the Captain of Marines from *Emerald* who was announcing to the company at the bar that his was the only ship to get home after the Japs had finished with the Eastern Fleet. He was, let it be said, a little in drink.

The Navigating Officer from *Emerald* also turned up, standing by a ship in the dockyard. He had been recalled from leave to take over the navigation of the force in the Dieppe raid. It was a beautiful day and he had spent it on the bridge of the Senior Officer's destroyer in his shirtsleeves.

'Bloody awful,' he said.

'Yes,' said I, 'they seem to have had a very bad time.'

He was not listening.

'I caught the worst cold I have ever had. It was nearly two months ago and I have only just got rid of it.'

Our funnels and guns were put back and we moved out of the basin to an alongside berth for the final touches. At lunch time Jimmy announced that he wanted all officers sleeping on board the next day. The ship gradually came to life, a happy and absorbing time for those involved in it.

When we arrived on the outer wall a boat was attached to us from the dockyard. It was manned by Wrens and in short time they had persuaded Jimmy their boat needed painting. We provided hands to do it and instead of them looking after us, which was the intention, we found ourselves looking after them.

Our departure was delayed by trouble with No 1 gun on the forecastle. Because the hull was old and weary the gun would not train and persistently stuck instead of revolving smoothly. Our lives might depend on it not sticking. The Ordnance Engineer Officer from the dockyard lived with the gun for days while it was craned in and out like a yo-yo. He passed it in the end, at the same time giving his views on the Naval Staff for attempting major conversions on old hulls.

The Young Doctor and the Captain of Marines had new wives, and the day before we left the WRNS bowman and I accompanied them on an expedition on Dartmoor. We blocked a stream and generally fooled about but after a while it dawned on both of us that the jollity was hard work for the others. We left as soon as we decently could and dined at the Morland Links. She had a terrier which she took everywhere; she tied her to our table while we were dancing. The terrier got jealous and bored and followed us on to the floor, bringing the table with her and the band to a halt.

I met a Canadian in the bar who had just finished a tour on Lancasters. He was one of four aircrew still serving from thirty who had entered together. During his operational training a Lancaster undershot at night and he was one of many who rushed to the crash. His greatest friend was trapped in the wreckage by a leg and they could not free him. The fire began to drive everyone back and he hit his friend on the head with a spade because there was nothing else he could do for him. He was trying to return to operations but they would not have him. He seemed near to a breakdown. I record this event because it seems to me to demonstrate, like Goya's picture of the soldiers executing their prisoners, the reality of war.

Leave expired fourteen days before we left and there were 75 men adrift. The number was whittled down to about 12, who had obviously deserted. We got them all in the end except for 6 from the Republic of Ireland who were beyond the reach of the Naval Discipline Act, even when reinforced by the constabulary armed with a warrant for arrest. One or two persuaded the priest to write letters excusing the inexcusable, which were unanswered. On 6 December 1942 we left for Scapa Flow to begin work up.

There was a northerly gale in the Irish Sea and progress was so poor that we went into Belfast Lough to shelter until the worst had passed through. Jimmy began the real work. I was talking to him at the foot of the bridge ladder, both of us holding on and shouting against the wind. She was washing down. A national service ordinary seaman passed us on the way to take his watch. He was green with nausea and misery.

'Enjoying the cruise, son?' said Jimmy.

The boy tried to grin.

'Screw down. You'll love it soon.'

Banal perhaps, but effective, and Jimmy knew how to do it.

While we waited for the storm to go through, the portable organ was rigged for the wardroom after dinner harbour routine. One of the work-up lieutenants played while we sang the songs that had been handed down from wardrooms and gunrooms before us. Some we had brought from our previous ships and there were few that were entirely new to us. During the long years when the Grand Fleet was in Scapa Flow the songs multiplied. Others came straight from the sailing days. Buck kept the music going as long as he had a congregation, and care was taken to make sure that his yellow china tankard on top of the organ stayed full.

When we felt like a change we asked the boatswain to give us a song. He never said no and there was no delay in choosing a work because he had only one song in his repertoire. He was young for his rate with a Devon accent that a foreigner could have spotted. He became Irish for his turn, and sang the 'Mountains of Mourne', with a deep baritone and heavy brogue. He did it well and we shut up to listen to him. When called upon he would stop what he was doing, stand up and burst out as if that was what he had been waiting for. We were proud of him and often got him going, especially when guests were there.

Someone tied an empty beer bottle to the deckhead fan and started the blades. This was childish but hilarious, and no one laughed louder than the second work up lieutenant, who was standing in front of the electric fire, holding a glass and smoking a pipe, no doubt reflecting with satisfaction upon the good job he was making of turning this rabble into men of war's men. Smoke rose from his trousers and we took care not to tell him. The smell of burning cloth and a warm behind stopped this part of the entertainment and someone put him out with a soda syphon. Meanwhile the fan and the bottle continued to rotate to the delight of all, including the Commander (E), a thin, saturnine figure and older than the rest of us, who had played rugby for the Navy. He had looked into the wardroom after visiting the engine room and was sitting in an armchair with his cap on. The line parted and the bottle shot away, knocking Chief's cap off and reducing the rest of us to incoherence. He found it no longer funny and closed the bar.

Scapa was stiff with warships and unrecognizable from the place I had visited in *Vindictive*. The Home Fleet had been reinforced with the King George V battleships and the new Fleet Carriers. This heavy force waited to cover the advance of the *Tirpitz* from Norway, or any other German big ship which tried to get into the Atlantic. None of this was our business and we were there, in the middle of winter, with constant bad weather and little daylight, to work the ship up in its anti-aircraft role. C-in-C's staff produced weekly training programmes but the weather was frequently unsuitable for the aircraft towing our targets and serial after serial was cancelled.

We shared the work up with *Belfast*, a 6-in cruiser that had spent most of the war in the dockyard, after being mined. We towed her aft and she towed us forward. We transferred stores and exercised night encounters with her. We got sick of looking at her and longed to go. Her Captain was slightly junior to ours and it rankled. Their Lordships had made it clear that by sending our Captain to the much older and smaller cruiser they had compared him unfavourably with the Captain of *Belfast* and we were reminded of it every day we spent togther.

The Fleet was ordered to exercise an anti-aircraft close range barrage. The dawn sky over the Flow was red with a canopy of flame and tracer while the guns ashore added to the show. A low flying aircraft would have been in difficulty. The islands were garrisoned by soldiers who had been given uncompromising orders. Three of us were walking along a road in the dusk after an expedition in plain clothes when a figure in a glengarry with a rifle jumped out of the ditch and shouted to us to halt. We told him we were naval officers and walked on. He shouted again and we heard the rattle of a rifle bolt. We stopped and parleyed; he was in earnest.

Cruisers and above had drifters attached to them to take libertymen to the cinema on Flotta. They brought off mail and fresh bread, whatever the weather. The skippers were quiet fishermen who enjoyed a chat in the warm wheelhouse, while the blast and spray tore at the drifter outside as she rolled through a black winter's night in the Flow. Whatever the conditions our drifter always found us and came alongside with ease. She brought the news from home and her contribution to our comfort was invaluable; she could be relied on.

Christmas came and the Wardroom were restive. We were tired of big ships and being the poor relation. After Christmas lunch Buck decided to exercise an officers landing party. Seven of us went away in a motor boat in pirates rig, armed with edged weapons. We aimed for one of the small islands, our bellies warm from the gin, claret, port and brandy. The expedition whooped its way ashore and formed a ragged line facing a hut about a hundred yards away. Buck drew his sword. He announced that the enemy were in the hut and we would assault it. It looked decrepit and seemed to be made of wood. Buck charged at full tilt with his sword arm extended. The hut, having been put there prepared for Orkney weather, was made of sterner stuff. Our leader's sword shot into the air and his right arm disappeared backwards past his ear. The same thing happens to matadors who hit a bone on the bull's neck. He yelled with rage while the rest of us rolled about in the wet heather.

After dinner we tried again. Pirates once more we took the portable organ to *Kent*, an 8-in cruiser with an admiral. The ladder to her quarter deck was in two parts with a grating half way. With difficulty two of us carried the organ in a position just adequate for Buck to play it on the ladder, while the rest sang. I cannot remember the song; it was probably 'One Eyed Reilly' with a chorus of ribald vulgarity. We made music across the quarter deck and into the wardroom. Four officers in mess undress playing bridge carried on as if we were not there. A group round the bar looked embarrassed. We put the organ down and Buck stopped playing; the singing died away. We had a drink with them and left, village carollers calling at the manor. From then on we gave up making advances to big ships.

The January weather was worse than ever and our work up fell behind schedule. Eventually the programme became unattainable. It happened while we were exercising damage control drills in the Flow with a gale force wind whipping the water to give a reminder of conditions outside. Captain's Requestmen and Defaulters were interrupted by the arrival of the Chief Yeoman with an intercepted signal. An old V and W Class destroyer had broken down off Lerwick and was asking to be towed in. We were already underway and near the entrance and the Captain reported that we were ready to proceed if required. The offer was accepted and ten minutes later we went through the boom in a dash to the rescue.

We steered east through the Pentland Firth and then north for the Shetlands into a north-easterly gale blowing across the tide. The ship turned into the wind and hove-to, unable to progress without risk that the sea would sweep the upper deck clean. Holm Sound, where Prien had taken U 47 into the Flow to sink *Royal Oak* in 1939, was under our lee and the spray was being thrown over the cliff tops. We were all right so long as the engines kept her head into the wind but there was no chance of avoiding damage. Upper deck gear not well secured was the first to go, followed by the whaler which had her side stove in. Although she did her best, with the help of her trawler bow, to ride the storm she could not avoid it all and one sea at least swept her from stem to stern.

I found the Young Doctor, like Hamlet's Ghost in a greatcoat, holding on to a lifeline by the funnels and nibbling a biscuit, probably following the advice he gave to the patients. I used my additional sea-time to persuade him that it would be prudent to go below, where I was immediately seasick for the first time in my life. Never make suggestions unless asked.

The Captain abandoned any idea of going on and his problem was how to turn round without broaching her. He made one attempt and her bow came off the wind as he altered course to starboard. She went over in a very heavy roll at once and he brought her back. We stayed like that for the next five hours until the tide turned and the wind moderated. Meanwhile the destroyer off Lerwick had got her engines going and was safely in harbour.

We went back into the Flow just before dusk having been out for six hours and travelled ten miles. The one heavy sea she had not shaken off had carried away a ventilator on the quarter deck and flooded the compartment below. The after high angle control system table, the equipment which had been fitted with so much trouble during the refit, had been flooded with sea water.

The Gunnery Officer was a reservist, an actuary by profession, and no fool. He realized that time was of the essence and his staff leapt on to the table with warm fresh water in the hope of saving it before the salt got to work. The treatment did not succeed and we were ordered back to Devonport for the table to be replaced and the other weather damage made good. The work-up was postponed.

The ship was late turning the corner because of another gale and approached Land's End after the Wolf Rock Light had been put out. The practice was to show coastal lights for the period when ships were expected to pass by and need them. This area was sometimes visited by E-boats and the rules were adhered to.

I had the middle watch in the navigational plot and noticed that the lamp under the table was not tracking to the west, as it should have been; the ship seemed to be on a course for the land. I shouted this news up the voice pipe and the Officer of the Watch, one of the work up lieutenants, suggested that the plot was useless as usual. This seemed to be a tenable opinion because at that moment it broke down; I turned it off and started up the bridge ladder to tell him. I heard shouted orders in the dark above me and felt the ship turn hard to starboard. He told me afterwards that we were close enough to see the seas breaking on the cliffs through the black night.

The ship was on passage round an unlit promontory under her

lee, at night, in a gale and in the middle of a war but both the Navigating Officer and the Captain were turned in.

The dockyard made good the weather damage but we were held up by the replacement fire control table, which was a complicated job. It was a month before we left for the second time and both watches got three days leave. The bowman and I were invited to spend it in London with the family of the coxswain of the bowman's boat. The three of us pushed our way into a crowded compartment on the night train. The coxswain had no seat but before I could offer mine she leapt like a monkey into a luggage rack and settled down for the night. She was small and agile and thought little of it. An American Air Force lieutenant announced that he guessed he had seen everything now.

I received a telegram from the wardroom which mystified my hostess. 'Indicate position, course and speed at midnight.' It would have been a waste of time to have sent a truthful answer.

The ship was repaired at last and we anchored in the Sound ready to leave for Scapa Flow the next night. No one was allowed ashore and we knew that we should not be returning to Plymouth. After dark a raid started on the city. It was not a hit and run affair but a sustained attack. We watched the gunfire ashore and heard the whistle of the bombs and the explosions while we remained silent in the Sound. The Captain was sick and Jimmy was on the bridge. He showed impatience.

'Guns, why are we not firing?'

'Nothing on the radar, sir.'

'What does that matter? For Chrissake get somethin' orf.'

Thus the first rounds fired by *Carlisle* in her last commission were directed harmlessly into the Devon night sky. It meant nothing to the enemy but lightened the burden on our Plymouth sailors who knew that their families were being bombed and there was nothing they could do. Jimmy saw it at once; it was sort of thing he never missed.

The proportion of days lost in Scapa for bad weather were the same in February as they had been in December and January. We did our best to prepare for war in the Mediterranean in the winter rain and mists of the Orkneys, while the ship shook down. In the vital matter of practice against targets towed by aircraft, we went on making do with dummy runs because the aircraft could not fly.

The Captain had another problem. The ship had been fitted with new and untried radar beyond the usual air and surface warning and gunnery sets. Thus we had a jamming set and equipment called Headache which listened in to enemy aircraft. The new outfits required more men to man them and more messdeck space, already reduced by the extra generators and controls the equipment needed. This created a snowball effect in a ship overcrowded with a full war complement.

On one occasion the Master-at-Arms leading the procession for evening rounds found the screen door to the forward seamen's messdeck barred, with all the wing clips fastened. The message was clear; the Captain banged away with letters and representations to authority and the useless jamming set, together with its power supply and crew were taken out. The Headache equipment remained and later on we were glad of it.

The screen door episode was exceptional. *Carlisle* had commissioned with conscripted Hostilies Only sailors forming the majority of the junior rates. Some of them had been civilians until two months or so before. Few had experience of the sea. Many were only just able to qualify physically. They came from every corner of society and by 1942 education was hardly a requirement. I remember an Irishman who told the Captain that he had never had a hot dinner until he joined the Navy. The Paymaster was a bank manager in a Devon country town. His writer had volunteered for service despite being 40 years old. He was a Nottingham journalist with heavy glasses, round shoulders and little hair. He exuded enthusiasm and goodwill and rejoiced that he was not going to die after an uninterrupted life of provincial monotony that he had expected.

Such men were not there because they wanted to be sailors, or hated the Germans, or sought honour and glory; both conscripts and volunteers did their duty because they would have been embarrassed to do otherwise. They knew none of the tricks of the long service men and were anxious to learn from them and do their best. It was upon their contribution that the professionals depended to keep the show on the road. We have an ability to produce modest unassuming men, with no interest in a military life, who behave with stoic determination in the face of the enemy. It was the same in the 74s, and on the the first day of the Somme, where only 7 of the 32 assaulting battalions with more than 500 casualties, were regulars.

At last we were ordered to the Clyde and we knew that the work-up was over. The Wardroom decided to celebrate our last night in the UK. We were surprised to have an unexpected guest onboard. The Reverend Tubby Clayton was a legend from the Great War, where he opened the first YMCA at Poperinghe in the Ypres salient, and became known to many soldiers he heartened on their way to the trenches. We had all heard of him and made him welcome as an honoured and respected visitor. We thought it impolite to ask him how he had become involved with the Navy or how he had found out that we were off the next day. It occurred to one or two that the presence of a parson might spoil the evening. In fact he made it memorable. He had a repertoire of amusing stories and party games. They were simple and entertaining and he made the evening for us.

We were going back to the Mediterranean to engage enemy aircraft but he said nothing about the prudence of invoking a little help from the Almighty before we entered the cauldron. He said no prayers and gave no blessing but when he had gone we realized why he had meant so much to the Tommies. His influence came from what he was rather than what he said. Simply put, he loved and prayed for front line soldiers.

On 11 March 1943 the ship landed the two RN work up lieutenants at Greenock and left for Gibraltar independently at 25 knots. I spent the five days on passage turned in with a high temperature, indifferent to the thumping of the screws, the motion of the ship or being alone in the battened down after flat. The PMO arrived once a day to paint my throat and my servant, Marine McLintock, brought soup. I put on a greatcoat the day before we reached Gibraltar and crawled up to sit on the after capstan. The sun shone and recovery was fast.

March 1943 was the best month of the war for the U-boats. For the loss of 16 submarines, 120 merchant ships were sunk. Nearly 200 U-boats were operational in the Atlantic alone. The

THE FLEET IN ALGIERS

Algiers, April 1943.

biggest convoy battles of the war against HX 229 and SC 122 were going on in mid-Atlantic while we cruised south in happy ignorance, rejoicing that we had left the North British winter at last. We re-fuelled at Gibraltar and passed Europa Point at dusk on 16 March into the Mediterranean, Nelson's station for honour.

Algiers was packed with shipping. The Captain was bidden to lunch by the Commander-in-Chief. Admiral Cunningham was surprised by our haphazard work up; he told the Captain that the only way to survive on his station was to be quick on the draw. He sent us to the French naval base at Mers-el-Kebir to sharpen up before being passed fit for operations.

Target towing aircraft were not available at Mers-el-Kebir or Oran. An American Liberty ship anchored in the next berth, with a torpedo hole forward and two Lightning aircraft in the deck cargo, twisted into a heap of spars and aluminium by blast. It gave us an idea of the form to be expected.

The C-in-C's plan for our further training was set aside under the pressure of events. We were required to start at once, the Staff having decided that we would have to learn quickness on the draw by getting into the saloon and taking our chance. After six days on the station we were sailed with convoy KMS 11 for Bone, the nearest port to the front line, where the 1st Army were engaged with the Afrika Korps. An RAF squadron leader joined to deter us from engaging friendly aircraft.

The convoy of about twenty ships formed up with *Carlisle* in the middle as anti-aircraft guard and senior Officer of the Escort of five Hunt class destroyers and corvettes spread out on the screen. The Hunts were half our size and complement but managed to mount six 4-in guns compared to our eight. They referred to us as the '8 gun Hunt'.

The first attack came at dawn the day after leaving Algiers. A Heinkel 111 torpedoed a merchant ship, the *Prince Wilhelm II*, and skipped away at wave top height apparently untouched by the barrage from the convoy and its escorts. Spitfires were called up from shore by our fighter direction officer looking at his screen in a compartment below. The first lesson learned was to get him out of his caboosh to the bridge where he could see what was going on and direct the fighters from there.

The attacks became heavier the next day. A mixed force of about 9 Heinkel 111 and 3 Italian S.M. 79 came in with torpedoes and were engaged with everything we had. My action station was on the bridge and I watched them at full throttle flying for their lives above the broken sea, trying to get close enough to make sure. The German Heinkels gave up first, dropped their torpedoes and turned away. The S.M. 79s with three engines and fabric bodies simply came on, dropped their torpedoes and flew past us and away the other side. It seemed that they would all be shot down. One of the corvettes signalled that she had picked up five from a crashed Savoia so that it was probable that the other two escaped. One merchant ship, the *Empire Rowan* of 10,000 tons was sunk and another escort picked up her people. We were told later that the shore Spitfires had accounted for more of the enemy on their way home.

The Italian airmen, in old slow aircraft, with no armour or adequate defence, showed courage that was an inspiration to see. If there were grounds for the propaganda put out about the military qualities of the Italians, it seemed undeserved by their Air Force.

Later in the day the weather freshened and a fast motor boat was seen approaching through the murk. We hauled out ahead of the convoy and challenged the intruder. There was no reply and No 1 gun forward opened fire. The shells burst nowhere near her because our heaving forecastle made accuracy hard to achieve. The shoot was interrupted by the Chief Yeoman. 'Message from *Ledbury*, sir. You are engaging an RAF rescue launch.'

We flashed an indignant signal to the motor boat asking why she had not answered the challenge. She replied that she was very sorry but had not appreciated that she was being fired at. Not only were we slow on the draw and unable to distinguish the cowboys from the Indians, but we could not hit the saloon piano.

Alongside at Bone the shell cases littering our upper deck were thrown into a lighter and replaced with fresh ammunition. Two hours later we were on our way back to Algiers as Senior Officer of the escort for convoy ET 16.

The Old Lady was in the ring again; happily for us, she was unable to express a view upon the crew that had been sent to man her.

CHAPTER 12

NORTH AFRICA AND SICILY

Three of the four bridge watchkeeping officers were RNVR sub-lieutenants, with little experience beyond that gained as Hostilities Only ordinary seamen. They were now standing night watches alone on the bridge in a zig-zagging darkened convoy awaiting the enemy, having been officers for about six months, the last three of which had been at sea. A Dartmouth cadet would have spent about seven years training from the age of 13 to reach a comparable level of responsibility. The RNVRs were motivated adults anxious to get the war over and carry on with their lives; by 1943 they ran the show at junior officer level.

The bridge in *Carlisle* was in three parts; the compass platform, from where the ship was conned, was a raised dais with room for about four people. Abaft was the chart table, main bridge and pom-pom director; then came the air defence position underneath the high angle director and the tripod mast. The ship went to action stations at dawn and dusk and one half of the armament was closed up when air attack was likely

On the day after leaving Bone a Dornier 217 began scouting ahead in poor visibility. The convoy was then attacked by six Heinkels without success. The Squadron Leader stationed himself on the air defence platform and bent, capless, behind the steel side with his hair blowing in the wind, and the noise of the guns about him, holding on to the screen and watching events. It seemed unlikely that there was a risk of shooting at our own aeroplanes, which had so far kept well clear of the convoys. I stood with him, to extend courtesy to a guest and be ready to deal, if I could, with any matters he wished to raise. He thought it unlikely that they would try again before we got to Algiers next morning. I said we looked forward very much to having him on the next trip to which he replied that he was an airman not a bloody sailor. At least that made the position clear. No one replaced him and we were left to our own watchfulness to sort out friend from foe.

Three days in Algiers were enough for a look around. The port was filled with British and American warships of all sizes and the streets bulged with Allied uniforms. I remember a queue about 100 yards long in the middle of the main street; they were USN sailors of all ranks and rates, the crew of a heavy cruiser, just arrived, waiting to get prophylactic treatment and be signed off for it, so that they would not be penalized if they developed venereal disease.

David, an old shipmate from *Revenge*, was serving in a submarine. I asked him what they had been doing and he said he could not say because their reports of proceedings went straight to the Prime Minister. I wrongly assumed this to be a joke but it was true. His submarine had jettisoned the corpse of a Royal Marine officer, dead from natural causes, off the coast of Spain so that the current took it ashore. It carried bogus papers to mislead the enemy about the next major Allied attack.

The wardroom had other front line visitors. There was an MTB officer who shortly afterwards went into Sfax harbour in daylight wearing German colours. Sadly the enemy were soon on to him and he was sunk by fighters and killed. There were the crew of a Wellington on the way home after over eighty missions over Libya and Italy.

The colonel of a parachute battalion called with two of his officers. I invited one of them to bring some of his soldiers to look round the ship. He arrived with a party of hard looking characters, members of the first of the parachute battalions raised. He lined them up on the iron deck; they looked like professional boxers who had wintered in the West Indies. Their faces were expressionless.

'We are here,' said their Captain, 'to look round this warship. We have been invited by this officer, who is a friend of mine. For that reason you will take nothing away from the ship and if I catch anyone who does I will take personal responsibility to ensure he goes to the glasshouse.'

He turned to me. 'I have to do that,' he said, 'otherwise you might lose anything up to a 4-in gun.'

They behaved impeccably. In my cabin my guest asked me if I was short of any kit as he might be able to swop for some he had acquired and did not want.

Carlisle was Senior Officer of the escort for seven more convoys running from Algiers to Bone and return. I have my office diary, now getting yellow. Mingled with entries such as 'Mr Hopkins, S206' and 'SCPO Hosgood, LS and GCM,' I have entered brief details of the attacks by torpedo aircraft to which we were subjected on every trip except one. This was nothing special as these things went at that time but the experience gave us a brisk introduction to the job.

On 5 April an SM 79 was shot down in flames ahead and the nearest Hunt reported that she had picked up one burned midshipman from the wreck. On the 10th a landing craft carrying German and Italian prisoners was torpedoed. The following day an attack by four torpedo bombers at dusk was beaten off by the use of smoke and the assistance of the Headache radar. The German-speaking public schoolboy working the set reported that one of the Heinkels had told another to drop a flare to the west and attack from the other side. I saw the flare come through the clouds but we had made smoke, altered away and probably confused the enemy. During the night a Beaufighter shot down a marauder but blew herself up in flames behind us. On the 21st after a dawn attack by two aircraft a Ju 88 was downed by fighters.

When the enemy came close the air was filled with tracer from the Oerlikons. The merchant ships, particularly the Americans, had little fire discipline and their gunners tended to keep a finger on the trigger whether or not there was a target within range. The Young Doctor and Leading Sick Berth Attendant Wainwright had the job of dealing with the casualties suffered in the Liberty ships from self-inflicted gunfire. On one occasion Doc had to persuade the Master to ask permission for his ship to leave the convoy to enable two seriously wounded men to get treatment ashore. In another ship the Mate had been hit; the Master refused to let him leave for treatment because he was the only other member of the crew besides himself who had been to sea before.

Doc and his assistant removed the shrapnel from the Mate's bottom to oblige.

One morning during a raid the sky was filled with the usual swirling red dots of confetti. A Liberty ship on the beam fired a burst at our bridge and it seemed that the tracer was coming straight for the Gunnery Officer, standing in front of me. I yanked at his oilskin and shouted, 'look out'. It would have been too late anyway and my reaction was instinctive.

He dived to the deck, followed by everyone else, including the Captain, who was not amused. 'We are up here to shoot down aircraft, not fool about,' was his reaction to the attempt to keep his Gunnery Officer's head on. Despite the sang-froid on the bridge in action, our two months on the station had livened our responses. We were learning the ropes.

The convoy duty was interrupted when the ship was ordered to embark Vice-Admiral Sir Algernon Willis at Bone for passage to Algiers *en route* to take command of Force H at Gibraltar. The ship was due to enter harbour at 0900 when a barge would take the Admiral to *Nelson* to call on the Commander-in-Chief.

I went to the bridge at about 0800 but Africa was nowhere to be seen and nothing broke the line of sea and sky. I asked the Officer of the Watch what was happening. He said he had steered the course he was given and knew no more. The Navigating Officer arrived and looked concerned. It had become overcast with no sun and a smudged horizon. The Captain and the Admiral's Chief of Staff, dressed in a smart uniform for the ceremony in *Nelson*, completed the party on the compass platform when the Chief of Staff asked the Navigating Officer the awkward question. 'What was our position when you took your morning sights?' Pilot confessed that he had relied on dead reckoning and had not taken any. The current had set us to the north and we entered harbour one hour late. The Commander-in-Chief and the guard and band on the quarter deck of *Nelson* had had a long wait.

The Captain did not break his rule of keeping out of the office because he knew there was nothing to be said there that would do any good. A commanding officer who kept both Algy Willis and Andrew Cunningham waiting for an hour on the same occasion had achieved a heroic double and an end to preferment.

The Captain decided to issue standing orders to the escorts to make them aware of his intentions in most situations. Some of the Hunts had been in the Mediterranean for two years and were commanded by officers who knew all the tricks.

I remember one with a famous Irish Ascendancy name, addicted to wearing a boat cloak, with a great black beard, a Mephistophelean figure with a gold watch chain round a broad middle. One end of the chain was attached to a piece of white bone like a hare's foot secured with gold wire, which he twirled about when talking. He had been washed over the side in a storm and washed back by the next wave, breaking a leg. The bone was a piece of his shin. Such characters were hard to disconcert.

The orders dealt with matters such as making smoke and communications. One, called Operation Starch, involved the despatch of a boarding party quickly to a stricken merchant ship to stop the crew leaving her before it became certain that she could not be saved. The orders were accepted in good heart and the word was that if that was the way he wanted it they would do their best to humour him. The trouble came from strangers.

Carlisle took over a convoy from the UK off Gibraltar which had had a hard time from submarines. The Captain decided to remind the Senior Officer of the anti-submarine escort who was boss, and ordered the screen to exercise making smoke. It was a clear day and the escorts, having spent a week in unpleasant circumstances, straining to make themselves invisible, acted predictably and did nothing. The Captain assumed they had not got the message and told the Escort Group Commander that there was something wrong with the communications in his Group. This was too much for this officer, who had probably had little sleep for a while, and felt compelled to make a tart reply. 'Our communications,' he signalled, 'were all right until you joined.'

This was diverting for the onlookers but unacceptable to the system. When the Commander came over the side to call on arrival at Algiers he was told by the Captain, before they left the quarter deck together, that his signal was to be cancelled and taken out of his log. I asked him thirteen years later, when we were both at the Admiralty and he was a rear-admiral, whether he had done so. He said he had not. He thought my Captain was mad.

Two American pilots appeared in the wardroom, and told us they were on leave from their light bomber squadron. Their squadron lost more aircrew from accidents than the enemy because the short wings made the bombers unstable, especially when loaded. I was talking to them outside the Aletti hotel when a middle-aged USAAF major, clearly a staff officer, came up. To my surprise they said that they were there to change a propeller and would be going back the next day. They had rooms in a French hotel but spent their nights in the Sphinx, the officers' brothel. They were both Californians who had been in civil aviation before the war. I found out later that when they concluded that the odds had become unfair they had simply walked away. They showed none of the usual signs of strain and were absentees who had weighed up the disadvantages of dishonour and court martial and accepted them.

The enemy had had little success with torpedo bombing and tried night raids. David and I had dined ashore and were in *Carlisle* when a raid started; I took him to the bridge to give him an idea of what we did. There was no one there except a signalman, and the box barrage in which the ship had a role was being fired by other warships in the harbour without our contribution. With some help from the *vin rouge* I called out the ranges and bearings from the barrage instructions, lying on the chart table, and David repeated them to the director. It may have been the other way round; I do not remember. The 4-in opened up and we engaged the enemy with panache until the Gunnery Officer arrived. He seemed satisfied and let us get on with it. When it was over we went back to the wardroom where David announced that he disliked the noise and preferred the quiet of a submarine.

For two convoys we were accompanied by a news cameraman. He wore breeches and a small moustache, a twenties figure from Hollywood and Ben Hur. He was allowed in the spotting top at sea, where he photographed the aircraft and the stricken merchant ships. In Algiers he bored the wardroom by repeated enquiries about our next engagement so that he could take pictures of it. He was a warmonger, not because he was wedded to the cause or loved a fight, but because he wanted to sell films and make money. This was a limited point of view which made it difficult for him to fit in.

One day, after he had been worse than usual, the boatswain offered to take him sailing in a whaler, hoping perhaps for a screen test to sing 'The Mountains of Mourne'. The boat capsized in a squall and the boatswain and the two seamen with him held on to the rails on the hull and showed the cameraman what to do. Unfortunately, he went to pieces and yelled blue murder. The boatswain was disgusted and did not keep it to himself when they got back. The media man asked to be transferred and solved the problem he had set himself.

The Army were doing well and when it became obvious that the Germans would have to give up or escape to Sicily the Commander-in-Chief ordered the destroyers to cut them off. It was thought unlikely that the Axis would leave their Army stranded, and would do their best for them in the same way that we had done for ours at Dunkirk, Crete, Norway and Greece. This was not to be and the worst the destroyers had to face came from Allied aircraft, despite the glaring red lead which had been painted over their forecastles to ensure recognition.

The Navigating Officer passed the word to me during a lunch time party that we were to lead the first convoy through to Alexandria. He had got the tip from the C-in-C's staff ashore. Like an idiot I assumed that the Captain was in the dark because he never visited the Staff, and thinking he ought to know, I told him. For once, he already knew and decided to track down what he saw as a gross breach of security. He asked me how I had found out. I was on a spot. I could not put a messmate in the cart and said that the information seemed to be generally known. This made it worse, and I was asked what ships I had visited. I had to say that I had dined in the submarine depot ship *Maidstone*. The Captain sent a personal letter to her Captain suggesting that someone in his ship had spoken out of turn. The letter was sent without my knowledge and could not have been based upon anything he heard from me. The reply from *Maidstone* was that he did not know what our programme was, neither did his officers, and he could not understand what it was all about. Happily the ship received her orders from the C-in-C in the middle of this nonsense and there were more important matters to think about.

The enemy surrendered at Tunis on 13 May and three minesweeping flotillas set to work to sweep the channel. In two days 200 moored mines were cleared and then it was our turn. We left Algiers on 19 May and anchored in a bay near Bone with the four destroyers who would be coming with us. One of them was a Great War 'W' class and her Captain arrived for the conference by whaler under oars. The convoy was the first to run through the Mediterranean to Alexandria for two years.

We met the four fast merchantmen of KMF 14X, and preceded by four minesweepers, set out for the Galita Channel and the Sicilian Narrows. The opposition had long gone and the passage was uneventful. The convoy went close to the shore off Cape Bon and we saw a giant glider with black crosses wrecked on the beach, surrounded by cheerful soldiers who waved at our procession. Bizerta, Tunis, Sfax, Sousse, Tripoli, Derna and Tobruk, so long held by the enemy, now lay captured under our lee as we made our jubilant way eastwards. The convoy entered Tripoli and we went on to Egypt with the Tribal Class destroyer *Ashanti* and the infantry assault ship *Queen Olga*.

Shortly after dawn on the day we reached Alexandria a heavy aircraft was detected on the radar and then appeared astern. We hesitated in identifying it until *Ashanti* opened fire and settled the matter. She turned towards us from about five miles on our starboard quarter and the Captain of Marines, who was the Principal Control Officer, opened fire with the after 4-in. As she got closer we saw that it was an Italian SM 79 intent on getting near enough to make a run at us with its torpedo. The multiple pom-pom now joined in, firing on an after bearing. The clatter on the bridge was considerable and the blast plucked at our heads. The Officer of the Watch answered the buzzer from the voice pipe and yelled out above the din. 'From the Captain, sir. Stop the pom-pom firing.' By that time the range was under two miles. From previous encounters we expected her to come on but she turned suddenly away, the guns were checked and after some parting shots from *Ashanti* it was all over.

The hands were falling in for entering harbour when the

Captain of Marines buttonholed me. He asked how he could arrange to see the Commander-in-Chief because he wished to state a complaint against the Captain. I told him to lie down for a while and the feeling would pass. It was soon apparent that he meant it. In his judgement the Captain had recklessly hazarded his ship in the presence of the enemy by ordering the pom-pom to cease firing for no reason other than the noise was disturbing him. I pointed out that it had made no difference to the outcome, his complaint would get nowhere save to put a mark on his career and the Officer of the Watch and I would be witnesses, not anxious to enter the arena in such a contest. He was not persuaded but let it go in the end.

It would have been unthinkable for the Captain to have been asked why he had given the order. It might have been that he saw the aircraft turn away through a scuttle and stopped the gun to save ammunition. That does not explain why he did not come to the bridge. I believe that the racket from the pom-pom outside his cabin pushed him over the edge for a moment and he stopped it on impulse without thinking of the consequences.

The strain of command could produce odd results. This was not the first, or the last, time that one of his officers had sufficient doubts about the Captain's judgement to begin a complaint procedure. Captain Queeg of *Caine Mutiny* fame was not to me the aberrant maniac his cross-examination makes him out to be. His behaviour matched the pressure he had to put up with. It was a young man's job but young men did not get it. *Caine* and *Carlisle* had things in common.

The ship had fourteen days to boiler clean, dock and carry out essential repairs. In the harbour the houseboats and yachts of the Egyptian well-to-do shared the facilites with Allied warships and merchant ships. An ancient Greek cruiser ferried a launch full of women ashore every morning after breakfast, encouraging speculation on the prospects of a liaison job with the Royal Hellenic Navy.

The two French heavy cruisers who had surrendered in 1940 were still there, covered by a duty British MTB with two torpedoes ready to fire. I met one of the MTB commanding officers later on and he told me that a soldier on board for a party cocked a firing lever and was fiddling about with the trigger when someone spotted him and aborted what would have been the most perfidious of all the deeds of Albion.

The Captain was a yachtsman and I crewed for him in a Dragon borrowed from the Ras-el-Tin Yacht Club. The boats were kept under permanent cover; a servant wiped them clean and dry and polished the cockpit seats before the ample Egyptian bottoms-in-waiting covered them. In those days the required reading for local colour was a book by a British army officer called *Oriental Spotlight* in which he declared that promotion in the Egyptian Army went by weight.

Transport was by gharry through the narrow streets round the dockyard. The locals sat outside their houses and ignored the wheels and the noise from these invaders. The city had been a septic tank of races since the Great Library was burned; they knew that they only had to wait a while and we would go away like the rest. The talk when we arrived was of a bomb hit on the brothel in Seven Sisters Street which killed some of the girls and their Australian customers. This seemed to show Allah at his most inscrutable; the damage elswhere was trivial.

The Wardroom decided that the Casino Chatby was to their satisfaction and we were often there. The premises were on the end of a pier and combined a bar and cabaret. Our favourite was a belly-dancer called Shirley who danced in bare feet and threw her long black hair in all directions. She was 16 and had the energy to repeat her performance if asked. After a while we became part of her turn and the customers knew there would be additions to the show when they saw us there. Our table was in front of the stage and at the climax of the dance, when Shirley threw her hair towards the audience in exhausted ecstacy Senior leapt to his feet to grab it. Two of us jumped on him to hold him down while he yelled in frustrated desire. Shirley had orders to play it to the gallery and, although our contribution must have been good for trade, we were given no reductions and a close watch was kept on us. Senior became so convincing that the proprietor probably thought he meant business and one night he would have a riot on his hands.

On 6 June 1943 we were sent through the Canal and anchored

late the next evening in the roads off Port Tewfik, south of Suez. An artificer who had been in the previous commission claimed that when the ship was there in 1941 a merchantman blew up in a raid and he saw a steam locomtive and fire tender from her deck cargo straddle her, the engine dropping one side and the tender the other.

We started badly, the Captain receiving a signal *en clair* from the Flag Officer at Suez asking why he had not called on him. The Captain climbed into a boat for the hour's trip to fulfil the demands of protocol, paying the price for his own rule of avoiding the office. We were particularly vulnerable, with a captain and wardroom unable to muster one name between us that mattered twopence to the great and good who determined our destiny.

The liner *Monarch of Bermuda* was in the anchorage and I dined there with a sub-lieutenant who had been a midshipman in *Emerald*. I found him living amid potted palms and white napery surrounded by the trappings of a peacetime ocean liner. The ship had been given heavy davits to carry infantry assault craft and his job was to take charge of a group of them and see the soldiers ashore. Dinner was served on separate tables in the main saloon by stewards who carried out the routine they used on the first class passengers. It worked all right provided their peacetime drill was not altered too much. This could lead to deputations to the merchant service Master and trouble with the union.

There were other liners there in the same role and it was obvious that there was a big landing in the wind. A plain language signal addressed to the Fleet from the Commander-in-Chief called for volunteers who were strong swimmers and could speak Greek. I doubt if there were any takers for this subtle stroke of counter-intelligence but from then on it was obvious that wherever we were going it was not Greece. On 14 June we left harbour with the liners and went round Sinai, arriving at Aqaba the next day.

Carlisle provided the anti-aircraft guard for five days while the Army and the boats practised opposed landings. Sometimes the wind blew the sand enough to darken the sun and bring a short sea which gave the soldiers a bumpy ride ashore. Sailing in a whaler could mean a double reef.

The finale of the exercise was a night attack in which the local garrison of Indian Army sepoys acted as German defenders. One of them became excited and took the pin out of a live grenade. The war ended then for three infantrymen who were buried a long way from home in the desert, at a place only known to their countrymen because of Lawrence of Arabia, who had taken it from the Turks in 1916 with a handful of men.

We went back to Suez where the army practised by day and by night with their boats, and our ship's company sat shirtless in the evening wind and cheered an *ad hoc* concert party, which somehow found room to perform round the forecastle capstan.

The soldiers we met ashore were 8th Army veterans. We looked at the flashes of the regiments on their shoulders and wondered what they might be in for the other end. Bertie, one of our lieutenants, was landed for a tonsillectomy at an Army base hospital. He chilled us with stories of the wounds and burns he had seen and we looked at the infantrymen in the Suez Club with respect. It was clear that those in the boats would be the first ashore with the dirty work to do.

Time began to hang heavily. In the wardroom Senior, a warrant engineer and the Assistant Paymaster began a whisky drinking contest which ended in an easy victory for the AP who began to talk rather more than usual. The Warrant Engineer passed out in an armchair and Senior staggered to his bunk. The Chief had to take the ship to sea the next morning because Senior was still out to the world and was not seen in the engine room until late in the day. It was a court martial matter but we all had other things to do and nothing happened. The rigours of the discipline the Navy was used to were often overlooked by this time.

Four months had passed since we arrived on the station and the ship had settled down. We were the only survivor of our Class, with nearly four years' front line service. The conclusion was evident but I am sure that no one thought about it. We were young, cheerful and beginning to learn.

An artillery captain and an RAF pilot joined us for liaison duties before the ship left next day for Alexandria, escorting the liner *Strathnaver* and her assault troops. Neither of our passengers knew where we were going. They had been told to identify aircraft and help engage shore targets.

At Port Said we slowed down to let a boat come alongside and an RAF flight lieutenant from intelligence joined. He had difficulty in getting up the jumping ladder because of the roll of paper under his arm. This turned out to be a grid map of Sicily which he showed to the nearest officer and asked where he should put it. He was told to shut up but the news was out.

We anchored in the roads outside Alexandria with shipping all round us. A boat brought off an officer and three bags of confidential mail addressed personally to the Captain. The First Lieutenant, Gunnery Officer and I spent the rest of the day round the table in the Captain's day cabin correcting the orders for operation Husky, the assault on Sicily. Most of it did not concern our sector but we put the corrections in, in case.

There was a spare day for last minute shopping and private affairs. One of the young RNVRs made a bee-line for Seven Sisters Street, determined not to risk a virginal death. I ate duck *à l'orange* at a restaurant in Sidi Bish before being stranded ashore with three officers and twenty sailors from the ship; the landing craft which should have taken us off left half an hour early. It was a long trip, the weather was not good and we made the decision to find a hotel because of the unlikelihood that the craft would be sent in again that night. We discussed the chances of them going without us and agreed that it could happen if boats could not run; our absence would not be a matter of consequence.

We booked into a rooming house near the dockyard, auspiciously named the Hotel Syracuse, where we shared the accommodation with two troopers from the New Zealand cavalry. They found us curious and we had many questions to answer. They were keen to know the chances of our being shot if the boat did not come in for us in the morning and we were found to have deserted.

We said goodbye to our friends at daybreak, rounded up the sailors and returned to the jetty. It was crowded with others who had also been left behind and we were back for breakfast. There was a distinguished guest onboard. Brigadier Chater, Royal Marines, the late commander of the Sudan Camel Corps, had decided to have a look at the war on his way home for leave.

The assault convoy left that night. The equivalent of three

divisions were embarked in seventeen large ships, bound for the eastern part of the island south of Syracuse. It was our task to provide air cover to the northern flank of the landing force, nearest to the enemy. The weather was warm and friendly and we knew that this was the end of the sideshows and another turning point of the war in the Mediterranean. Subdued but cheerful, I turned in.

The duck à l'orange hit me during the middle watch, having been trampled on by Egyptian flies before I ate it. I could not stand, my temperature soared and my inside was a rat's nest. The Captain visited the sick and gave me sherry to drink which excited the rats and annoyed the doctor. He kindly lent me the only book he had onboard entitled A Short History of the United Service Club. I was on my feet by the evening of the 9th, in time.

The convoy had altered to the north before being joined off Malta by armoured units in LSTs and LCTs from Sfax and Tripoli who formed up astern ready to land after the assault infantry. The weather became overcast and a north westerly brought a short sea and a miserable passage for the soldiers in the landing craft. The first wave was due to land at 0245 and the ship was at general quarters all night ready for the big day. We turned westwards and ran in.

The summer sky was speckled with Dakotas and gliders heading for the shore with the 1st British Airborne Division from North Africa. The enemy flak began to come up in earnest; we were expected here, not Greece. The head wind and the tracer caused inexperienced pilots to let go their tows too soon and the gliders were coming down in the sea. By this time it was getting light and the landing craft were well inshore.

The Captain decided that we had time to help and took the ship alongside a glider with soldiers standing on the wing. They sat in a huddled group in blankets in the Captain's day cabin, quietly drinking rum, waiting to get their bearings. Out of 1200 British airborne troops who set out only 200 were able to take part in the operations ashore that day; most of them ended in the sea.

I left the soldiers and went to the quarter deck. The glider was still afloat, bobbing alongside within reach. I secured her properly to the stern with some idea of saving her, or at least keeping her there until the dead could be taken out. It was an unsound plan, no doubt induced by lack of sleep and the excitement of events. The ship got under way, the line pulled a piece out of the glider causing it to fill and sink, taking the drowned men with her. I went back to the bridge.

The shore batteries were being hard hit by the destroyers. Their positions had been marked on our plans and it was not long before shell fire from the land stopped altogether. Aircraft were our business and we did not expect to wait long for customers.

A fighter came down in a screaming vertical dive and there was a cheer as it hit the sea. 'That was a Spitfire,' the RAF pilot said. Ashore another fighter began an umistakeable dive to destruction and we groaned. 'That is an Italian Macchi,' said the airman and the bridge brightened up. The pilot got out but his parachute did not open and the watchers shouted in anticipation; our early curiosity about enemy aircraft was turning to malevolence as the threat increased.

We could see the vehicles and tanks pushing off the beach near the small town of Avola. The soldier with us asked to be put ashore to report to his headquarters and the RAF pilot and Brigadier Chater went with him. The soldier come back an hour later and said that despite some unburied dead here and there things had gone very well and he had been told that Syracuse would be taken next day.

The ship anchored but soon had to get underway. There were two Ju 88s in line astern, hard black pencils against the blue sky, diving steeply to make their one pass before the odds engulfed them. I saw them pull out and hurtle away at full boost watched by their host of enemies, diverted by this forlorn hope. The bombs missed the merchantman they were meant for and went on missing at each of three more raids before dark. *Carlisle* anchored and reduced to defence stations for food and sleep before the next episode.

I shared the flag deck with a signalman and the RAF intelligence officer, still with us. The arrangements were uncomplicated, the bedding being a rolled lifebelt for a pillow and night attire a pair of overalls and sandals. Sleep came easily and induced a lasting rapport with hard beds.

The alarm rattlers brought the Signalman and me to our feet, putting on tin hats and racing for the bridge ladder, while the ship vibrated as the cable came in. I shouted to the airman, who seemed immobile. I saw the Signalman bend down and shake his shoulder as I ran up the ladder. The ship got underway, awaiting a solitary aircraft detected by the radar.

About a mile away on our starboard bow we could see the bright lights of the old hospital ship *Talamba*, a reminder of the Java Sea the year before. She was at anchor with wounded being ferried out to her. A landing craft lay off her gangway waiting its turn. Large brightly lit red crosses marked her sides and upper deck and she shone like an electric bulb in a dark cellar. After nearly four years of blackout she provided a dramatic tribute to the Geneva Convention and civilization. The rules for the protection of wounded had been agreed a hundred years before, after the horrors of the battle of Solferino. It seemed inconceivable that they would be broken by the countrymen of Beethoven, Goethe and the rest.

Jimmy announced to the silent, watching bridge that he wished she would put those bloody lights out, but he would, wouldn't he? I was sure that the Germans would not bomb her. This was a line that would be crossed only by barbarians on a rout.

An aircraft in a steep dive passed over *Carlisle* towards *Talamba* and pulled out and away without bombing. They had seen the red crosses and were following the rules. We heard the engines in a dive once more and again the aircraft went over us. The scream of a bomb left the hospital ship smothered by a cloud of spray from a near miss aft. She began to settle by the stern at once; by some grim chance of engineering her bright lights continued to demonstrate her innocence to the end.

It took about ten minutes and gave some of them time to get into the water, although the severely wounded in beds must have had little chance. We got the whaler away with the Young Doctor and as much gear as he had time for. *Talamba's* stern went slowly under and then the end was quick. Her bows rose upright and we heard the crash of escaping machinery and collapsing bulkheads, the death rattle of a sinking ship. I tried to put the havoc inside her out of my mind. There were one or two boats in the oil slick and some heads, though not many. We had not fired a shot.

The ship edged slowly towards the survivors. Our whaler could be seen hauling them in. Some of the wounded were clinging to wreckage and Doc swam to them and shouted to the coxswain of the whaler a course to steer through the darkness to pick them up. Having been in the Navy for less than a year he had not mastered the jargon and surprised the coxswain by referring to 'bowside' and 'stroke' rather than 'port' and 'starboard'. He manoeuvered a raft under *Carlisle's* bows with the army hospital ship colonel in it and two female nurses, one with a broken leg. They were got inboard with difficulty while Doc was left hanging on to a scrambling net, dead beat. The ship then got underway. He was pulled up by a sailor who went down to get him. The man concerned had been punished shortly before for malingering, on evidence given by Doc. You never know who your friends are.

The landing craft that had been lying off before the raid came neatly alongside. The wounded were lifted out and taken to the sick bay, or made comfortable on stretchers near to it until they could be looked at.

Her Leading Seaman coxswain had been hit in the bombing and we found him by her wheel when the casualties had gone. He was brought inboard and died on our iron deck. He was the only one we picked up who died in *Carlisle*. The Leading Seaman was taken to the wardroom bathroom and Jimmy and the Master-at-Arms sewed him into his hammock. A splinter had taken away a large part of his right chest. Jimmy could not understand how he had stayed on his feet long enough to steer an awkward craft, at night and loaded with wounded, through the debris after the sinking and bring her safely alongside a darkened ship a mile away. He must have guessed that he had been mortally hit and needed immediate help.

In the hubbub we did not want the hindrance of a funeral and sent his body, with the survivors, to another ship the next day. That was the way of the world at that moment. In courage and self sacrifice the Leading Seaman was with Roope of the *Glowworm* or Esmond in the attack on the *Scharnhorst* and *Gneisenau*, but we who saw it neither reported what he had done nor had time to bury him. It may be that these words are his only record of that night.

About one hundred were picked up from *Talamba* and issued with the standard survivor's kit. The wardroom was full of Lascars, delighted to be rescued and beaming with pleasure at their new towels, overalls and shaving gear.

The Army nurses were put into the sick bay, partly because one was injured, and also because Jimmy thought it a convenient place to mount a sentry. He had a gloomy view of sailors when women were about, whatever the circumstances. They were with us for three days until we could move them.

The doctors were at it all night keeping the casualties alive, indifferent to two further raids. The PMO was a GP who typed novels in his cabin and was alleged to recoil at the sight of blood. The Young Doc was a distinguished physician in the making who had been obliged to acquire surgical experience in the Blitz. Thus the repair work fell upon him, with assistance from two doctors who were lent to us from the Admiral's headquarters ship, *Bulolo*. Having spent much of the night dragging wounded men out of the water, he then operated on them. He could not get rid of the oil fuel and looked like Al Jolson. He was given the MBE for his efforts, the only decoration given to the ship while I was there; a surgeon lieutenant on the Dieppe raid, for similiar services, was awarded an immediate DSO.

We oiled from a Royal Fleet Auxiliary, *Emmerdale*, the next day and anchored again. The Chief Yeoman of Signals came to see me on serious business. The Signalman who shared the sleeping billet on the flag deck had reported that he had been unable to get the RAF officer to his feet. He had spent the time during the raid with his head in his arms in a corner. If the Signalman had done that the Articles of War ordained that his life could be forfeit. He wanted something done. The Chief Yeoman told him to keep his mouth shut and the First Lieutenant would deal with it. For once Jimmy looked troubled. He ordered one of our motor boats to be lowered as he went aft to see the Captain. Within thirty minutes the Intelligence Officer was on his way and we did not see him again. Perhaps justice was not done but that was not the aim; Jimmy could not ask the ship's company to accept an officer who, for whatever reason, behaved openly in a way that others had to control.

Carlisle entered Syracuse, the first major warship there. The harbour and town were deserted. The Captain of Marines and I explored the main street but there was no sign of life. We went into a wrecked shop and shouted but there was no answer. We heard the noise of a motor cycle and a German Army bike arrived outside ridden by a commando sergeant. He had made the bike more comfortable by adding a large black silk cushion to the saddle and called at the shop for more loot. He told us that he had been captured in the assault but managed to escape on the bike.

The ship was ordered out before nightfall and we went back to the anchorage. There were two raids on the harbour before we left but no damage was done.

The merchantman *Ocean Peace*, anchored nearby, was hit during a raid by two Ju 88. A small fire was started but she showed no signs of serious damage. We were astonished to see her lower a boat and bring it to her stern. The crew clambered quickly down a rope ladder to the boat. Last was the Master, carrying a brief case and holdall. By this time the unattended fire had gained a hold and the anchorage was marked by a billowing cloud of black smoke. This was unhelpful to our affairs and *Carlisle* was ordered to sink her. We banged away with 4-in and saw the shells bursting on her but she showed no signs of sinking. The Captain decided to change the bearing and try again. He gave the engine orders and as we moved off there was a loud explosion, her bows and stern rose into the air and she sank at once. A Tribal class destroyer the other side had despatched her with a torpedo. It was effective but risky because we lay in line with the target, had the torpedo run deep. In the flurry of the early days of the operation such an episode was soon forgotten.

During the morning watch we picked up a German airman who had been in his dinghy for some thirty hours. It was possible, though not certain, that his pilot had sunk *Talamba*. The doctors would not allow him to be interrogated because of his condition and he remained in the sick bay.

Back in Syracuse *Carlisle* anchored while tanks and vehicles poured ashore from the landing craft. Except for the duty watch the ship's company collapsed into sleep. A signal was made to the Admiral asking what we should do with the prisoner. The reply was 'Give him to the Army. Remember this is a combined operation.'

Jimmy gave me the job of landing him. I took McLintock and another marine in the skimming dish. Both had Sterling sub-machine guns and it was clear from the prisoner's face that he thought we were taking him ashore to execute him for *Talamba*. There had been no trial, or vote upon the sentence, but I suspect that he did not regard such preliminaries as essential to the outcome. So far as he was concerned the proceedings were to be a re-run of the last page of The Three Musketeers, with himself in the role of M'Lady and me the Headsman.

We landed over the beach, the prisoner gathered up his parachute and dinghy, and an unmilitary procession stumbled over the shingle towards a White Ensign near the harbour, where we expected to find the Naval Officer-in-Charge. The victim cheered up when it dawned on him that his chances improved with every step away from the beach. He was a lad of 19, short, with fair hair and an address in Cologne. His name was Peter Reinhardt and he was the gunner of a Ju 88 and the only survivor.

We found a group of officers from the Naval Port Party standing about in their building, waiting for something to happen. The senior one was an evident dead beat with two and a half straight stripes and a complete set of khaki kit, including cap cover, that looked as if it was straight from the Army and Navy Stores. I told him who I was and what I wanted. He made some remark about the Captain's clerk and I turned my attention to an RNR who seemed to be closer to events. He suggested that I took the airman into the town. Before we left I handed over the Belgian francs that had been found in the boy's pocket. He had three tickets for a Brussels brothel which were given back to him, amid the sniggers of the Port Party officers. I heard that the dead beat was replaced the next day as soon as he was spotted by a senior officer.

The centre of the town was a storm of dust and dirt from a procession of heavy tanks from the 4th Indian Division, disembarking from their LSTs. I reported my party to a captain wearing a black beret and he agreed to take our prisoner. He saluted him and the airman clicked his heels in reply. I had the hospital ship in mind and did not take part in this exchange of honours among fighting men, although I knew that an airgunner would not have made the decision to sink her. Nevertheless, had I told the marines to shoot him I believe his chances would have been no better than evens.

The ship acted as A/A guard that night, anchoring near an ammunition ship waiting to unload. The raids caused the harbour to thicken with gunsmoke, the muzzle flashes showing up rolling clouds of it around us. The walls and old fortifications contained the noise and fumes; the general effect was Trafalgar at 1330. There was a hangfire or premature burst in one of the close range guns in the ammunition ship and the screams of a wounded man pierced the racket, to the unease of those on our upper deck who heard it.

There was one more raid the next morning before we were sent north to act as A/A guard in Augusta, captured the day before. The first round was over.

CHAPTER 13

MALTA

Augusta was taken two days before we got there and we were not harassed from the land. The place had provided the Italians with a naval base and good anchorage but indifferent facilities for unloading stores; most of the merchant shipping continued to discharge either in Syracuse or, temporarily, over the beaches near Avola. Augusta became a base for coastal forces operating at night in the Straits of Messina, and a jumping off point for commando raids to the north. Of the territory then occupied by the Allies in Sicily it was nearest to the Italian airfields on the mainland, home to the Ju 88 and SM 79 squadrons we had come to fight.

Carlisle was the only warship there bigger than a destroyer. The MTBs and MGBs made use of the back-up in the stores, repairs and medical attention we could offer; for them it was Hobson's choice because they had no other logistical support. The shore batteries and searchlights in the Straits of Messina made life hard for them, and when they came back they berthed on *Carlisle* to get our help in repairing their action damage and treating their wounded.

It was known by that time in the war that blood and plasma made all the difference between life and death to serious casualties but the Navy had no Blood Transfusion Service. Our doctors had to beg, borrow or steal from any hospital they could reach to keep up their record of not losing a man while he was with us. The Young Doc told me he was going to do something about the Crimean arrangements for the navy wounded when he got home, and knowing him, he probably did.

Air raids were frequent by day and night. The Italians put all they had into one night attack with SM 79s, straddling *Carlisle* and the Infantry Assault ship *Ulster Monarch*, anchored about 200 yards

HEADLONG INTO THE SEA

away. *Ulster Monarch* was near missed and we could see the flames inside her through the holes in her hull. She was loaded with heavily armed commandos setting out on a raid. The bombs exploded ammunition about them, causing many casualties on her forward messdeck.

It was a stream attack and *Carlisle* had every gun in action with only the whistle of the bombs audible above the racket. The Navigating Officer, Officer of the Watch, Chief Yeoman of Signals and I decided that no useful purpose would be served by remaining on the compass platform, where our chances of receiving a splinter hit were marginally higher; we retreated to the bridge below and gathered round the chart table, sheltering behind a canvas dodger. The Captain stayed on the compass platform, alone, not to set an example, because we were the only ones near him, nor to see better what was going on because there was little chance of influencing events in that inferno, but simply because it was right and we knew it, but allowed our animal instincts to hide to take charge for a moment.

The sky blazed and an SM 79 with her three engines on fire went in off our starboard bow. The Captain told me to tell the ship's company; I used the bridge microphone to broadcast the success to all quarters below. To our amazement we saw a second flaming bomber crash and then a third. I broadcast what I had seen; my audience were entitled to conclude that either I was affected by drink or the ship had become quick on the draw at last. It was neither. Beaufighters from Malta had massacred the enemy, being equipped with a new radar enabling them to lock on to and destroy the slow Italian aircraft as they pressed bravely on to attack the anchored ships. I believe at least eight bombers were so destroyed and an Air Force officer who had done most of it received a DSO.

When it became clear that our contribution was not having much effect the Captain ordered the eight-barrelled pom-pom below the bridge to stop firing, to reduce the smoke and noise and enable him to get a better view of events. The director passed the order but nothing happened. After a third failure the Captain ordered me to go down and stop it. I found the Petty Officer Captain of the Gun standing stiffly behind it; two of the blast caps were blown apart by premature bursts, while the crew continued to feed it with ammunition, acolytes in a frenzied ritual. These guns were nicknamed Chicago Pianos; Chicago Apocalypses would have been better. The muzzle flashes from No. 1 gun just below, the choking gunsmoke, the blast and clatter from the pom-pom and the whistling of the bombs could turn the crew into automatons if it went on long enough.

I put my face close to the Petty Officer's ear and shouted to him to stop it firing. He seemed in a trance and ignored me and I had to punch him on the arm to get his attention to my gestures before he came to and obeyed the order. The blessed lull was well received in the sick bay, directly underneath the gun, where a major operation was in progress to save a young MTB officer with a stomach wound. The vibration and racket from the pom-pom and No. 1 gun caused the operating table to shake. An Army officer with dysentry crawled repeatedly across the deck to get to the heads behind the operating table.

The surviving Italians left and we ceased firing. An escort asked for medical attention for a wounded airman they had picked out of the harbour. Jimmy lowered a boat amid the din of a fresh attack and the Young Doc went off with his bag once more. He came back an hour later after a disagreable journey, his errand of mercy unperformed. He had found the Italian very dead. He enquired from the escort why they had asked for medical help and was told that when the airman parachuted into the water someone on their upper deck thought that they had heard him grunt.

We were shelled by an enemy light craft which approached the harbour during the raid. The gun was almost certainly fired over open sights and as we were anchored, and a sitting target, we were relieved to hear the shell pass over the forecastle. An unsuccessful attempt was made to return fire before the enemy cleared off north.

On Monday 19 July our direct involvement with the Sicilian operation ended and the ship was ordered to Malta, having survived eighteen raids in eight days without loss or damage. On the way out of harbour we had the new experience of being attacked by six Me 109s in the fighter-bomber role. They came in low, bombed and were away before we knew what was happening. A low level aircraft could get under the radar and was hard to counter.

Our arrival at Grand Harbour, Malta, nearly brought disaster. The Navigating Officer took the shortest course to the entrance and we crossed a British minefield. We should have been mined and the fact that we arrived untouched probably worried the Staff as much as our indolence in using an uncorrected chart. A sharp signal from Vice-Admiral Malta ordered us to give our reasons in writing and submit a track chart before sailing.

The ship was sent to Marsaxlokk to oil and then to sea to join an eastbound convoy. I began the reasons in writing but had to wait for Pilot for the track chart; he was occupied until we had joined up with the merchantmen. Thus the order could not be complied with for some time and we expected trouble. In the event no disciplinary action was taken against either the Captain or Navigating Officer although they had taken the ship on a course which should have doomed her.

After two more convoys from Malta to Syracuse we left Sicily on 24 July, arriving at Alexandria four days later. *Carlisle* had done what was asked of her in Sicily but any modest satisfaction among the ship's company was soon removed by our Admiral, ashore at Ras-el-Tin, who did not greet our entry as an occasion for favourable notice, but used it to point out that there were hands on the upper deck fallen in for entering harbour whose dress could have been smarter.

The ship went straight into dry dock for a bottom scrape while the Wardroom headed for the Casino Chatby, leaving Pilot as Officer of the Day, the only officer onboard. He turned in to make up for lost sleep while the dockyard workmen began to pump out the dry dock. Towards midnight he was shaken by a distraught Egyptian who announced that the ship was about to be destroyed. Pilot struggled back to conciousness and went to the dockside to find that the yard foreman had made an accurate diagnosis of what might have been a terminal problem. The bows and stern were supported by the wooden blocks in the dock bottom but the middle ones were missing so that as the water was pumped out the whole weight of the ship was taken increasingly by the blocks forward and aft, advancing the moment when the unsupported midships would collapse under its own weight, and break her back. The pump out was stopped and water returned to the dock at the rush; it was just in time by about ten minutes. The cause of the near disaster was soon determined.

On our first visit to Oran there had been a false alarm over an underwater attack by frogmen. The Officer of the Watch in a Fleet carrier thought that he had seen one and opened fire. Later in the war I met the Italian Admiral responsible for underwater attacks by frogmen and he told me that they had never attacked Oran. As a result of the scare ships were ordered to rig bottom lines, ropes going under the ship's hull and secured each side amidships. The purpose of the lines was to enable our own divers to hold on to them to get below and remove limpet mines. Our lines had been rigged but no one had remembered to unrig them so that when she entered drydock they snagged the midships blocks and pulled them over, leaving the ship unsupported when the water was pumped out. A humble Egyptian foreman rigger had saved us from destruction.

In view of her age, time and resources would not have been spent on the major re-build that would have been needed to repair her, even had that been possible. She had earned her luck; it would have been unfitting for this ship to have ended her days by accident in a Near Eastern dock.

We escorted a through convoy to Gibraltar and brought one back, returning to Alexandria on 29 August. Shirley had left the Casino Chatby in our absence and the Wardroom walked out in gloom. Senior was particularly downhearted by the loss of our personal belly-dancer; on the way home he ordered the gharry driver to change course.

We found ourselves in a room lit by oil lamps while Senior explained to Madame that the officers present desired to be entertained by the best exhibition the house could provide. She left to see what could be done, giving him a free hand in the peripheral arrangements. He invited the gharry driver and his horse in for the show. The driver had been over this sort of course before and, provided the money was right, would have engaged in the ritual slaughter of his grandmother.

The horse was taken out of the shafts without difficulty. Senior led him in while the rest of us brought up the rear. He would probably have refused to go into a horse box, had he ever seen one, and had no intention of going through a brothel door, despite the shove we gave him from behind. The driver said something in Arabic and he backed out. For them it was probably an old trick. We persuaded Senior that the horse had already seen the show, held our aching sides and invited Madame to begin.

The saturnalia was interrupted by a crash of boots and two military policemen came in, bulging with authority. One of them brought off a resounding salute in front of Senior, accompanied by more sonorous boot work. Madame and the girls slid out.

'Sir!' said the M.P.

'Good evening,' said Senior.

'These premises are out of bounds, being in a black brothel area.'

'Good Lord!' said Senior, 'how could we have made such a mistake.'

'I do not know,' said the policeman, 'because there is a large illuminated sign at the end of this street marking it out bounds to all ranks.'

Our luck was changing.

We left for Gibraltar with a convoy on 4 September and off Bone were passed through by the surrendered Italian Fleet from Spezia. There were 2 battleships, 6 cruisers and 8 destroyers escorted by *Warspite* and *Valiant* and 7 destroyers. The flagship *Roma* had been sunk the day before by Do 217 aircraft from France with radio controlled bombs. When *Roma* blew up she took with her the Italian C-in-C as well as the naval families taking passage.

The great ships made a famous sight but otherwise meant little to *Carlisle's* crew, for whom the Italian Navy had been a remote threat. The ships were powerful and threatening but their guns and directors were part of the old gunnery world we knew to be on the way out. The projectiles with which we were concerned were not lobbed by cordite from floating platforms travelling at 25 knots fifteen miles away, but bombs and torpedoes dropped from aircraft close at hand. The future lay in the air.

Later that day a minesweeper from Malta brought out mail

and delivered my relief. It was a station appointment and the RNVR who took my place did not deny that he had engineered it from his desk in Valetta. I had to take his job in exchange.

The ship made a brief call at Algiers the next day. I had left my best uniform at home and McLintock soon got my modest kit into the boat. I went ashore with Jimmy, on his way to sort out a drafting problem. He hurried off after a short goodbye, engrossed by urgent business in which I could no longer claim to be involved. We now belonged to different unions and membership of mine was likely to last longer. No doubt this accounted for the fortitude with which the Good Lord provided me to overcome my regrets at leaving my friends.

My time in *Carlisle* was a year without complication, when we were all for one and one for all, united in a journey to a predictable end. I was not privileged to stay with her; she has, however, stayed with me.

I joined a dirty French steamer for the passage to Malta. She had been engaged in peacetime on the Algiers–Marseilles run with recruits for the Legion on the outward trip and Algerian *vin rouge* the other way, for sale to indigent alcoholics. The food was uneatable and shunned by the cockroaches. A Royal Marine lieutenant and an artillery captain, returning to their units after wounds in Sicily, joined me in seeking out the First Officer and there was a marginal improvement, provided the food was judged at the point of raving hunger.

The Royal Marine had been a recruit with a Bren gun on top of the coal tip the night the *Paris* was taken. In Sicily he had been hit on the morning of the assault by an Italian machine-gun firing on a fixed line; his life had been saved by a cigarette case which stopped the bullet before it reached his liver. He had the case with the hole to prove it.

The siege was over in Malta but the clearing up had a long way to go. I found a way through the stone debris to a billet in Mint Street, Valetta, for my first night in a shore job, and remember ten hours of dreamless sleep before waking to the sun on my face, and the amiability of a condemned man told that the hangman had missed the train.

I pushed my pen in a chamber in the old Lascaris fortress, the headquarters of the Vice-Admiral Malta. The secretaries wrote their hearts out for seven days a week, shuffling the papers with attentive devotion. It has been truly said that ships are not required if sufficient secretaries and staff officers are available to take in each other's washing and answer each other's questions. The dockets came round, we drafted the answers and the Staff approved them. It was dangerous to make unusual suggestions and fatal to be funny. The treadmill helped the officers condemned to service ashore in coming to terms with their lot.

The set up was too much for a splendid Royal Marine major with a black beard, conscripted into this monkey house, who showed his determination to be detached from it by pitching a tent on the walls of the fortress, and living there with his servant until someone got the message and sent him back to active service.

After a week of the routine I told the Secretary that as it was Sunday afternoon I intended to go for a swim. I expected to be treated like Oliver Twist but the Secretary was no workhouse master; when the nonsense was challenged it collapsed. From then on we all took an afternoon off.

On 9 October 1943, the Staff Officer Operations met me outside the operations room and asked me to go in. He handed me a signal and I knew what it might be.

She had been jumped in the Scarpanto Strait between Crete and Rhodes by twenty Ju 87 and He 118. The Gunnery Officer had been killed and 5 of the Wardroom wounded; 22 sailors and marines had been killed and 11 seriously wounded. She had survived 4 direct hits and 3 near misses and was being towed back to Alexandria to be written off, a casualty in one of Churchill's last bloody interventions—the pointless assault on the Germans left in the Dodecanese. One of her escorts, the fleet destroyer *Panther*, had been sunk in minutes.

SOO said he was sorry to have to give me the news. I went to the top of the wall and looked over Grand Harbour. Absurdly, I felt disconsolate that I had not been there. I expected the feeling would pass, but it has not.

She was the last to go and joined her sisters *Cairo*, *Calcutta*, *Coventry*, *Curacoa* and *Curlew*, Staff answers to the air threat which were at once cheap to convert, old and expendable. All lacked the radar, fire control and close range weapons to give them much chance against bombers flown by high grade airmen; their real purpose was to inspire confidence among the ships they were sent to protect. They were twice the size of a small destroyer, and therefore prime targets, with only two more 4-in guns, less manoeuvrability and twice the number of men to be pulled out of the water. Their fate, if it achieved anything, brought the day nearer when Whale Island could no longer pretend that the gun was the answer to the bomber.

I shared a flat in Isouard Street, Sliema with an Air Force officer who commanded the airstrip at Safi. He had been shot down in the Battle of Britain and after flying to Malta from *Ark Royal* in the middle of the siege was shot down again, and wounded for the second time. He had accounted for five of the enemy in his flying career so the books were balanced. I learnt most of this when I read his *Times* obituary. He left in early 1944 and thereafter a succession of birds of passage moved in and out until I got away myself.

Donald, ex-*Emerald*, arrived, the third hand in an 'S' class small submarine *en route* for the Eastern Fleet. I lent him a clean shirt and we had one good evening before he went on his way, taking my shirt with him. His war came to an end soon after when his ship was sunk by a Japanese escort in the Malacca Straits. He was the only officer survivor and lived through the prison camp and got home.

The Admiral was a keen horseman; he instructed his Flag Lieutenant to go to Sicily to find two horses. Flags found two fine greys and rang the Admiral to report that the Sicilian aristocrat wanted a great deal for them. He was told to requisition them for nothing and arrived with the horses and a load of hay in a landing craft. When the Admiral wanted something he could not find in Malta he used a personal Beaufighter and pilot to organize it from Italy. In the words of the Naval Prayer, he was enjoying the blessings of the land with the fruits of his labours.

A Ju 88 arrived to take photographs. We left our desks to watch the thin trail miles high as she flew for her life north. A Spitfire shot her down and the last raid on Malta was over with a victory, although the Spitfire was lost on the way back.

The headquarters were visited regularly by Lord Gort, the Governor, accompanied by his two ADCs, who complained of

HMS Carlisle hit, Scarpanto Strait: 1943.

hunger because the Field Marshal seemed not to acknowledge the end of the siege and sparse rations were served amid the grandeur of the Governor's Palace. He paid a brief visit to Italy to present his spare VC ribbon to his son-in-law, one of the heroes of Anzio. The other visitors were commanding officers keeping abreast of events; the Captain of the Fleet destroyer, *Laforey*, only came once before his ship was blown apart by a gnat torpedo, taking him and most of his crew with him.

Some had earned their lotus days in Malta; we had a lieutenant-commander RNR who had decided to leave the merchant service after being torpedoed twice in the North Atlantic, getting away the second time with some difficulty from a burning tanker. He decided to join the Navy for a rest, and must have said so in the wrong company, because he found himself at St Nazaire, where he commanded the only motor gun boat to get back.

When the Admiral was away the personal staff entertained their friends at Admiralty House. I remember one evening which began with a seaman lieutenant-commander boring everybody with a diatribe against air officers who were allowed, wrongly in his opinion, to compete against the rest for promotion and command. He meant it. I had heard this special pleading before and my attention wandered.

A civilian was sitting opposite to me, an expert in the service of the Admiralty. He secured my whole attention when he began dipping his fingers in his whisky and soda and drinking from his finger bowl. He had been well lunched in a destroyer and had now begun to lose touch with events. Flags escorted him to the door and into the large American car in which he had arrived. He told us that the expert had driven up the street like a comet streaking from human ken. Everyone laughed. I continued a conversation with a French naval officer who told me that he expected to be in a bed in his family home the next night after landing in France by parachute.

I had to wait until morning to hear the outcome of the party; the expert had killed two people on the pavement, one an RAF sergeant. I never heard what the Admiral did about it. They could hardly have kept it from him.

An infantry battlion of the Loyal North Lancashire Regiment

HMS Carlisle *and HMS* Panther. *Taken from the bridge of HMS* Rockwood. *Scarpanto Strait: 9 October 1943.*

provided the only serious soldiers in Malta and they were often
to be met on the roads, marching hard from one end of the island
to the other, keeping ready for their call to the line in Italy. They
went after Christmas and took with them the last reminder of the
war on the island.

The Young Doc from *Carlisle* arrived in the old hospital ship
Maine and I heard how she had gone. They expected an air escort
of long range American fighters and when a number of aircraft
appeared on the screen not showing friendly radar identification
it was assumed that it was the Americans, who had not switched
on their sets. The hands reduced from action to defence stations
just before the attacks and she was caught unawares. *Coventry* had
been lost off Tobruk in 1942 in similiar circumstances, a mix-up
over identification radar in friendly aircraft, but the lesson had
not been passed on.

The first bomb landed on No. 4 gun, the Marines gun, killing
all the crew, and reducing the quarter deck to a bloody shambles;
Senior, Bertie, and two of the RNVRs had been hit. McLintock
had been killed with No. 4 gun's crew. The Gunnery Officer was
killed on the bridge by a splinter. The Captain of Marines had
taken the massacre of his detachment badly and engaged the
enemy with a Bren gun as long as there was a chance of reaching
them. The Assistant Paymaster had seemed all right until one
evening in a restaurant in Alex he announced that he intended
to inspect the kitchens and had no difficulty in condemning them,
being the secretary of a London club in peacetime. Unfortunately,
he sacked the manager too, and went for a rest.

In due course the action was analysed in the Admiralty and I
have a copy of the comments from the Director of Gunnery and
Anti-aircraft Warfare. They are critical. *Rockwood*, one of her
escorting destroyers, saw the enemy about a minute before the
rest, showing that the other ships had put too much reliance on
radar; the escorts were not given radar sweep sectors and there
was no avoiding action. Had the wheel been put hard over it is
unlikely that the enemy would have secured four hits and three
near misses very close together on *Carlisle's* after end. Admiral
Cunningham's prophesy had been fulfilled; you had to be quick
on the draw on that Station to survive.

HMS Carlisle taking tow from HMS Rockwood. Scarpanto Strait; 9 October 1943.

By mid–1944 Malta was back to peacetime. An RNVR pay-master-commander from the base greeted his wife with the first draft of WRNS. This was held to be over the top and he was sent to Naples and told to wait.

Grand Harbour was no longer bursting with warships. An ex-RNVR Mid from *Revenge* turned up wearing two wavy stripes, in command of a Fleet destroyer. His Captain had gone sick and he found himself Lord of All until they could find someone to take over. He told me that he was unsure which was the more frightening, the power he had over the 120 sailors or the horsepower driving the screws. I went to the welcoming party to his new Captain which began at 1130 and ended at tea time when we had a last liqueur with the tomato sandwiches.

The old destroyer *Echo* set a happy precedent; she was destined for hand over to the Greek Navy. Her Captain hoisted a Gin Pennant inviting any officer onboard for refreshment while stocks lasted. He kept the pennant up and by the time the Greeks got her there was not much left.

Normandy D-Day found me in Bighi Hospital for a tonsillectomy. The opposite bed was occupied by a dypsomaniac who beat the bulldogs every time and always had a drink somewhere. A submarine engineer officer with TB occupied the isolation ward. The place seemed empty until some Frenchmen arrived, casualties from a failed landing on Corsica. Help, however, was at hand; the day I was discharged I was appointed to join the Ancona Port Party, being formed to organize the naval base when the Army had taken the seaport.

My goodbyes were as quick as good manners demanded and I left Malta at the end of June 1944 in the sloop *Black Swan*, on passage for Taranto. My time in the Admiral's office had not gone well and I was lucky to get away while the going was good. The Admiral's Secretary was tolerant of my lack of interest in the life of the secretariat and it must have been his finger that pointed to me when the Admiral was asked to find a paymaster lieutenant for a Port Party. It was a good turn I had not earned.

CHAPTER 14

ANCONA

In a country of beautiful buildings Taranto in 1944 was common-
place, with dingy main streets and shabby houses, the first Axis
city on the mainland to be liberated. The axe and fasces symbols
of the Party that were still about clashed with dingy brass plates
on the peeling walls, the nameplates of practitioners skilled in the
treatment of venereal and skin diseases, *Venere e Pelle*, last hopes
for the desperate. The bar signs begged for business - *Pizzeria
Napoleone 5 Lire*. 'Piss on Napoleon for sixpence' spelt out a wag
in the draft.

Happily the Ancona Port Party was not here; I joined it onboard a Landing Ship (Tank) of the Greek Navy at Bari twenty-
four hours later, after a drive through Calabria in an Army
3-tonner. The noise of mating cicadas in the olive trees competed
with the engine and conversation.

The party were led by the First Lieutenant, a passed over
regular who had commanded a Yangtse gunboat. My boss was a
reserve paymaster lieutenant-commander. There were about a
dozen other officers, nearly all specialists, who joined in the daily
chore of checking stores and exchanging signals with the Naval
Officer-in-Charge, waiting near the line with the advance party.

When Ancona was taken the LST would go with the first
convoy. It was then our task to organize the base for the Liberty
ships. Until the Germans were pushed out the 8th Army had to
rely on the long haul north by road from Bari, supplemented by
stores landed over the beach nearer to the front.

The Greek officers ate at a separate table in the wardroom and
when they had fed, divided into two camps for a political shouting
match, ill-tempered and embarrassing to hear. It happened after
nearly every meal. We could understand none of it and guessed

that the better turned out ones were royalists, and the others, republicans. It was probable that they did not strike one another, not from good manners, or self control, but because they did not want to spoil it all by going too far. Their First Lieutenant was a large man with a black beard and an archimandrital presence who expressed his opinions in a loud monologue, to the evident irritation of the smaller, plebian, officers on the receiving end.

On the second day I suggested to Number One and the Paymaster that I might be of more use with the advance party, where I could look out for suitable storage buildings amongst the ruins we had seen on the aerial photographs. I was surprised to receive agreement, upon the condition that I looked also for a wardroom and barracks, before the Army and RAF beat us to it. Number One, although no soldier, correctly guessed that creature comforts had a significant part in land operations.

The signal was sent, the approval of NOIC obtained, and having bought a pair of brown subaltern's boots from the Bari officers' shop, and drawn a revolver, I set out the next day in a Humber staff car with my kit and a corporal of Royal Marines to take the car back.

The advance party were at Porto San Georgio, a fishing village 400 miles north of Bari and about twenty miles behind the line. Progress was good because the road was clear; we crossed the Sangro, negotiated the ruins of Ortona and reached Giulianova about lunchtime. I drove towards the harbour and was surprised to see a White Ensign on the mole, and some vehicles. They were a Coastal Forces Mobile Base working their way north to operate from Ancona when the moment came.

Snaky and Chum, the Commanding Officer and Engineer Officer respectively, provided a welcome lunch of corned beef, olives and *vino rosso* while we exchanged information. They told me that the fighting was being done by the Poles, who were held up by the German rearguard, skilful soldiers able to make up for their lack of numbers by the help they received from the natural barriers in the countryside, the pride they had in their own arms and the contempt they held for their polyglot enemies. The Poles had tried to outflank them and received a bloody nose at Filotrano. My new friends whiled away their waiting time with the local landowners, with whom they had established measurable relations. This was encouraging and I continued my journey with an awakening interest in life on campaign.

I found the advance party in a villa at Porto San Georgio in crowded but comfortable style. The building had been a German field hospital and there were enough beds and furniture to supply the needs of our four officers and twenty sailors. The Naval Officer-in-Charge, Signal Officer, Bomb Disposal Officer and a Polish liaison officer made up the wardroom. We lived well on army compo rations, issued to front line troops, who usually had little time to send vehicles looking for food dumps.

The villa was near the beach. We met after breakfast, before adjourning to the sun and the sands, where we swam and sun-bathed between meals until it was time to turn in. If this was life in the field I felt that I was for it.

The NOIC was a lieutenant-commander, axed from the Navy in the twenties and given the acting rank of commander for this job; he was about 50 and, in an age when the Navy bred them, was entitled to be regarded as a character, kind and rude in turns, a disciplinarian with a charming modesty, and a retentive memory for aphorisms and Dickens, a great deal of which he seemed to know by heart. He was a bird watcher and able to name most birds with the help of a small pair of binoculars which he wore when in the countryside.

He attributed his lack of success in the Service to two successive commissions in the Persian Gulf, where he met nobody, and to keys. It was keys that did for him. While he was on week-end leave from his first command the Officer of the Day ran a bugger to earth in a provision room, to which he had obtained access because the key routine was slack. He was criticized by the Board of Enquiry and axed shortly afterwards.

He had a spell as a whale inspector and then served as an official in the non-intervention patrol during the Spanish Civil War. He loved the Navy and longed for the old days which had left him forever. As a young officer he had taken part in a plate smashing guest night in the Austrian Flagship when visiting Pola in 1910. In the Great War, while serving in the Otranto Patrol, he claimed that yesterday's *Times* was always in the wardroom at breakfast when his ship was in harbour. His memory was full of off-beat information of that sort.

On the morning after my arrival I decided that I had a duty to be frank and told NOIC that, as a regular officer, I should be at sea, rather than sunbathing on an Adriatic beach. His reaction to this piece of impertinent arrogance was to sign my written request and send it upwards, without comment. This was not what I had expected but it was typical of his understanding of both the Navy and all sorts of men with whom he had dealt in his varied career. He saw at once that by putting no obstacles in my way I would thereafter feel that I was in his debt. My request disappeared without trace. I had had four years at sea and the official line was that it was someone else's turn.

We kept in touch after the war and I went to his funeral and acted as trustee of his estate. It was sad for him, and for the system in which he had been brought up, that it was unable to make better use of him. He had a substantial belly, gold rimmed glasses and a black beard. His summer uniform was usually a disgrace.

Our Liaison Officer visited the Polish Corps Headquarters every morning and returned to report, while we gathered round a table with the latest aerial photographs and maps and made plans for our arrival. The liaison officer had an unpronouncable name and was referred to as Messerschmitt, the nearest we could get to it. The Polish Corps had come from Russia via Palestine, where they had been trained. Their politics were their own affair. Informatiion of any kind was difficult to obtain and Messerschmitt's reports were invariably no more than 'Not to-day' or 'Not this week'. We were not told where the headquarters were and NOIC was never asked to go there, being left to organize with the intelligence we could scrounge.

The plan was uncomplicated; when we got into Ancona NOIC and the Signal Officer would make for the harbour and report what they found to the Admiral at Taranto; the Bomb Disposal Officer would look for a barracks and check it for booby traps, while it would be my task to find suitable storerooms in the harbour area and a building for the wardroom.

Thus prepared we continued to live like the seriously rich, abiding events. There was a tremor in our happy life when a near-by DUKW pond was bombed while unloading stores, and lost some men. There was nothing we could do and we went back to sunbathing and counting out our fighter bombers in the evening, while we sipped our vino; by the time we were ready to eat they were back without their bombs and long range tanks. We gave them a boozy cheer and rejoiced in our good fortune, while NOIC set the mood with one of his melancholy pieces of Arabism from his long years in the Gulf. 'There is a boy across the river with a bottom like a peach, but alas—I cannot swim.'

The audience groaned in sympathy at such misfortune.

He had been the Senior Naval Officer in *Queen Mary* ferrying soldiers across the Atlantic and sometimes he sounded nearer to the Bronx than Basra. 'The blacker the berry the sweeter the juice; I should like a black goil for my personal use.'

He was a store of the humour distilled by the Navy from years in distant places by men living their lives without women, making jokes out of the loneliness and despising their own weakness. His generation solved the problem in practical ways. When he was a watchkeeper in a ship in Malta before the Great War, the three members of his union took a flat and installed a Maltese girl in it to look after them. One was always on watch and another onboard, standing by. This left one to spend the night in the flat, one night in three. He claimed that the system was a delight for all, particularly the girl.

On 17 July 1944 Messerschmitt arrived back earlier than usual, bursting with importance. He took NOIC to one side with a message of unbearable secrecy. NOIC held his tongue long enough to grin and then whooped at us to pack our kit and get into the vehicles, the Germans were going back and we would be there the next day.

I travelled with the Bomb Disposal Officer in a truck, loaded with his complicated gear. He was an Ulsterman of few words who wore a George Medal, earned by dangling with a line round his ankles in the hold of a ship in Belfast, while defuzing a parachute mine, hung up by its cords. It was an experience to kill small talk for some time.

Our little party joined a convoy led by the Brigadier who was to be the Area Commander, and we headed north. The night was spent in a vineyard under the cathedral on the hill at Loreto, where angels flew with Mary's House from Dalmatia in 1294 after the Crusaders had recovered it from the Holy Land. I looked through the mosquito net at the Cross on the tower and decided that I had no difficulty in believing that the angels had made their journey, particularly if one of them could spare the time to keep an eye on us during the next few hours.

We set off at dawn and were soon in the outskirts of Ancona. Polish armoured cars went ahead and there were bursts of machine gun fire and bullet-riddled walls and statues and the odd wrecked vehicle. It was all make believe; the enemy had decided to go, in his own time and in good order, and there was nothing there to shoot at.

The harbour installations were shattered by ceaseless bombing into mounds of debris, with capsized ships in most of the berths. In the Cantieri Reuniti, a yard capable of building a cruiser, a party of German sappers had spent a month destroying the machinery with surgical skill.

I left the truck and went towards some undamaged archways with stores underneath them. Polish sappers were sweeping for mines and putting down white tapes. I found three empty stores, wrote out requisition notices and attached them to the doors; it was a start. In fact they were never used because better places were found. I began looking for a wardroom mess.

The enemy had blown the main sewer near the entrance to the dockyard, where the tunnel junction collected waste from the town. The result was a stinking cauldron of pullulating filth which took the engineers weeks to repair and spread fly blown infection everywhere. A bulldozer driver dropped fifteen feet through the top of a tunnel and grinned up at us through the dust and muck, still seated behind the wheel of the machine.

NOIC found a building with superficial bomb damage near enough to the port for a naval headquarters. About 400 yards into the town I found a hotel which was undamaged. It looked substantially built, albeit scruffy and rundown. I walked in and called for service. There was no one in sight; although the place seemed used, it was empty. I looked about and went back into the hall where I found four people who had come up from the cellar.

There were three nervous chambermaids and a major domo who announced in English that his name was Remo and he was at my service. This was not strictly accurate because we found out later that he had been left behind to spy for the Germans. I told him that the hotel was requisitioned and that if any other officers came in after I left he was to tell them to push off. He sensibly asked me for a *permisso* and I wrote out on a signal pad that the place was the wardroom mess of HMS *Fabius* (Ancona) and gave it to him.

The Bomb Disposal Officer found an intact bank building which he requisitioned for the barracks. The Chief Boatswain's Mate, being very old navy, began scrubbing out at once before setting down his bedding in a place that had been occupied by Eyeties and God knows who else. His efforts were interrupted because a school was found which was more suitable and we gave the bank to the Army. One wing of the school had been bombed but we had Royal Marine engineers in the main party to rebuild it.

I reported to NOIC and he sailed into the wardroom, lately the two star Albergo Roma, like Caesar, and pronounced himself satisfied. That night we slept between clean sheets. In the drawer of my bedside table I found a copy of the *Volkischer Beobachter*; it was 2 days' old. It had been a piece of cake.

The line stabilized at Senigallia, about ten miles north, and stayed there until the next push. There was some desultory shelling by an 88 during the second night but it was not seriously meant and there was little damage.

The minesweepers swept a channel and the LST with the main party arrived on the fourth day and was soon unloaded. Unfortunately she was mined on the way out and the Greeks had to forget politics for a while. NOIC's secretary had come up in the LST; he and I were ordered to swop jobs because he had no secretarial experience. This was an agreeable change for both of us; I was still not as sure as I should have been how Jack got his dinner let alone his pay or slops.

NOIC, the King's Harbourmaster and I occupied three offices in Navy House overlooking the harbour. NOIC was conveniently placed in the middle and able to goad either of us at will. Each day began with a conference chaired by NOIC and attended by the Brigadier, at which the Army were represented in strength while we discussed the task of clearing the wrecks from the berths, the rubble from the streets and the mines from the harbour. The Army had the resources, and many of their officers had done the job before. The Port Commandant had done it about ten times, beginning in North Africa.

It was soon apparent that the naval officers were amateurs in dealing with the sort of problems that faced us. NOIC was content to let the Army get on with the major engineering tasks of clearance, leaving the Navy to deal with the operational movements of the ships, harbour defence and minesweeping. The top priority was clearance of the alongside berths, reduced to rubble by the bombing and German demolition. The chaos was so universal that some berths were still blocked when I went back in 1960. The tanker berth was vital, fuel being next to ammunition and food in the Army list of priorities.

The night after the first tanker began to pump her load of petrol into the pipe lines waiting for her, the harbour was attacked by E-boats, probably from Pola. The oiler and the mole were indistinguishable at night and the boats fired their full outfits, no doubt believing that their target was at anchor. The torpedoes tore chunks of concrete out of the mole and blocked the road but the oiler was undamaged.

The assembly of convoys and the general control of shipping was left to specialist departments, including experts in stevedoring and loading of merchant ships, the Sea Transport Officers. The Coastal Forces Base arrived and operations were begun in the Northen Adriatic. Two Fleet destroyers supported the army with shellfire, and returned to Ancona after their daily bombardment. A captain RN with the grand title of Senior Naval Officer Northern Adriatic was put in charge of the air and sea operations and set up an independent headquarters. Various training organizations began work, together with a Naval Provost Marshal and a Welfare Officer. We had an Officers' Club and the Army built a squash court. The harbour became crowded with merchant ships and the number of officers in the Port Party grew to over 130. The boatswain and I were the only two on the active list. We were approaching the point when there were enough officers ashore to enable us to run happily without the ships.

While the line was at Senigallia two of us paid it a visit. We threaded our way through the lorries heading north on the coast road. The pipe line with the petrol ran by the ditch; we were astonished at the size of the ammunition dumps, also by the roadside. This Army did not need a Lloyd George to get them shells to plaster the enemy. The traffic began to diminish until we seemed to have the road to ourselves. The only sign of life was a light aircraft flying idly back and forth.

We reached Senigallia and went slowly on. The town had been the summer home of the Popes since the Middle Ages and we looked forward to an interesting look round. The whole of the Marche province, of which Ancona formed a part, was Papal territory at one time.

The road bore right and we stopped outside a villa. There was a whistle and a bang and a soldier ran out of the house towards us. I asked him if it was all right to go on and he said that he did not mind what we did as long as we did it somewhere else. The canal that divided the town was about 150 yards up the road. We decided that that might be interesting and told our friend that we thought we would have a look at it.

'Up to you,' he said. 'We hold this bank. Jerry is the other side.'

I let the clutch in and the jeep crept quietly away. I do not know what we had expected but we were disappointed. It was nothing like Journey's End.

In October there was a diphtheria epidemic and NOIC went down. I visited him at a Base Hospital, overflowing with wounded from the last attempt on the Gothic Line. We tip-toed between stretchers in the corridors and found him in a small isolation ward which he shared with a private soldier, also a diphtheria case, who was evidently a mate. I suggested that he would not be needing his jeep for a while and that I might borrow it to visit Rome, liberated that summer. He croaked that he really did not care and I left him in deep conversation with the private soldier, who was describing, with Anglo-Saxon emphasis, the rigours of life in an Army Detention Quarters.

On the way out I asked a young officer what had happened to him. He told me that he had made the mistake of going into a house, which was demolished by shell fire before he could get out.

Among the close packed beds I saw one with a German infantry
lieutenant in it; his tunic hanging near by bore the Russian medal
and the Infantry Medal with a Close Combat Clasp. He was the
first German officer I had seen and I felt a need to say good
afternoon, and perhaps wish him well, but he was white faced and
beyond reach. It seemed then, and now, that the stricken lieutenant in the Abruzzi military hospital, and our wounded who were
his enemies, had more in common with each other than with their
politicians, but it will need a generation to pass before the true
history is written. The young men were unable to decide for
themselves, unlike Yeat's Irish Airman.

> Nor law nor duty bade me fight,
> Nor public men, nor cheering crowds,
> A lonely impulse of delight
> Drove to this tumult in the clouds;
> I balanced all, brought all to mind,
> The years to come seemed waste of breath,
> A waste of breath the years behind
> In balance with this life, this death.

I took the Staff Officer Operations with me and, huddled in
great coats, we crossed the Apennines in the jeep and clocked in
at the Albergo Nationale, requisitioned for officers on leave in
Rome. We appeared to be the only ones from the Navy. I took
out the rotor arm and we went in with our kit. I went back to
make sure that the lights were off. In the three minutes which had
elapsed two jerricans of petrol, chained to the chassis, had disappeared over the surrounding barricade. It was an early lesson in
Roman morals but we did not benefit from it.

I visited the Coliseum, and saw *Madame Butterfly* at the Rome
Opera House. At the Vatican I got caught up in the audience the
Pope gave to servicemen. The city had been steeped in bloody
wars for 2,000 years and the present conflict hardly made a ripple.

The night clubs were packed with British and Canadian infantry and American airmen, on leave and determined to have the
best time available. The drink was usually vermouth and it was
hard work.

Our last night arrived and we spent it at the Nirvinetta, the best of the night clubs. I parked the jeep and took out the rotor arm. I found a soldier who had been at school with me and began a conversation. SOO arrived five minutes later and asked why I had not come in the jeep. We rushed outside but it had gone forever. According to the Military Police about six a night were stolen, usually by front line troops who were encouraged by their officers to bring one back after leave. Jeeps were being withdrawn and sent to Burma and the Army in Italy were short of them.

The war was ending and the pins in NOIC's map of Russia moved westward daily. The Adriatic was a sideshow but that did not stop the killing. Four MTBs were mined while operating from Ancona and three names were taken off the squash ladder. The Hunt *Aldenham* was mined, the last British destroyer sunk in the war against Germany. It was said that one of her RNVRs had been sunk six times before and was anxious about a growing reputation for being a Jonah.

My relief in *Carlisle* turned up in one of the bombarding destroyers as Secretary to Captain (D) and I opened negotiations with him to swop jobs. He owed me one. He was interested but talks had to be broken off when his ship was mined and disappeared south for repair. I resolved to accept the rigours of my job, miles from an outnumbered and beaten enemy, where the main hazard was falling off my motor bike on the wet pave roads.

There was a *frisson* when the Intelligence Branch got on to Remo. I was ordered to sack him and the Field Security Police would arrest him outside the wardroom. I loaded the Luger for the interview in case he overreacted but he left like a lamb and the only excitement occurred when I took the magazine out and pressed the trigger. The bullet left in the chamber went through the floor. So far as I am aware Remo did not get shot though he probably deserved it. He certainly risked it at the interview.

The prisoners' cages near the harbour filled up at shorter intervals; the soldiers were of two main kinds, either SS and parachutists, or Mongolians recruited by the Germans from the East. It was an odd mixture but effective, judging by the slowness of the advance. Although Rimini had been taken on 21 September the Gothic line remained unbroken at the end of the year and the Venice port party continued to wait in idleness in their billets outside Ancona. During the Christmas period we lost three men through drink or drink related accidents.

The enemy under Kesselring were still full of fight. Our side was supposed to be holding the Germans down in Italy but we so outnumbered them now that it seemed to be the other way round.

CHAPTER 15

VICTORY EUROPE

We were over 500 miles from Taranto, where our Admiral flew his flag. This enabled NOIC to run his own show with little interference. The Port Party sailors behaved well, being away from the rigours of shipboard discipline. This was the rule, proved often in times past when bluejackets were landed to back up the Army. When out of routine Jack could be relied upon for cheerful co-operation.

It was otherwise with the merchant seamen in the Liberty ships who were, by 1944, often rejects for the fighting services, with little motivation and less discipline. A coaster fell astern of her convoy because a fireman got drunk and barricaded the door into the boiler room. A surly deckhand felled the Mate and abused the Master. It was fruitless to threaten such people with prosecution before sympathetic justices at the ship's first port of call on return to the UK. NOIC decided to smarten up merchant seamen by setting up a court to try them at Ancona.

The appropriate tribunal was a Naval Court, introduced by the Merchant Shipping Act of 1894 for the trial of merchant seamen abroad. A naval officer of commander's rank acted as President, sitting with two merchant service Masters as Members. The Court's powers were similiar to those of magistrates, with a maxmimum prison sentence of six months, which in our case had to be served in Army detention quarters. Although unhampered by a legal qualification I became Clerk of the Court. In that capacity I could dissuade NOIC from having them hanged or shot.

It was soon evident that the labyrinthine procedures of the Victorian Act would take too long to follow. We claimed jurisdiction by using the buckshot provisions of wartime Defence Regulations, which declared an open season on criminal behaviour.

With the help of the Naval Provost Marshal, whose party contained ex-policemen used to petty sessional procedure, we opened for business.

Two masters of British merchant ships in the harbour reported to Navy House on the day of the first trial. One was overcome by the ceremonies of office and, like the captain of one of His Majesty's ships, referred to himself by the name of his command.

'Good morning, sir,' he said to NOIC, 'I am the Duke of Sparta.'

'Good morning,' said NOIC, 'I am the Queen of Thebes.'

Thereafter the Court dealt out justice in fines and detention, giving some back-up to the Masters, who had a hard task in keeping their riff-raff in hand. One day the system broke down. It was my fault.

I was lunching in the Officers' Club with an officer I knew in the SAS. I asked him what had happened to a chum of his I had met. He looked at his watch and told me that at that moment he ought to be floating down on to the Venice Causeway. He added that it was really his turn but he had a cold.

Lunch went on for some time while we did our best to cure the cold. It ended when a sailor arrived in the dining room with a message from NOIC that the Naval Court was waiting to start.

I hastened to Navy House and took my place, as if delayed by urgent business. The defendant was the Mate of a Canadian merchant ship who had put his Captain in hospital. Such behaviour was certain to earn the maximum from NOIC, and the Mate was soon tried and sent to the Army detention quarters to serve his six months. I had a feeling that there was something different about this one but could not decide what it was.

Four months later, when he was about to complete his sentence and the record of the Court proceedings had reached the Admiralty, we received a priority signal from Their Lordships ordering us to obtain the immediate release of the Mate, whose sentence threatened an uproar in the UK's relations with Canada. Under the Treaty of Westminster, which established Canada as a Dominion, the jurisdiction of British courts over Canadian citizens abroad had been removed forever and we had had no right to try him.

NOIC announced that the blighter had got what he deserved; he had nearly finished his sentence and he cared not what the Admiralty thought. His own position was cast iron; he would never be on the Flag List and Their Lordships could not put him in the family way so what had he got to worry about? We heard no more. If the Government paid an out of court settlement for damages for wrongful imprisonment we were never told. I resolved to keep a closer eye on the diary and lunch time gin and French.

In their slow journey north with the Coastal Forces Mobile Base Snaky and Chum had led a full social life and been passed on from one Italian family to another. They took me to a party at Osimo, a small hill town about fifteen miles south of Ancona, where I made firm friends with people who had been there for some time; their arms are on the doors of thirteenth-century Loreto Cathedral.

Piero had been a friend of d'Annuzio, the Italian poet and airman and had flown with him against the Austrians in the Great War. His Countess was Austrian. Their house in Osimo occupied one side of the Piazza, with one room after another of fading antique furniture and ancestral oils.

A German company had held the Poles up here and the Polish artillery knocked a hole in Piero's roof. There had been civilian casualties and some had been brought to his cellar. A woman had died on a blood-stained sofa, comforted by Piero's younger daughter, while they waited for the shelling to stop. The Germans left but the shelling went on, until the Poles could be persuaded to send a patrol up the hill to see for themselves. They could not get reinforcements and had to avoid casualties. This must have caused the destruction of many beautiful things in Italy.

My new friends had none of the condescension of some of the English aristocracy and, unlike them, made little effort to adapt with the times. They lived in the same way and at the same pace that they had always done. They were used to invasions and whether surrounded by Austrians, Germans, Poles or English, they behaved with the same good manners and waited for it all to be over. Meanwhile they kept busy exchanging news of their friends and relations, and ceased worrying.

Their eldest daughter was married to an Italian cavalry officer but they were separated and she was left with a 6-month-old baby, nick-named Tidaldo, who was cared for by the women living in the house, who seemed to be Piero's poorer relations. The two other children, Maria Grazia and Fabio, had both helped the *partagiani* before the Germans moved north. Fabio then returned to Macerata University. His tutor was an aged Anglophile, who surprised me when we met by asking why Evan-Thomas had been left behind during the run to the South. I realized that he was talking about Jutland and did my best to keep up with him but I was soon at a loss. He was an expert on the battle and understood its intricate history.

Piero's friends had, like him, lived in the Marche for ever in the same houses. There was a young man in his twenties in the big house at Offagna, a hill village near Osimo, who must have been about twenty-five stone. His house was run for him, as seemed to be the custom, by a less fortunate female relation with two daughters. One was beautiful and madly in love with Chum and the other rather plain. The plain one had retired to a Spanish nunnery but before she finished her novitiate she gave it up and came back to Italy, anxious not to miss the fun.

The household lived in dread that its master would demolish the furniture by sitting on it and 'Doucement Alessandro!' was a constant cry. We spoke in French. Maria Grazia was an exception. She had had an Irish nurse and spoke fluent English with a Donegal brogue. The nurse taught her a piece of doggerel.

> I am a girl of innocence,
> Who shows my legs for forty pence.
> If you give me fourty-four, then
> I'll show you something more.

I became attached to their feudal existence and used NOIC's jeep to visit the lotus eaters in their dream world. For the simple sailor it was not temptation from Scylla and Charybdis on either hand, but the sirens dancing a ring-a-roses.

I remember a lunch under the trees in the courtyard at Offagna when a great pie was served. It was delicious, although full of small bones. I was told it was made from larks; I hope it was not skylarks but it probably was. The *condotierri* in Alessandro's blood would not have made him squeamish.

Two hundred yards from the house, on the roadside near the Calvary, a carved wooden cross marked the grave of a Panzer Grenadier, aged 16 when his comrades put him there, alongside the ditch. There were always flowers by the Calvary but none on the boy's grave; lonely and unadorned it had a message for the traveller:

> Go, tell the Spartans, thou who passest by,
> That here obedient to their laws we lie.

By March 1945 the prisoners were coming back in strength. The Mongolians were turned out into wire encircled compounds with a few bivouac tents, in a density suited to a cattle yard. The ground became mud. Their natural hardiness kept them alive but the politicians sent them back to Russia later, and probably did for most of them. The German para, SS and mountain troops were defiant to the end, looking contemptuously through the wire.

The Royal Marine commandos ordered to attack across Lake Commachio used Ancona as a base; we lent them an officer to give them a course to steer in their swimming tanks. They lost heavily in an operation that was difficult to understand, bearing in mind that the war was almost over.

The unnecessary killing was not confined to the land. About a week before VE Day Navy House was rocked by an explosion which broke the windows and brought the plaster down. An Italian coaster going alongside exploded an oyster mine laid before we got there. The mine had been passed over many times but only became armed after a pre-set count. When the next ship passed it exploded. It was a disgusting weapon which might have stayed in inactive lethality until after the peace.

She turned over and four survivors were entombed in her upturned hull, tapping on the steel while they were able. We could not cut into her, which would have drowned them at once; nothing else was any good and we had to leave it to the dockyard to right her and bury them.

We picnicked in the woods near Iesi and drank wine with our

Maria Grazia.

backs against the cork trees while we watched a swarm of American Fortresses sail overhead to bomb Bologna.

The Italian newspapers were full of the first pictures of Belsen; after six years of total war there was little surprise and no one then foresaw that the massacres would become the main story of the war.

This was the time of the breaking of the nations but NOIC had some details that demanded his attention. The base Stores Chief Petty Officer had been caught out exchanging service provisions with the locals for wine. I remember a part of the evidence.

LSA Mudd: 'I reported to the Chief that we were out of marsala.'

Prosecutor: 'What did he say?'

LSA Mudd: 'You must go ashore with a little sugar, Mudd, and swop it for some more.'

The wine was sold at a 100% profit to local Army messes with no questions asked. The Staff in Taranto were horrified. NOIC was ordered to arrange a court martial to deter entrepreneurs.

I prepared the papers and went to Bari in a Dakota and then on to Taranto where I presented them to the Admiral's Secretary, whose job it was to run the trial in Ancona. He had other ideas. I was taken before the Admiral, who had been briefed. He told me that acting as Judge Advocate in your first court martial was like taking command of your first ship and he expected me to do it. I had to wait another thirty-seven years before taking command of my first ship, a twenty-eight foot sloop, so that, in retrospect, it was a good offer, and I accepted with alacrity. I set out for Bari and home, eager to set the wheels of justice turning without inconveniencing the Staff.

Bari airfield was solid with mud and we four passengers were glad of a lift with the crew to the aircraft, loaded with dried blood and plasma, flown daily to the line. About fifty miles from Ancona we hit a front and flew into a blizzard. The cabin went dark and the Dakota bucked about but it seemed no worse than a ship in a seaway and I took little notice until I looked at the officer next to me. He was an RAF pilot and it was clear that he viewed with concern the arrangements being made for his safe arrival. The

Red Cross official in charge of the blood, who must have been well used to the trip, gave up the cheerful repartee with which he had entertained us during the hours in the air. I wondered what I had done to get myself into this situation; I was a sailor, not a bloody airman.

Monte Conero was directly between us and the airfield at Falconara, and I was delighted when the wireless operator put his head round the door and said that we were not going to risk it. We landed back at Bari having spent most of the day droning about to no purpose. I hitched a lift in the Hunt destroyer *Ledbury* the following morning.

The trial took place on VE day and the day after. The Chief put up a spirited defence, helped by his advocate, but we had the Italian suppliers there and an interpreter to reveal all. He was convicted and disrated to Stores Petty Officer. A month later he came back in the cruiser *Orion*, having been advanced to the acting rank of Stores Chief Petty Officer, and no doubt pleased with the opportunity to renew old connections. He sported a long cigarette holder, looked like Alfred Hitchcock and had beaten the system by a wide margin.

While this state trial was in progress the VE celebrations took place. A soldier in drink fired a burst with a Bren down the main avenue but no one was actually killed and NOIC was pleased with the outcome, although he complained about my Yorkshire leading writer, who barged into his office and put up the black out, before telling NOIC in a fuddled voice that it was all over and he should go home.

We had seen something of the communist partisans from the other side of the Adriatic when they came to Ancona, looking for equipment. They were armed to the teeth and negotiated from their position of weakness in an insolent way which irritated us. They made it clear that they were making sacrifices by talking to capitalist scum rather than shooting them. It was no surprise that Germans in Yugoslavia did their best to surrender in Italy.

An E-boat flotilla and some flat barges loaded with troops found their way across. The boats' crews saluted their flag and each captain broke the ensign staff before they marched off to a prison camp, leaving behind a marked chart of the German minefields in the Northern Adriatic. The chart turned out to be accurate and I have little doubt that it was left there deliberately. They were not all savages.

The soldiers were white-faced with hunger and sea-sickness and crawled up the ladder from their barges to the jetty, where they laid down their arms. There were about 100 of them, from a mountain battalion. I saw each one wait his turn, as if on parade, before saying goodbye and shaking the hand of their *Oberleutenant.* The officer had a few words and a joke for each one; it was obvious that they would have followed him anywhere.

A large harbour launch with a Red Cross came with them. We found a German army doctor onboard and four dead men. The doctor had some duelling scars which proved too much for the Provost Marshal, an officer whose lack of either intellect or charm was sufficient to be noticeable to other policemen.

'What do you think of of old Hitler now he has shot himself, eh?' he said to the doctor who replied in a quiet voice that he regarded the end of the life of the Fuhrer as the death of a hero. For this honest answer he was made to stand all day in the sun without food or water until the other prisoners had gone, no doubt reflecting during his wait upon the merits of the cause which had

Ancona 1945. Author and NOIC.

laid waste his country, if the fight had been against the likes of the Provost Marshal.

A heap of small arms, field glasses and cameras left on the jetty were sorted by the officers from the base, hyenas round a kill.

Snaky decided to take his friends for a trip in one of the E-boats. We waited for an RN crew to get her going, but they could not start the diesels. Two Alsace Lorraine engineroom ratings were found. They busied themselves below before announcing that they only understood their own boat. We were about to transfer when there was a cloud of black smoke and a roar; we were ready to go. In a slight sea at 30 knots the glasses of sherry on the bridge were hardly affected. NOIC and I went to Trieste shortly afterwards in one of our MGBs and the comparison favoured the E-boat, which was quieter and more stable.

It was difficult to sustain interest after the surrender and NOIC observed, accurately, that I was getting slacker and slacker. I asked for two weeks off and set out with Maria Grazia for Venice, Bologna and Florence, where she had relations. I borrowed an open Mercedes staff car, looted in Catania by our engineer officer, who claimed it had belonged to the Herman Goering division. This division, although formed from *Luftwaffe* airmen without full infantry training, had done well in Sicily under a general from the Russian front. A fictitious War Department number had been painted on the bonnet to ensure that fuel could be drawn from army dumps. The car had had a hard life and drank oil in increasing amounts. It was fitted with elaborate filters for the desert and although the engine was nearing the end, the suspension remained excellent.

Venice was crowded with the New Zealanders who had taken the city, enjoying the facilities of the Danielli at sixpence per day. We visited St. Andrea Island in the Lagoon as the guests of Lionel Crabb, an underwater specialist who was killed when diving secretly on the Russian cruiser *Ordzonikidze* in the fifties. I had met him in Ancona. I last saw him in Malta in 1950 where he arrived to dive on *Breconshire*, sunk during the siege. He heard somehow that the Duke of Argyll was thinking of looking for the Spanish galleon in Tobermory Bay and sent him a telegram offering his services free.

St. Andrea was the headquarters of the Italian 10th MAAS Flotilla, a band of intrepid divers who had achieved much. They attacked the battleships *Queen Elizabeth* and *Valiant* in Alexandria in 1942. Their leader, de la Penne, could be seen in the Officers' Club at Taranto after the war, wearing a gold brooch in his lapel, to show that he held the Italian equivalent of our VC. The operation was done with maiales, two men midget-submarines, and both battleships were put out of the war for months. A similiar force had attacked the shipping in Gibraltar harbour from a converted merchant ship in neutral waters at Algeciras, on the Spanish side of Gibraltar Bay.

The Italian divers were prisoners and spent the day around a large swimming pool, in which they continued to train. Crabb was on very good terms with the officers, most of whom he knew by name or reputation during the years when they had opposed each other at Gibraltar. He introduced us to an Italian lieutenant who had made three attacks on Gibraltar. At lunch we met an octogenarian who had invented the maiale. He claimed that it could have destroyed all the British big ships in the Mediterranean at one stroke, and thus changed the course of the war, had the Italian Navy used it properly. The weapon should have been held back until there were enough of them with trained crews to strike the finishing blows. It was the same argument as that advanced by the inventors of the tank, who despaired when the new weapon was frittered away on the Western Front in piecemeal attacks, instead of one all out assault. It was a fascinating day and Maria Grazia established rapports with both our host and the brave Italian lieutenant. We went away in a fast motor boat in the nick of time.

On the way to Bologna we passed the boarding school where she had been educated until the nuns told her father to take her away. One of the pilots at a military airfield near by bet his friends that he would take out one of the girls. He had found out that each pupil had a school number and thought he was on to a racing certainty. He arrived at the door in his dashing uniform and asked for No. 180, his niece by marriage, whose name he said he had forgotten, although he had written down the number given to him over the telephone when he spoke to her mother. He expected to get one of the sixth-formers but unfortunately for him the girls were numbered the opposite way and he was faced by a child of 8 or 9 who burst into tears when she saw her new uncle, and lost him the bet.

Bologna had been heavily bombed and we had trouble in finding an aunt whose palazzo was flattened. She was in a three roomed flat, too embarrassed to speak about it and begging with her eyes for us to leave her.

In Florence, cousin Alfredo and his charming wife were living as well as could be expected after no bombing, but two years under the Germans, and were delighted to have us.

A visit was paid each morning to a bar near the Ponte Vecchio where the Florentines in the blue book gathered to discuss each other. We ate delicious pigeon in a restaurant at Fiesole overlooking the valley. We called on yet more relations, including a marchesa in an exquisite eighteenth-century country house. She had lost touch with her husband in the war and was in sole charge of five lively daughters in their teens and early twenties. The house had been used as an officers' mess by the New Zealanders and some of the antique furniture had gone for firewood. Despite these misfortunes the unprotected girls and their mother were bubbling with good humour, no doubt setting down their calamities to experience.

It was otherwise at a villa overlooking the city with a beautiful terrace and cypress trees descending the hill before it. The unmarried daughter of the house, who had an English mother, showed us her bedroom, which had been occupied by German parachutists. They had knocked a hole through the roof for a Spandau and when they left she found the room like a pigsty covered with empty schnapps bottles and general detritus. A drawer with her clothing in it had been used as a lavatory.

Alfredo announced that he would like to pay his uncle a visit and they piled into the back of the old car, to be set down at Osimo after a long dusty journey which they bore without complaint, and indeed claimed to have enjoyed it.

The balcony outside Piero's house had been used by the communist mayor to address a crowd. The two pillars were daubed 'Viva Lenin' and 'Viva Stalin' in red paint. I asked him why he had let it happen and he shrugged his shoulders. 'It is what they want,' he said, 'if I refuse they will take the house.'

Every morning a convoy left Osimo with workers for the Cantieri Riuniti in Ancona. The lorries bore red flags and the passengers sang the 'Internationale' at full throttle. Being Italians, they sang in tune, and always found a good-looking pair of young men to hold the flags, their hair streaming in the wind and clenched fists held on high. It was hard to take these romantics seriously; while they might paint graffiti on the big house it seemed improbable that they would engage in bloody revolution. Fabio asked me whether I could find him a sub-machine-gun for a friend in the *partagiani* who wanted one to defend his factory. This was more opera and he was not surprised that I did not take him seriously.

NOIC, because of his age and length of service, was one of the first to go home to his Sussex Georgian house. He had been sent photographs of each room and every part of the garden, which he looked at frequently after he came out of hospital. I went in the Humber with him to Rome to catch the aeroplane. His RASC corporal, who had driven him in Italy throughout, and his Maltese steward, completed the party.

I took him to the Nirvinetta for his last run ashore in the uniform he had first put on as a boy of 13. We drank too much and were asked by the management not to throw corks on to the floor, where the solo dancer had to do the splits.

When he was dying, years afterwards, I wrote a codicil to his will in longhand because time was short and the doctor and I witnessed it. The doctor was an old destroyer lag and the three of us drank gin in the sick room and laughed at the old jokes. NOIC was the only one who was not sorry he was leaving.

It was August before I was told to go home and I decided to go by road. The Admiral in Caserta gave permission and I set out in the Mercedes with written orders I addressed to myself to go to Calais via the 8th Army leave route, report my address to the Admiralty, and wait for instructions. I had a vehicle work sheet covered with official stamps to ensure that I got petrol. My kit covered the back seat, and as we were ordered to be armed, I kept a Thompson sub-machine-gun with the stock removed between the front seats. The gun had been given to me by an officer from

Cantieri Riuniti, Ancona, 1945. Author, NOIC, Constructor Officers.

Road to Rome, June 1945. Driver, steward, NOIC, author.

the Port Party at Ortona, where the line had stagnated. He used it to shoot stray cats in the ruins when they kept him awake.

Maria Grazia came as far as Voghera, south of Milan, in order to stay with her sister. It was off my route but all Europe was on the move and I would not be missed.

The journey took all day and the lights on the old car were weak. We arrived at about ten o'clock and found a note telling us to go on to a house where they were having dinner. We spent an hour wandering around Piedmont, unable to find our way. By this time the lights were dim. We came to a village and resolved to ask for directions. A man on a bicycle came from the shadows and the car sent him flying.

He was a big man and made a lot of noise, as he was entitled to do. A crowd came out of an adjacent bar and gathered round in boozy indignation making it impossible to get out of the car. Two of them picked up the casualty and his broken bicycle. He sat on a wall groaning and the others turned their attention to us. They saw my uniform, which made them worse. They kicked the car and began rocking it. I shouted at them in English to shut up and help the victim into the back so that I could take him to hospital. They did not understand and my attempts in poor French and worse Italian were ignored. One of them stood out as spokesman and waved his arms about and shouted offensive remarks which seemed to the mob's taste. These people had been occupied by the Germans until a short time before and whether Fascist or Communist by inclination, they had no room for an English officer with a well dressed Italian girl who had just knocked down one of their pals.

I was thinking about leaving when Maria Grazia lost her temper. She pushed out of the car and I followed her, hoping for the best. She spoke to them in an angry voice and they shut up at once. The Italian was too fast for me but I could see the effect; the crowd became silent; the ringleader obeyed sheepishly when she ordered him to help the injured man into the car and come to the hospital. Two of them put him into the back and comforted him while the rest gathered round, contrite and anxious to help, naughty children after a rebuke.

Our passenger complained that he could not breathe properly

and it was a relief to hand him over to the Sisters of Mercy. He appeared to have broken a rib. I was asked who I was and wrote down my name, rank and address before we went back to Voghera to find that the house party had come back.

As well as the family there was a Calabrian marquis and his mistress and a British captain serving with the Allied Military Goverment. He held sway over an area the size of an English county. I wrote a report of the accident and give it to him.

The villa was modern in the worst of 1930s fascist architectural taste with pretentious rooms and staircases, concrete everywhere and large grounds, with a swimming pool surrounded by a pergola hung with scented flowers. In the gardens a *partagiani*, loaded with weapons, was on constant sentry-go, uncertain I think whether he was there to stop any coming in, or to stop us going out. Later on he was taken away and we did the rounds.

We visited the Visterinis where our hostess, who was determined to think the best of everyone, referred to us as the *fidanzati*, or betrothed. It was explained to her that we were not but she took no notice. Italians do not allow facts to spoil things. After dinner a projector was rigged in a bedroom and an old film shown on a screen in the garden, with fifty estate workers sitting on a lawn to see it. I asked my hostess why they took this trouble, assuming that there were cinemas nearby. Her husband thought it good policy to provide the entertainment on site, thus keeping his people away from the towns and communist influence. The Milan Chief of Police was one of the guests at dinner; they were determined to survive.

The 8th Army leave route began at Villach in southern Austria. I lost the way outside Milan when I followed a lane and saw the autostrada in front of me, with no access to it and no way of turning round. I was stuck. The local peasantry appeared at once, surrounding the car, staring at me and the kit on the back seat, leaning on their rakes and spades and saying nothing. I told them in my 8th Army Italian that I was trying to get on to the autostrada and go to Brescia. There was no response. There were about fifteen of them, pushing closer in their rags and peering at the show, visitors to a zoo. One or two had their heads over the side of the car and for an idiotic moment I thought about picking up the Thompson and soon decided that not picking it up was the better policy.

I played a subtle card and announced, '*Io Inglese, officiale di Regio Nautica.*' They nodded their heads and beamed and a dozen of them got their hands under the car, lifted it with me in it and turned it round to face the other way. One shouted, '*mare, signor!*' and pointed a finger, upon the reasonable assumption that as I had told them I was a naval officer I wanted to know the way to the sea. I decided I had a suspicious nature and gave them cigarettes and many '*molto grazie*' before I drove on.

Near Vicenza the light had nearly gone; the car was no longer drivable at night for long. I went through the biggest gates I could find. The village was Castello del Franca, and my host welcomed me and insisted on locking the car in a stable and giving me the key before we sat down to an excellent dinner. This part of Italy had been in the German theatre for five years and despite his hospitality, I wondered where his sympathies lay. I found out many years later when I called there with my wife to thank him. As we went up the drive I saw a grey haired and well-dressed old man disappear through a doorway in a wall next to the house. I asked a servant if I could speak to the Count. He said he was not there and I knew he was lying. I could not understand it but my wife suggested that he did not like Germans. We were in a BMW car. I hope that was it.

The 8th Army leave route was set up in 1945 to provide a quick way home for soldiers in the Mediterranean. There were five staging camps across Europe providing food, petrol and shelter for the leave parties, who travelled in 3-tonners. The first camp at Villach was an infantry barracks with dramatic murals of eighteenth-century grenadiers designed to ginger up the recruits. I appeared to be the only traveller enjoying the luxury of a car, and the only sailor.

At the second camp at Innsbruck I noticed a cavalry officer with an MC carrying a fishing rod, who seemed familiar. We had been in the same form at school and he kept me company. We stopped on the autobahn to look at a jet fighter in the trees and he asked me if he could drive for a bit. I accepted with pleasure and we set off with some difficulty, which I attributed to his inexperience with that sort of car. That was not the reason as I soon found out when he ran us off the road—he could not drive. The Army were content to let him rush over the countryside in a tank, where there was more margin for error, but he had never been taught to drive cars.

We waited to cross the Danube by landing craft at Ulm and a knot of ragged German boys began pushing each other about. One of them seemed to be getting the worst of it and we thought of interfering when they ran away, and I saw that the victim had lost his left hand. 'Typical Jerries,' said the tank man, who knew more about them than me, and was less appreciative of their better points. The accommodation in the ruins of the city was poor and we crowded into two semi-detached houses. Two black-dressed old women there looked at us in frightened hostility.

Stuttgart was a heap of orderly blackened hard core, one of the killing grounds where between 300,000 and 600,000 Germans lost their lives in exchange for those of 55,573 aircrew. In the end the bomber offensive was not a famous victory and the survivors remain unhonoured by the politicians, for whom it looked better to eulogize soldiers who triumphed against an enemy overwhelmed by numbers and American materiel, or in defeats suffered with phlegm. Stuggart and Essen and the rest do not rank with Dunkirk or Alamein in the annals of our wars.

At Mainz we spent the last night in Germany and reached Sedan the following day, where we were put up in wooden tier bunks in a barracks used by the soldiers of BAOR, lucky to have served in the shortest campaign of the war, when the *Luftwaffe* was exhausted.

I was awakened in the early hours by the usual maudlin sounds and a party of subalterns staggered to their beds. One of them must have seen my reefer hanging from the top bunk with the white stripe between the gold lace. 'Look at this!' the boy piped to his pals, 'he's not a fighting officer at all.'

I only record this trivial incident, almost buried in my memory, because it is a perfect epilogue to any ego trip about war service.

The Mercedes was on its last legs and just made it to the Channel. The pistons were worn out and the engine needed constant lubrication. I had jerricans of oil tied on to the front wings; during the last 200 miles she would not go for more than a half an hour without a stop for some more.

The Royal Navy at Calais had been reduced to a skeleton contingent and the Resident Naval Officer was surprised to see me. I was given a splendid dinner at a country restaurant near a VI site; for the journey back the car was driven by a French naval officer in the party.

She had other tricks besides the oil, including a loose driving seat. I did my best to point this out but no one paid attention and we set off. When the Frenchman applied the brakes in earnest the seat left its moorings and he arrived with it on the back seat, where he and I and the RNO's wife became a giggling heap of arms and legs, leaving it to the RNO, alone in the front, to stop her, which he did with some dexterity and no casualties.

When I left the next day he asked what he should do with the car. I told him it was his in exchange for the dinner, and for a bonus I handed over the Thompson and ammunition. He seemed overwhelmed and said he would sell the car for me. He took little notice when I explained that it was not mine, but loot from the German Army, and presumably belonged to the King. I was delighted to get rid of it and forgot all about it. Nearly a year later I received a letter in Ceylon from the RNO's wife enclosing a cheque for £75 'to repay the loan'. The French were short of cars and no doubt it finished up in some quiet corner, probably with a farmer, one with access to oil.

I joined the Dover ferry, loaded with soldiers taking leave from Germany. A subaltern told me that he had managed to fire one shot in anger the day before the war ended, when he had stopped a railway engine on a level crossing with a round from his tank. I said that it seemed tough on the engine driver and he looked at me in disbelief. He asked where I had come from and how long I had been away and when I told him he made an excuse and wandered off; he took me for a nut case.

My father had got back from India and it was good to see him after four and a half years. I remained on leave for three months and then received an appointment to the base in Ceylon for disposal at the Commander-in-Chief's discretion to relieve a reserve officer waiting to come home.

CHAPTER 16

RETURN TO THE ISLANDS

I took passage to the East in *Ranee,* an American built escort carrier which had seen service in the Pacific. The wardroom refrigerator was decorated with the squadron insignia of an American Air Group. She was being used as a trooper with drafts of Australians and New Zealanders going home, and an RN contingent of reliefs for Hostilities Only sailors anxious to be de-mobilized. The journey from Portsmouth to Colombo took four weeks and the officers in the draft were hard pressed to occupy the time.

Bridge was played in four available sessions, forenoon, afternoon, dog watches and after dinner. Three sessions were enjoyable, four made the game a chore. My partner was an Irish doctor who claimed to be unlucky. He was; in the weeks we played together he had an opening bid twice. During the hours he spent as dummy he told yarns about the Giants of County Sligo who prospered by slaughtering passing pilgrims. Blarney, told by an expert, lightens the long sea miles.

He had been a student in the Rotunda in Dublin; while waiting for maternity calls he had assembled a repertoire of medical jokes. He liked to sing 'Seated One Day at the Organ', apparently the anthem for Trinity College students so occupied. He had a literary variation.

> Lunching one day with Charles Morgan
> And feeling ill at ease,
> He began to quote from Sparkenbroke
> Before we reached the cheese.

The Captain entered Malta in some style by executing a pinwheel turn in the middle of Grand Harbour. In the evening we accompanied the Commander to the Gut, known to the Navy for

generations as the street for fun and games in Valetta. He had
not been to Malta since the twenties and had happy memories of
the wine and roses. Unfortunately, the girls had not changed
because the Church would not allow new recruits to the Island.
We made the best of it and the middle aged ladies were cheerful
company. The Commander did not give up easily; he danced The
Sampan Man and they joined in with ripe agility.

In Port Said the Irish doctor, an RNVR sub-lieutenant and I
decided to ride and we climbed on board three horses on the
beach. We trotted away and the Sub was bucked off. The Irishman
could not persuade his mount to go on and was taken back
willy-nilly to the start, despite his efforts to keep him on course.
My horse gave up trying to turn back and I kicked him on. The
result was an uncontrolled gallop for about two miles. We came
to rest near some workers' houses, where the owner caught up,
and accused me of trying to wreck his horse like all the other
feelthy British. He found support from some locals, who gathered
round in muttering confrontation.

It seemed that these horses liked going home, and had been
trained to do so in order to make better profits. When I pointed
him back down the beach and called for action there was another
electric gallop, pursued again by the shouting owner, until we got
back to the start, where the animal pulled up, sweating and
foaming. The attitude of the proprietor now changed and he
became ingratiating and suggested a large tip for the excellent ride
I had been given. The other two heard the argument and suggested I gave him a good kick on their behalf instead. We left,
followed by shouts for baksheesh..

That evening I bought a Longine watch I wear now from Simon
Artz for £18 and arrived back onboard with the Irish doctor, in
excellent fettle. Our four berth cabin was shared with two newly
qualified doctors who had so far been unable to adapt to their
new lives, and gave the impression that they had left home for
the first time when they joined the Navy.

The Irishman produced an Austrian hunting knife and our
companions watched wide-eyed. He threw the knife up by the
blade and caught it by the handle. I buried the point in a notice
board. This was a challenge he could not pass by; he put the back

of his hand against the board and dared me to throw the knife so that it would land between his open fingers. I aimed off and mercifully it stuck in the wood six inches from his thumb. He said that I had missed and challenged me to do it again; I refused and conceded defeat. The Irishman was disappointed; the two recruits had their heads under their sheets, pretending to be asleep and not wondering how to deal with a wound from an edged weapon.

Christmas was spent in the Red Sea; bridge gave way to faro and I lost more money than I could afford to the Sub-Lieutenant who came riding at Port Said. I gave him a cheque and have not played since. The Sub was dead within three weeks from some lethal tropical disease. I opened my next bank statement with uncustomary optimism but the cheque had been presented.

I left the ship in Colombo on 27 December 1945 and reported to the Fleet Supply Officer. I was taken in by a Wren personal assistant who stayed there for the interview. While the Captain was going through the list and deciding where to send me, the Wren and I exchanged a look and I gave her a wink because she looked delightful. I was told to wait outside, then called back and ordered to join HM Landing Ship (Tank) *3028* as secretary and supply officer to the twelve ships in the 50th LST Flotilla. I have reason to believe that FSO thought that he was sending me to the naval equivalent to a penal battalion.

I joined LST *3505* for the voyage to Singapore; we left Ceylon on 2 January 1946 with forty officers on passage. She was American built with diesel engines and cooler in the tropics than the British built ones with steam frigate engines.

I went into the wardroom and found it full. A youngster in a red football shirt sat beside me on the club fender with a glass of beer and I asked him where he was going. He told me that he was not going anywhere because he was one of the wardroom stewards. She turned out to be that sort of ship, officered by second raters who had allowed discipline to decline to such a degree that almost nothing was done properly. The Captain was unable to find the entrance to the Malacca Straits, and we wandered about like the Marie Celeste until the weather cleared. We reached Singapore a day late and I left with alacrity.

The Captain of *3028* was a charming professional, an RN

commander who had been Senior Officer of the Dover MTBs when they attacked the *Scharnhorst* and *Gneisenau* on their way up Channel in February 1942. The ship was run like a destroyer. My every want was taken care of by an aged Chinaman whom I hardly ever saw. 'Give me my ease,' NOIC often announced, as one of the basic needs in life, 'Maltese, Goanese or Chinese, and I am a contented man.'

The Wardroom had a liking for the Happy World Chinese fairground in Singapore and developed a party trick. Chinese wrestling was popular and we had a variant of our own. Two of us would pretend to have an argument and make enough noise for a crowd to gather. One would then strike the other on the jaw and fell him. The trick was to aim the blow into the victim's open hand, held near to his face. It was a drill followed by stunt men in films and the noise and fall looked real, and brought cries of indignation from the spectators. This childish diversion gave the Wardroom great pleasure. I do not know why, unless it was the beginnings of the *cafard*, or beetle in the brain, endemic in the Foreign Legion when kept too long in the desert. It went wrong on one occasion when the victim was slow in putting up his hand and was knocked out. The rest had to drag him off quickly before becoming involved in explanations to the Malayan constabulary.

The Japanese heavy cruiser *Myoko* lay near to the Causeway with her stern blow off in a midget submarine attack. Japanese working parties were everywhere, clearing up the mess in the dockyard and loading and unloading the LSTs running to the islands and returning British troops to Singapore for passage home: *3028* had just come back from Saigon with the guns and transport of an artillery unit. We embarked a REME formation and sailed for Bangkok on 22 January.

I was asked to help out with watchkeeping at sea and undertook standing dog watches. The Captain decided I needed a navigation course and began with a sun sight. He said the theory was quite simple; it had been explained to him at Dartmouth by a schooly who used an orange for demonstration. The Captain held the orange between his finger and thumb and began the lesson, but had to give it up. He suggested I ate the bloody orange and relied on the tables and sextant like everybody else.

I was happy to stand on the bridge, partly because I enjoyed it but also to strike a blow at the Branch apartheid system, which needed it. There was a sequel for me in 1956 when the draft of a new Naval Discipline Act was published. No doubt persuaded by the dear old salts who gave evidence the Committee recommended that the President and half the members of a court martial should always be officers with a bridge watchkeeping certificate, as if an ability to follow the Rule of the Road or put a running fix on the chart were qualifications for understanding the Judge's Rules, or the difference between false pretences and larceny by a trick. This was too much, even for politicians, and the proposal was soon dropped. Meanwhile I obtained a watchkeeping certificate from my old Captain in *3028* and sent it in; I was told that it was in the wrong form. The clause manifested the determination of some of the senior officers of the executive branch to hang on by hook or by crook. I have included a copy of my certificate here to remind the reader of the absurdity of the old branch system, which was surely doomed when steam took over from sail.

The soldiers and vehicles were discharged at Paknam and the lightened ship was able to cross the bar and go alongside in Bangkok. The city had enjoyed a boom during the Japanese occupation but now seemed half full. The night clubs were empty and begging for business; Jack had the unusual experience of being greeted on the pavement outside the lanterns and music, and offered the first bottle of sake free if he would go inside.

The Engineer Sub-Lieutenant announced in the wardroom that he had been to bed with a Siamese princess; three officers present said 'Snap' and consoled the engineer by reminding him that under the local rules all mothers took the father's title. (I have no idea whether this is true—I only report what happened.)

We went down river next day to load and embarked the HQ of the 7th Indian Division for passage to Singapore. During my watch we passed over the position where *Prince of Wales* and *Repulse* had been sunk, but there was nothing there to mark it.

The Moslem soldiers would not use the same heads as the Christian sailors and had their own facilities, consisting of a special box in the chains on either side of the ship. As a gesture to privacy a canvas dodger was rigged round the outside. When the visitors left the Chief Boatswain's Mate had a simple way of tidying up; a heaving line was attached to the box and the pin knocked out of the grating causing the whole contraption to fall into the sea. It was towed there for a few days until Christian scruples permitted it to be hoisted inboard.

The Indian cooks spent hours preparing curry which the soldiers ate twice daily. The Chief and I became addicts, with the help of one of their officers, who made the arrangements with his driver. In a burst of good will, which I regretted later, I gave this officer an excellent German bridge coat, taken from an E-boat in Ancona, and received a return gift of two Japanese officer's swords. There was an immediate field trial after dinner, when the three volumes of the Navy List were laid on the deck in the wardroom. I got three-quarters through Volume One, the thinnest, which seemed an indifferent result.

A Japanese working party came onboard at Singapore and I asked their English speaking officer how old the swords were. He took the first one out of the scabbard and lifted it over his head in a way which seemed to me unnecessary for the purpose of a simple dating exercise. I was relieved when he put it down and showed that he had no intention of making a foolish gesture. He took the peg out of the handle and pulled it off, showing a Japanese inscription half hidden by rust. He told me that he could not understand the writing but it looked at least 300–400 years old. Thereafter I regarded the swords as heirlooms until I had one valued, with the help of one of my daughters-in-law who had a job at Spinks. The finding was that they were replicas of a kind issued to Japanese Hostilities Only officers, who did not belong to the samurai and had no swords of their own. They were worth about £50 and I use them for vigorous garden clearance.

Two other ships from the flotilla were in company at Singapore and I paid them my duty visit as a member of the Staff. I found one commanded by the RNR Second Lieutenant from *Hermes*, the boats officer who picked up crashed airmen. He had become eccentric and it showed itself in the décor with which he adorned his bridge, which he fitted with a striped awning and a carpet. There were wicker tables and chairs and a plant or two. At sea he wore a large Panama hat, sipped drinks and smoked cheroots

while the world went by. He kept to this way of life until he was
sent a first lieutenant, ex-Burma police, with a mahogany com-
plexion and one gold wire earring of the sort which used to be
worn by seamen, who could out drink him with ease. In the face
of this challenge one of them had to go, and it was the Captain.

On 9 February 1946 we embarked a force of Dutch soldiers,
described as 'stoottroepen', or stormtroops, armed with British
equipment, and set out with the minesweeper *Pincher* in company
for Banka Island, where the Dutch had the job of taking over
from the Japanese battalion there. The next day we were joined
by two more minesweepers, a motor launch and a Landing Craft
(Gun) for support if needed. The force was under the Captain of
3028. We anchored off Tanjong Kelian light and the Captain,
who had not beached the ship before, decided that the shore
should be surveyed before we went in. It looked superb, with white
sand for miles and green jungle behind. Although the town of
Muntok was near by, no one appeared.

The motor cutter was lowered and the Captain went in to carry
out the survey in person, equipped with a pole to show the depth.
For defence, the bowman was given a rifle and told to hide it in
the bottom of the boat, in case any unseen watchers in the jungle
became provoked by such a display of arms. The political situation
was tricky; it was no part of the United Kingdom's job to help
the Dutch to regain their colonies, but without our help they had
no means of reaching them, and our long term interests were not
served by allowing the Japanese to hand over to left-wing rebels.
When the Japanese took Singapore Island they stopped the colonial dance for ever but it did not seem quite that in 1946. Our
role was confined to giving the Dutch passage and leaving it to
them to sort out their differences with the Indonesians, who had
no intention of having them back if they could avoid it.

It was a bright day and we saw the boat reach the shore. The
LCG had her gun's crew closed up ready to respond, but nothing
happened. The Captain poled his way along the beach and the
signalman put a marker flag into the sand. The boat was recovered
and we worked up to 8 knots and aimed for the land. The Captain
announced to the bridge that he had spent the whole of his service
avoiding going aground, and this seemed like asking for a court

THIS IS TO CERTIFY that
Lieutenant-Commander R.A. Clarkson, Royal
Navy, while serving as Lieutenant (S) in
H.M. L.S.T. 3028 under my command took
charge of a watch at sea as Lieutenant and
performed efficiently the duties of that
rank.

(E.N. PUMPHREY)

CAPTAIN

30th December, 1956.

Bridge Watchkeeping Certificate

Bridge Watchkeeping Certificate.

martial. She was just about to beach when the Yeoman reminded him that he had not let go the kedge. This was a stern anchor, dropped during the run in to keep the ship in the correct position on shore, and help haul her off. It was too late for that and she grunted into the sand. The follow-up wave coursed past her and the doors were lowered at the rush, because this was an operation.

The Chief Stoker was first ashore, to check her trim, followed by the First Lieutenant to look for hull damage. Chief and I then wandered out because it looked inviting and we had nothing much to do. We sat down on the sand and enjoyed the view. About five minutes later there was a clatter of boots and some Dutch soldiers came down the ramp, rifles at the high port, crouching and ready to engage the enemy. They were without helmets and the rifles were their only arms. Shortly afterwards the first 3-tonner appeared and crawled up the beach. The infantry were still standing about, looking at the jungle. 'This,' said Chief, who had had some experience of landings, 'is going to be a cock-up.'

While the ship discharged two of us went in a Dutch lorry to Muntok to see what was happening. The stormtroopers were digging rifle and machine gun pits in the road intersections; they had no armoured vehicles and I did not see any heavy weapons. We went on to the headquarters of the Japanese infantry battlion which garrisoned the island and would stay until the Dutch took over. The Japanese had been made responsible by the British for the Chinese population, under threat from the Indonesians.

There were two smart sentries outside the headquarters, in clean uniforms, carrying rifles and fixed bayonets with the ease and alertness of trained soldiers. One was a little slow in giving an answer and received a slap in the face from an NCO. We were met by a captain who spoke American and told us that he had lived in the United States. He adopted a nauseating, chummy demeanour and we were glad to leave him and return with the empty lorries to the beach.

The Japanese had massacred civilians on this beach in 1942. There were large dumps of tin ingots neatly piled on the sand, put there by the enemy for their ships, which never arrived: *3028* would soon be unloaded and the chance seemed too good to miss, but we were told to leave it alone. The staff thought that if the

HM LST 3028 Banka Island: 10 February 1946. Chief, author, Dutch soldiers.

tin stayed there it would be filched by Chinese boats from Singapore and find its way into the Malayan economy; if we took it away the Dutch would claim it. It was worth about £1.5 m at the prices then prevailing.

At 2 am we finished discharging and managed to haul off and anchor near the rest of the Force, despite the absence of the kedge. The Captain, First Lieutenant and I landed next morning and walked to Muntok. We equipped ourselves with .30 carbines lent by the Dutch. No one was about and the stoottroepen had dug themselves in deeper in the town. We had the feeling that we were being watched from the jungle but nothing happened; it is probable that the risk we ran was more from an accident with the carbines, about which we knew nothing, than anything the Indonesians might have started. We learned afterwards that the rebels waited until the Navy left and then attacked the unfortunate amateurs we had taken there, giving them a hard time.

We were swept out by the three fleet minesweepers we had with us. The LCG and the motor launch fell in astern. It was my dog watch and I was surprised to find myself sharing the bridge with the Yeoman Signals. Our course took us over a position where mines had been laid. We knew they were there because a British submarine had laid them. Most captains would have been on the bridge until we were clear, but ours stayed in his sea cabin on the deck below.

I kept an eye on the flags on the orepesa floats ahead, marking the sweeps, tried to keep her on course, and hoped for the best. Signal flags appeared on the yard of the leading minesweeper and the Yeoman sang out that they were altering to starboard. They went round and I waited for their bearing to change to the new course so that I could follow in succession.

I told the Captain down the voicepipe that we were altering and gave the wheel order to bring her to starboard. She began to go round and the stern swung out. Simultaneously, two orepesa floats went under and two mines came to the surface fine on each bow. We were bound to hit the one on the port side with our stern with the wheel I had got on. I told the helmsman to put the wheel amidships and reached for the Captain's buzzer. I heard his voice behind me before I got to the button.

The ship passed between the mines leaving them about fifty yards on each side. Floating mines cut from their moorings should be safe, but these had been there for some years and the system had been known to fail. The Captain had taken the ship over, and I retired to the back of the bridge and shot at the mines with the rifle we kept in the charthouse, hoping to sink one. I missed and the empty cartridge cases rattled through the open engine room hatch, irritating the Chief, who complained that each one had to be picked up. There were no other episodes and we cleared the island for Singapore.

It was typical of the Captain that he kept abreast of events by looking out of his scuttle rather than show any lack of confidence in his Officer of the Watch by taking over the ship. He was able to swallow the alteration of course but when he saw the floats go down he was on the bridge in a flash.

He left us in Singapore and we gave him the best dinner the messman could muster. After the port and liqueurs and a loving cup drunk out of a salad bowl, he told us that the worst moment in his life was when he realized that he had no hope of getting through the screen of E-boats and destroyers round *Scharnhorst* and

Gneisenau, and had to order his MTBs to fire their torpedoes outside it. He had an electrifying effect on the crew of *3028*, who did not expect to get the best to command them. She soon went off the boil after he had gone.

The ship went to the Naval Base to carry out essential repairs for the passage home. The new captain was an RNR commander who had been in combined operations from the beginning, and claimed to have taken part in all the big landings. He told me on his first day to get him a Sterling sub-machine-gun and ammunition, which he intended to keep in his cabin. I must have looked surprised, because he thought it appropriate to explain. 'I had a mutiny at Salerno,' he said, 'I do not intend to have another.'

He abhorred beards, worn by nearly all the officers and a majority of the ship's company. He told the Wardroom to remove them and refused all future requests from sailors to cease shaving. Fortunately, he did not order those who already had beards to shave off; that might have brought him the mutiny he feared. We did not think him anything out of the ordinary; it was a time of eccentricity.

The Captain was ordered to take three LSTs under command and sail for the UK on 31 March. On that day a signal was received from the shore Admiral ordering me to be discharged before the Flotilla left, to enable me to attend an enquiry. I hastened to the office. It was the accident at Voghera. Letters had been sent to the address I had given to the Mother Superior but I had never received them and they concluded that I was avoiding the issue. I explained and wrote out my reasons in writing there and then. I got back to my ship in the nick of time.

The Flotilla was due to sail from Keppel Herbour at 1600 and at 1545 the Captain was still drinking in the wardroom with the rest of us. Happily the Sub-Lieutenant RNR, Navigating Officer, was not at the party, except on occasions when he put his head round the door and asked for permission to come to immediate notice for steam, call special sea dutymen, and order the Flotilla to be ready to sail at the time ordered. To each of these requests the Captain signified his acquiesence by nodding his head, thus avoiding the need to articulate.

When the Sub came in to remind him that we were going in

five minutes, he turned to me and asked if I would like to take the Flotilla to sea. This seemed a splendid idea and I headed a procession to the bridge. I did not take her out, neither did the Captain. I think it must have been the Sub, a hard working young chap, who deserved better than employment in a madhouse. The other three ships followed dutifully astern and the four of us set out for home.

We called at Trincomalee to oil, arriving in the early evening. The Port War Signal Station was flashing us as we entered harbour and I remembered enough from the endless Morse exercises in *Vindictive* to recognize my own name. I looked over the Signalman's shoulder and read that I had to be landed before sailing and would stay there. No reason was given and I assumed it was Voghera again. By this time I was getting fed up with that episode, which had been partly the fault of the victim for riding an unlit bicycle after an evening in the pub.

I went ashore ready to say my piece but Voghera was not the problem. The C-in-C's Staff had found out that the Flotilla had an RN Lieutenant (S) and decided it would be a waste to let him go home when he would be useful here. Thus for the third time I left my ship while serving on a foreign station. It mattered not; I had few ties, and from the little I had seen of wartime UK, it was better abroad.

The Wardroom gave me a dinner in the Officers' Club. The Chief insisted on wearing his bowler hat, which he had taken with him everywhere since 1939, throughout the evening. I was probably the only one who would still be in the Navy in three months time and in sympathy they gave me the best wake they could. For my part I was sorry that they would be cast into civvy street without jobs and not much fun.

Back onboard, the Captain, Chief and a chaplain on passage continued the party in the wardroom until 0600 when the Padre announced that he had decided that I ought to train for the Roman Catholic priesthood, and offered to write to someone to start me off. This was an offer to which it was difficult to respond without hurting his feelings; he had given me his white uniform, which he would soon need no longer, and people become serious in all-night discussions. I said that I had spent nearly seven years trying to learn the job I had and did not feel able to change my religion and start another yet, despite the advantage of having had an audience of the Pope. (There were about 200 American GIs there too but I left that out.) We parted the best of friends and they saw me over the side *en route* for my office while they made do with the rolling deep.

> Stick close to your desks and never go to sea,
> And you may all be Rulers of the Queen's Navee!

I watched them leave and threaded a way through the jungle to Naval Headquarters, intent upon getting out of it somehow.

I was invited for a drink by my predecessor and wandered about, looking for the mess, when I saw a Wren officer I recognized as the personal assistant from Colombo. I asked her how to get there.

She said she thought she could put me right.

She did.

She still does, thank God.